TACIT KNOWLEDGE

Also by Neil Gascoigne and published by Acumen
Scepticism

Also by Tim Thornton and published by Acumen
John McDowell

TACIT KNOWLEDGE

Neil Gascoigne and Tim Thornton

ACUMEN

NG – For my girls!

TT – For new colleagues in the School of Health with thanks for their warm
     welcome.

First published in 2013 by Acumen

Acumen Publishing Limited

4 Saddler Street
Durham
DH1 3NP, UK

ISD, 70 Enterprise Drive
Bristol, CT 06010, USA

www.acumenpublishing.com

ISBN: 978-1-84465-545-8 (hardcover)
ISBN: 978-1-84465-546-5 (paperback)

British Library Cataloguing-in-Publication Data
A catalogue record for this book is available from the British Library.

Printed and bound in the UK by MPG Books Group.

CONTENTS

INTRODUCTION

It is so difficult to find the beginning. Or better: it is difficult to begin at the beginning. And not to try to go further back.

(Wittgenstein, *On Certainty*)

MAKING IT TACIT

We live in an age of explicit rules and guidelines; of aims and objectives; of benchmarks and performance indicators, standardized tests and league tables. Systematization abounds in the criteria specifying good practice and the delivery of public services; in the charters that outline rights and responsibilities in both civic society and in society's microcosms. A university's once unspecified expectation that its students will attend lectures and prepare work is often now formalized in contracts, and in return students are informed of the explicit "outcomes" of their learning activities. Likewise, in the UK at least, patients' expectations of the quality of care from the National Health Service (NHS) are increasingly constituted by waiting times and the availability of choice. Such reforms aim to replace a tacit or implicit understanding of practices with something explicit and codified. They are expressions of what Max Weber calls "intellectualization": the sentiment that one can "in principle, master all things by calculation" (1946: 139).

Weber traces the "disenchantment" (*ibid.*) of the world that this presages to the very origins of systematic epistemological inquiry, and in *The Craftsman* Richard Sennett similarly identifies as longstanding a suspicion of merely implicitly understood standards:

> Plato views it as too often an excuse for mediocrity. His modern heirs in the NHS wanted to root out embedded knowledge, expose it to the cleansing of rational analysis – and have become frustrated that much of the tacit knowledge nurses and doctors have acquired is precisely knowledge they cannot put into words or render as logical propositions. (Sennett 2008: 50–51)

As Sennett suggests, the "Platonic" drive towards systematization manifests itself equally in the move to obviate dependence on the skilful judgements of

1

individuals by formalizing the knowledge and making explicit the rules that experts purportedly employ in making them. In medicine, for example, the rise of the influence of evidence-based medicine (EBM) has been accompanied by a general codification of the relative merits of different forms of evidence in the shape of the EBM hierarchy, which prescribes that meta-analysis of randomized control trials are to be preferred to randomized control trials or merely descriptive studies. All are to be preferred to the clinical judgement of respected authorities.

One reason for wanting to expose the practical wisdom of experts to "rational analysis" is the fear that it otherwise remains hidden from those who manage them and are held to account for their activities. Others are the reasonable hope that expert judgement is objective, and the widespread assumption that objectivity and codification go hand in hand. It is a platitude that if a judgement concerns something about which we can be right or wrong then it must answer to some standard of correctness that has nothing to do with mere opinion. And it is tempting to infer from this that tacit or implicit forms of judgement or of understanding can be "cleansed" of subjective factors and rendered objective – and therefore genuine exercises of rationality – only in so far as they are codifiable in a principle or set of principles.

From this perspective, prospects for a form of knowledge or judgement that is not codifiable but is still genuinely answerable to features of the world appear limited indeed, and this conclusion seems more pressing still in the case of practical knowing. The intellectual difficulty here is brought out nicely in an exchange between Sennett and Grayson Perry, the Turner Prize-winning artist and craftsman–potter. Perry's report that he had the saw "Creativity is mistakes!" cast into the concrete of his studio elicited a delighted response from Sennett: "Oh very good! Oh I like this!". But then the conversation continued:

> PERRY: There is no right way to do it and it is always about my judgement: what is good.
> SENNETT: You've got an objective standard though, of course? You are judging yourself.
> PERRY: Yes [doubtfully] – but it can move. I have an aesthetic standard. You can't measure it. You can't put a ruler next to it and say it is good. (BBC Radio 4: 2008)

Perry's slogan suggests a normative standard for potting: it is possible to make mistakes and thus, learning from them, to become more skilful. However, he also denies that there is a *right* way to do things and rejects Sennett's suggestion that he exercises judgement against an objective standard. This may be because Perry aims to make works of art through his pottery and thinks that aesthetic judgements are not answerable to features external to the sensibility of the artist. But even if one thinks of the manufacture of pottery not as art but as a *craft* – by contrast with the industrial manufacture of identical items – it would be implausible to think it might be judged with "a ruler". But that need not imply it cannot be judged according to some standard. Contrary to what Perry's doubtful response suggests, there is no implication from *not* being able to use a rule to codify judgements to such judgements *not* being right or wrong. What is required here is the concept of a form of knowing that is not codified, because not "calculable" with some analogue of a ruler, but which answers nevertheless to a genuine standard of correctness. This is what we will call "tacit knowledge".

"WE CAN KNOW MORE THAN WE CAN TELL"

The idea of tacit knowledge (or "tacit knowing", as he preferred) was first promoted by Michael Polanyi. A more detailed account of Polanyi's contribution to the topic will be offered in Chapter 1, but two of his suggestions concerning the nature of tacit knowledge run throughout this book and are worth noting in advance. We will look at one in this section and the other in the next.

The first suggestion comes from *The Tacit Dimension* (Polanyi 2009) and is, if not quite a definition, the purported fact that forms the basis of his own investigation: "we can know more than we can tell" (*ibid.*: 4). As Polanyi is quick to acknowledge, "it is not easy to say exactly" (*ibid.*) what this suggestion means. It does, however, imply that one can approach the nature of tacit knowledge through a form of "*via negativa*". What is tacit is what is not "tellable" under a suitable understanding of what that means. According to this method, one clarifies what "tacit knowledge" means by directing attention at some suitable antonym.

Let's consider a few intuitive examples of knowledge that might fit this criterion: recognizing someone's face, or a few hastily drawn lines *as* a face; throwing and catching a ball; operating a complex piece of machinery; riding a bicycle; being a concert pianist; reading a book or map; "reading" a patient or a set of complex data; navigating the shoals of interpersonal relationships; understanding a language; excising a brain tumour. These phenomena seem to involve normative, intentionally directed activities that might readily be characterized in terms of knowledge, but at the same time might seem to involve something that cannot be (at least fully) put into words.

Without further exploration, however, the suggestion that tacit knowledge can be investigated via some contrast is underdetermined. One might, for example, take Polanyi's talk of tellability to suggest a contrast between tacit and explicit. But consider the fact that people often draw on knowledge, whether practical or theoretical, without being *aware* of it or consciously attending to it. One can drive home with one's mind on hard philosophy, rather than the journey, and successfully negotiate other traffic and the intervening junctions without being consciously aware of it. Nevertheless, the success of the venture implies the possession of knowledge, for example, of where to go as well as how to operate the controls. Should this be counted as tacit because the knowledge involved was not explicitly entertained?

Two accounts of less everyday examples are worth setting out because they are often used as paradigmatic examples of tacit knowledge. The first relates to the economics of poultry farming, which are such that it is a great advantage to be able to determine the gender of chicks as soon as possible after they hatch. In the 1920s, Japanese scientists discovered a method by which this could be done based on subtle perceptual cues with a suitably held chick. It was, nevertheless, a method that required a great deal of skill, developed through practice. After four to six weeks of practice, a newly qualified chick-sexer might be able to determine the sex of 200 chicks in 25 minutes with an accuracy of 95 per cent, rising with years of practice to 1,000–1,400 chicks per hour with an accuracy of 98 per cent (Gellatly 1986: 4).

The second story is that of skilled Polynesian navigators who were found to be able to navigate small out-rigger canoes "across two or three hundred miles of open sea; and do so in almost any weather, and even when less than fully sober. How is it done?" (*ibid.*: 5). Investigation suggested that the skill took years to master and was context-specific; that is, they were only able to navigate the seas in the natural conditions of their familiar part of the world.

What makes the first story particularly significant is that early Australian investigators were unable to determine the nature of the skill involved. Further the story has developed that the chick-sexers themselves were unable to express the nature of their knowledge (aside from saying which were male and which female). Likewise, the Polynesian navigators had mastered techniques – still, to this day, taught in the Wilson Islands – that they were unable to put into words. According to their folkloric reception, then, chick-sexers and navigators alike are unable to tell *how* they do what they do (how they know that *that* is a male; that *that* is the way to head). Hence they have both been held to by prime instances of tacit knowledge according to the first of Polanyi's key claims: that tacit knowledge is untellable.

These examples seem to undermine a view of knowledge sloganized by what we will call the *principle of codifiability* (PC):

PC   All knowledge can be fully articulated, or codified, in context-independent terms.

If the Polynesian navigators are unable to explain in general terms how it is that they are able to navigate, and if such navigation is a matter of knowledge, then it seems that not all knowledge can be articulated in general terms. One can imagine them, under anthropological questioning back on land, being quite unable to describe what it was about the wind or tide which enabled it to guide them home. Their knowledge might resist general description on the shore.

But there is a stronger interpretation, especially of the first story, suggested by the common exaggeration according to which the chick-sexers themselves do not know how they determine sex. That reading suggests that there is knowledge that cannot be articulated at all. Call this the *principle of inarticulacy* (PI) of knowledge:

PI   There can be knowledge that cannot be articulated.

It runs counter to a nuanced view of knowledge, summarized in the *principle of articulacy* (PA):

PA   All knowledge can be articulated, either in context-independent terms (i.e. it can be codified) or in context-dependent terms.

Thinking of tacit knowledge in this general way as violating either PC or PA (and affirming PI in the latter case) may seem, however, to raise a difficulty. It may seem to threaten its status as *knowledge*. Roughly, if what is known cannot be carved out in words – if it is untellable – in what sense is there anything known? Both to answer this, and to refine the options, it is helpful to turn to the second suggestion from Polanyi.

THIS TIME IT'S PERSONAL

Polanyi's second suggestion relating to tacit knowledge is that it is *personal* knowledge, involving an "active comprehension of things known, an action that requires skill" (Polanyi 1958: vii). This suggestion forms part of his broader criticism of the notion that knowledge can aspire towards a degree of objectivity in which the features of the knowing subject drop out entirely. Polanyi's account of personal knowledge is an attempt to overcome the traditional opposition between objectivity and subjectivity by showing that the only coherent account of objectivity is one in which the personal plays an essential constitutive role. In this respect, the concept of personal knowledge suggests a rebalancing of what are often taken to be in opposition: theoretical and practical knowledge.

Polanyi's idea of personal knowledge has two aspects, both of which will be important in the body of this book. The first is the idea that it involves *active* comprehension. Personal knowledge is practical knowledge connected to skill and ability. We will argue, later, that performance and the judgement of performance are connected. An audience member might be able to distinguish a good tennis player from a poor one, or an off-tune performance from one exhibiting fidelity to the melody, but be unable to make the finer discriminations we associate with expertise in an area because he or she does not have the appropriate skills or abilities. Having greater skill is having greater practical knowledge, which like all knowledge can be manifested in a number of ways including both performance and judgement.

The second aspect is that personal knowledge is connected to the exercise of a skill in particular contexts. There are two dimensions to this context-dependence. Part of what it *is* to be able to cope in a skilful way is to be responsive to the demands of particular situations. One example of such context-dependent knowledge is what Aristotle called "*phronesis*", which involves perceiving the moral demands that particular situations make on rational subjects. But just as for Aristotle the ability to make such judgements is a matter of the *character* of the *phronemos*, we will also take "personal" to flag the centrality for such knowledge of the skilled agent him or herself. Since personal knowledge and ability go hand in hand, the particular person is an important part of the context.

The personal perspective may be taken to suggest a more radical interpretation of Polanyi's "untellability" criterion. If knowledge can be personal – can depend on aspects of a subject's subjectivity – perhaps that explains why we can know more than we can tell. Perhaps some features, at least, of our subjectivity cannot be shared with others, cannot be clothed in language because merely public words cannot capture the private scene. This thought prompts an explanation of why we can know more than we can tell because the (putative) knowledge in question simply belongs *outside* the realm of articulation, the view we have labelled PI, the *principle of inarticulacy* of knowledge. While it seems clear how this may merit the description "tacit" by emphasizing the "personal" dimension, it is, as remarked at the end of the previous section, altogether less clear how it combines that with the objectivity required for "knowledge". How can states that cannot be articulated count nevertheless as knowledge? What is the content of such knowledge, for example? What *is* it that is known?

There is, however, space for another option here suggested by the connection between personal knowledge and both practical ability and context-dependence. One can take what is genuine in the stories of the chick-sexers and Polynesian navigators to illustrate the falsity of the more specific view (PC) that all knowledge can be fully articulated, or codified, *in context-independent terms*. Denying that all knowledge can be codified in context-independent general terms need not commit one to claiming that there is knowledge that cannot be articulated at all. That is, one can deny PC while still maintaining that if there is knowledge then it must have some sort of demonstrable and articulable content (PA). We will argue, then, that the logical space for an account of tacit knowledge can be found by denying PC and PI, and affirming PA, taking tacit knowledge to resist articulation through codification – and hence answering to Polanyi's first suggestion under a particular interpretation – because it is *personal* knowledge, according to his second suggestion.

On the account promoted in this book, tacit knowledge is personal or practical in the senses conveyed in the above examples. It is untellable in so far as the tellable is equated with what can be codified in general terms. In this respect, tacit knowledge contrasts with explicit knowledge only in so far as the latter implies such context-free codification. But tacit knowledge need not lack an articulable content. It need not be *ineffable*. The contrast with explicit knowledge relates to the context in which such knowledge is made manifest and to the *persons* who – in so far as they exhibit the appropriate abilities – in part comprise that context. It can be articulated, then, but only practically and in context-dependent terms employing demonstrative concepts.

As we saw in the exchange between Perry and Sennett, thinking about practical knowledge (the cognitive basis of skills and abilities) tends to be conditioned by a limited sense of the conceptual possibilities available. Viewing tacit and explicit as opposites, and only the latter as answering to independent standards, encourages the temptation to see the former as knowledge in name only. But, following Polanyi, one can instead grant that tacit knowledge construed as personal knowledge depends on a knowing subject – since it is practical knowledge – while still answering to standards independent of the subject. So care has to be taken in fixing the proper interpretation of what contrasts with the tacit. In a slogan, the aim of this book is to steer a course between codification and ineffability: between the intellectualistic reductionism of PC and inflationary mysticism of PI. Tacit knowledge stands opposed to what can be codified in context-independent general terms, but it does not stand opposed to what can be articulated in any way at all.

THE ANTONYM OF "TACIT"

We can get a clearer picture of the potential dangers of approaching tacit knowledge through contrast with an antonym by outlining one strand of another recent book on tacit knowledge: Harry Collins's *Tacit and Explicit Knowledge* (Collins 2010a). Collins also approaches the nature of tacit knowledge through a contrast with what is explicit. He describes his strategy in a pithy summary: "explain 'explicit', then classify tacit" (*ibid.*: 1). But his particular interpretation of "explicit" distorts the account of tacit knowledge that flows from it.

A clue to the difficulty comes in the first sentence of the first chapter of his book. "Tacit knowledge is knowledge that is not *explicated*" (*ibid.*: 1, emphasis added). Now, this might be terminologically innocent if "explicate" is taken to mean *make clear*. If so, tacit knowledge is knowledge that cannot be made clear, which has echoes of Polanyi's first slogan. But Collins also slips into using it to mean *explain*. Thus tacit knowledge stands opposed to what can be explained. Even though he allows that this can be a matter of degree, it yields a much stronger claim. As we will describe, one consequence of this assimilation is that it undermines the idea that his subject matter is a form of personal knowledge – knowledge *for* a subject – at all.

We can begin to explain this by contrasting two claims Collins makes. He says, on the one hand, that:

> the idea of tacit knowledge only makes sense when it is in tension with explicit knowledge, and since cats and dogs and sieves and trees cannot be said to "know" any explicit knowledge, they shouldn't be said to know any tacit knowledge either. In fact, they don't "know" anything. (*Ibid.*: 78)

But he also goes on to suggest a comparison, which is supposed to render tacit knowledge less mysterious, between genuine tacit knowledge (e.g. possessed by human subjects) and just these non-human cases:

> In all the ways that do not involve the way we intentionally choose to do certain acts and not others, and the way we choose to carry out those acts, the human, per individual body and brain … is continuous with the animal and physical world. We are just like complicated cats, dogs, trees, and sieves … Sometimes we can do things better than cats, dogs, trees and sieves can do them, and sometimes worse. A sieve is generally better at sorting stones than a human (as a fridge is better at chilling water), a tree is certainly better at growing leaves, dogs are better at being affected by strings of smells, and cats are better at hunting small animals … That teaching humans to accomplish even mimeomorphic actions is a complicated business, involving personal contact, says nothing about the nature of the knowledge, per se. (*Ibid.*: 104–5)

So aside from the fact that we can *choose* to do some things rather than others, and can choose to do them in particular ways, while cats, dogs, trees and sieves cannot, the performance of the tasks, which for us is expressive of tacit knowledge, is just the same. In that respect, we are *just like* those animals, plants and artefacts, according to Collins.

A clue to how Collins addresses the apparent incompatibility between the claims that cats, dogs, trees and sieves *know nothing* while the way they "do" things is *just like* the way we do things when we express tacit knowledge is his focus on what he calls (in the last quote) the "nature of the knowledge, per se". In fact, this does not seem to mean the way humans *know* how to do the task, their knowledge, which is the focus of this book. Rather, it seems to mean the nature, not of the knowledge, but of the task itself. That is how it can be a common element between humans and non-humans. Thus taking the contrast to tacit to concern whether a task can be explained distorts the subject matter of the book away from tacit *knowledge*, the cognitive state of a subject, and towards a worldly *process* however it is carried out and whether the result of knowledge or not.

A second consequence is that Collins takes "tacit" to admit of degrees. Thus having said that "tacit knowledge is continuous with that possessed by animals and other living things", he goes on to say that "in principle it is possible for it to be explicated, not by the animals and trees themselves (or the particular humans who embody it), but as the outcome of research done by human scientists" (Collins 2010a: 85). This comment is relevant – is not a *non sequitur* – because such scientific explanation tends, on his account, to undermine the tacit status. It renders the examples highlighted via cats, dogs, trees and sieves merely "medium degree" (as opposed to strongly) tacit knowledge.

Elsewhere the opposition between being tacit and being scientifically explicable and the relative status of the former is made even more explicit:

> In *The Logic of Tacit Inference*, Polanyi argues persuasively that humans do not know how they ride, but he also provides a formula: "In order to compensate for a given angle of imbalance α we must take a curve on the side of the imbalance, of which the radius (r) should be proportionate to the square of the velocity (v) over the imbalance $r \sim v2/\alpha$." While no human can actually ride a bike using that formula, a robot, with much faster reactions, might. So that aspect of bike-riding is not quite so tacit after all. (Collins 2010b: 30)

So the fact that the task can be explained by others – whether or not they have practical knowledge how to do it – counts against it being fully tacit for a different subject, however he or she thinks about or grasps riding a bike. Explanation elsewhere has action at a distance here for the status of a subject's tacit knowledge.

This assumption is also operative when Collins notes that, for skilled typists, consciously following the rules they originally learnt by slows them down. He comments that "this seems to bear on nothing but the way humans work; it does not bear on the way knowledge works" (Collins 2010a: 104). "Knowledge" *simpliciter* does not denote the personal knowledge or know-how of human typists, then, but rather a thoroughly generalized account of the task of typing that could be given. This assimilation is also suggested in a later comment on the limits of human typing: "The constraints on the methods available for efficient typing by humans (by contrast eg with machines) are somatic limits; they have everything to do with us and nothing to do with the task as a task – nothing to do with knowledge as knowledge" (*ibid.*: 104). That last line makes plains the real subject matter of Collins's book: not the *knowledge* a particular subject has but a *task*, whether carried out by humans, animals or even trees or sieves, independently of whether or not any knowledge is actually involved. Construing the antonym of tacit the way he does has far reaching consequences for his account and undermines the claim that it is an analysis of a form of knowledge at all.

Our analysis, by contrast, seeks to preserve a connection between tacit knowledge and the subject who has it, through the idea that it is personal knowledge. The fact that a task might be accomplished algorithmically by a machine via explicit programming, or by a human via explicit rules, does not undermine the fact that it can also be carried out as an exercise of skilled know-how by a person with relevant tacit knowledge. If so, it is tacit for the subject who possesses it.

CHAPTER OUTLINE

Chapter 1 focuses on arguments from two other philosophers in addition to Polanyi: Gilbert Ryle and Martin Heidegger. All three share an emphasis on the importance of practical knowledge ("knowledge how", or "know-how"), for understanding theoretical knowledge ("knowledge that", or "know-that"). Furthermore, all argue for the priority of practical knowledge by deploying a form of regress argument against a particular understanding of theoretical knowledge. We argue that Ryle's and Heidegger's views complement those of Polanyi to suggest an initial assimilation of tacit knowledge to practical know-how.

Chapter 2 explores Ryle's regress argument further and defends it against recent criticism. Although we argue that the regress argument is sound, and indicates the priority of knowing how over knowing that, that fact does not show that practical knowing how cannot be expressed. It can be articulated using context-dependent concepts in practical demonstrations. Consistent with PA, we suggest that tacit knowledge is best understood as such context-dependent but still conceptually articulated personal knowing how.

Chapter 3 begins by outlining Wittgenstein's discussion of rule-following and the conclusion that there is a way of grasping a rule which is practical.

It then looks at two responses to this argument, which might be used to support a view of tacit knowledge distinct from ours. Saul Kripke's sceptical interpretation suggests that following a rule has to be a tacit skill because there is no pattern of correct use that an individual can grasp. Adrian Moore's interpretation suggests that understanding a rule is a form of ineffable knowledge because it answers to nothing. Neither view, we argue, helps support a notion of tacit knowledge that is both tacit and knowledge.

In Chapter 4 we look at how John Searle deploys a version of the rule-following regress to argue for the existence of a "Background" of non-intentional know-how that makes possible our knowledge-that. We show that although this would give us an alternative account of the status of tacit knowing it is premised on an unsatisfactory account of rule-following. We conclude that a correct understanding of the challenge of the regress warrants no invocation of a Background to our practices, and thus no suggestion that our tacit knowing is somehow "hidden" from view.

Chapter 5 takes up the phenomenological challenge to our account of tacit knowledge as knowing how. This combines considerations discussed in Chapter 1 in relation to Heidegger with attempts, inspired by the work of Gareth Evans, to make good on the notion of nonconceptual content. Since our exploitation of demonstratives owes something to John McDowell, it might be confused with the latter's conceptualism. We consequently evaluate attacks on McDowell's conceptualism by Sean D. Kelly and Hubert Dreyfus, to demonstrate the failings of the phenomenological alternative and to clarify the extent to which our account of tacit knowing can be classified as "McDowellian".

Chapter 6 looks at the relation between tacit knowledge and language and asks two questions:

1. To what extent is language mastery a matter of tacit knowledge?
2. To what extent does tacit knowledge depend on linguistic mastery?

Tacit knowledge has often been deployed by philosophers to answer question 1. The task they have undertaken is to codify the understanding of a language that a speaker possesses in a grammatical theory. Since, however, speakers cannot articulate anything more than a fragment of such a theory, they must have merely tacit knowledge of the theory. Because the idea of tacit knowledge is not embedded in ordinary usage, an account of it is in part a matter of stipulation as well as analysis. Thus we do not argue that it is simply wrong to call grasp of a hypothetical theory of meaning "tacit knowledge". But we do show how different such a conception is from ours putting considerable strain on the claim that it is any form of knowledge. We reiterate the moral of Chapter 3, however, to argue that because language mastery involves context-dependent know-how it is an instance of tacit knowledge as we define it.

Question 2 is prompted by some recent sociological work by Harry Collins and Robert Evans, who argue that mastering the language of a particular practice, whether tennis or gravitational wave physics, involves a form of tacit knowledge they call "interactional expertise". We criticize this idea, but, by outlining a sketch of an externalist model of testimony, we highlight the connection between know-how, practical demonstration and linguistic articulation.

1. THREE SOURCES FOR TACIT KNOWLEDGE

1976 AND ALL THAT

In this chapter we will offer a preliminary explication of the concept of *tacit* or *personal* knowledge by focusing on aspects of the work of three thinkers: Michael Polanyi, Gilbert Ryle and Martin Heidegger. Having given this book its theme, the inclusion of Polanyi requires little justification; likewise that of Ryle, since, as we remarked in the introduction, there are good prima facie reasons for associating tacit knowledge with both knowing that and knowing how, yet it cannot seemingly be both. For some readers Ryle's anti-intellectualist argument for the primacy of knowing how will be sufficient to explain the introduction of Heidegger. To this can be added both the interest Ryle took at one time in the development of phenomenology and the isomorphism between Polanyi's work and that of one of Heidegger's scions, Merleau-Ponty. However, what follows is not intended as mere background. Polanyi *et al.* share a *concern* and a *method*, which serve both to illuminate the concept we are proposing to elucidate and to diagnose why competing views fall into the trap that (we will in subsequent chapters claim) they do. It is in the account given of Heidegger that this becomes clearest.

At its most basic, the *concern* is to rebut what is construed as an unacceptably Cartesian or Intellectualist conception of knowing. The *method* then has two characteristic moments: a *negative* phase involves the deployment of a regress argument against that conception, and a *positive* phase: the instatement of some progressive alternative. One important feature of this is the relationship between the two phases, of which two interpretations are immediately forthcoming, one *sceptical* the other *transcendental*. According to the former, the opposed conception of knowing is shown to give rise to a regress because it presupposes a process or activity of cognition that is itself question-begging. According to the latter, the conception of knowing is taken to be legitimate only in so far as its purview is restricted and the progressive alternative acknowledged as an account of how things must be at a "deeper" level. On the *sceptical* interpretation the progressive alternative is proffered as just that – as an *alternative*. On the *transcendental* interpretation it is advanced as a *solution* to the regress problem. Crucially, then, although the transcendental strategy can radicalize our understanding of knowing in so far as it shows that the opposed conception is incomplete, its authority derives from redeeming some element of that conception.

Key to the position advanced in this chapter is the idea that the regress arguments to be examined take their form from Kant's in the schematism chapter of the *Critique of Pure Reason*. The schematism concerns the way concepts are applied in experience or, in Kant's term, to intuitions. The worry is that any account of how this can be a rule governed application of the concept to the intuition threatens a regress when it comes to selecting the right rule to match the right concept and intuition. As we will see (§"Schemata"), the account of the schematism of concepts is presented by way of a (transcendental) *solution* to the threatened rule-regress. But the form that the regress takes is in turn conditioned by the specific character of the understanding's judgements that Kant desires to legitimate. From this perspective, Heidegger, Ryle and Polanyi are viewed as undertaking the same task: offering their own versions of how to think about the work of schematism by offering their own responses to the rule-regress. As noted, this is most evident in the work of the early Heidegger (see §§"Being in the world" to "A world well lost?" below); but what is obvious there serves to clarify what is less so in the work of Ryle and Polanyi. It is to Polanyi, however, that we will turn first and to the view that the path to understanding tacit knowledge is signposted not "know thyself" but "we can know more than we can tell".

VARIETIES OF OBJECTIVITY

Michael Polanyi[1] made important contributions to several areas of physical chemistry before turning his attention to economics, politics and – increasingly – the philosophy of science.[2] To reflect this change in his interests he resigned the chair of physical chemistry at Manchester in 1948 in favour of a specially created professorship in social studies. Although occasionally cited by contemporary philosophers (cf. Johnson 2007: 4), Polanyi's work has not been given any significant critical evaluation;[3] although since even the most ardent of his admirers concede that his writings are at best "rather rapid-fire sequences of insights ... without much pause for examining ... possible counterarguments" (Sen 2009: 15) and at worst "often obscure, sometimes mistaken, and couched in a rhetoric that most philosophers find it hard to tolerate" (Grene 1977: 167), he did little to obviate such a fate. Nevertheless, Polanyi was much admired during his lifetime, not least for his defence of science's speculative autonomy against the rival conceptions of two rather contrasting opponents: on the one hand, that of the Stalinists; on the other, that of the positivists. Since these "defences" offer a convenient way into the topic, we will examine them briefly.

In relation to Soviet science, the issue is with how, given the logical gap between evidence and theory, one might distinguish a Lysenko from a Dobzhansky (see *TD*: 3; Dobzhansky 1955). For Polanyi, the understanding of the "nature and justification of scientific knowledge" (*PK*: vii) that made the crude Soviet instrumentalization of inquiry possible is itself based on the presupposition that "believing what I might conceivably doubt" entails a "self-contradiction" that is more than just "apparent" (*PK*: 109). The key to exposing Stalin's pseudo-scientific abettors, then, is to undertake the "conceptual reform" (*PK*: 109) required to resolve the apparent self-contradiction that makes their position seem plausible. That reform turns on the "novel idea of human knowledge" (*TD*: 4) summarized in the slogan referred to in the introduction, to the effect that our knowledge outruns the limits of what we can report.

Since the underlying worry here is a variant of the demarcation problem that exercised, among others, the logical positivists and Karl Popper, one might suppose that Polanyi would find common cause with such approaches. However, when critics write admiringly of Polanyi's post-empiricist philosophy of science, they have in mind the following sort of stance: "I agree that the process of understanding leads beyond ... what a strict empiricism regards as the domain of legitimate knowledge; but I reject such an empiricism" (*TD*: 21).

For Polanyi, the reductive empiricist's blindness to the creative, non-codifiable dimension of inquiry turns out to be yet another manifestation of the cultural malaise that found expression in Lysenkoism. In the terms introduced above, the *concern* is to overcome an intellectual worldview still in thrall to the quest for the "purity" of an objective conception of knowledge in response to a global sceptical doubt: "The method of doubt ... trusts that the uprooting of all voluntary components of belief will leave behind unassailed a residue of knowledge that is completely determined by objective evidence" (*PK*: 269).

The implication here is familiar from pragmatist and other narratives of the distorting effect of a Cartesian "quest for certainty": an *un*reasonable doubt determines epistemic criteria that set the bar for knowledge beyond the reach of finite, embodied creatures. Since this undermines any cognitive distinctions among dubitable beliefs, the threat is that one is left with no criterion with which to disambiguate genuine scientific inquiry from ideological usurpation. Of course, this threat would be obviated if one could regroup around the idea that the *subjective* is the source of doubt, to be contrasted with a realm of *objective* observation statements; that scientific theories are economical summaries of experience, which by definition they can never transcend. For Polanyi, the exacted cost of this false dichotomy (cf. *PK*: 300) between a disavowed subjectivity and a "strict objectivity" (*PK*: 18) is a conception of science that denies the *"personal participation* of the knower in all acts of understanding" (*PK*: vii).

Crucially – and we will return to this below – the consequence of this denial is that it renders inexplicable the very objectivity towards which it aspires. For Polanyi, then, the *genuinely* objective is not the converse of the subjective; rather, it is that towards which we understand ourselves to be striving when we undertake responsibility for our attempts to comprehend the world. According to this "conceptual reform", once we recognize that objectivity only becomes intelligible through its relation to the *personal* we will come to acknowledge the extent and ineliminability of the tacit dimension of knowledge; of all the mute skills, expertise and connoisseurship that cannot be made explicit and yet without which no explicit knowledge would be possible.

At this point it will be useful to recall the three principles that might be invoked in characterizing a position on the status of tacit knowing:

PC   All knowledge can be fully articulated, or codified, in context-independent terms.

PI   There can be knowledge that cannot be articulated.

PA   All knowledge can be articulated, either in context-independent terms or in context-dependent terms.

Although from the foregoing it appears that Polanyi would reject PC, we are not yet in a position to fully classify his position. In order to do so we must first determine *why* an "objectivist" "ideal of scientific detachment" is held to be both self-defeating and to "falsif(y) our whole outlook far beyond the domain of science" (*PK*: vii). The reason for this is obvious enough: if tacit *knowing* is in some sense *personal* knowing we need to ascertain how, in opposing the *personal* to the "objectivist ideal", Polanyi avoids it becoming merely the (old) *subjective* and thus undermines its cognitive bona fides. Referring back to the point about *method*, then, he must

(a) *negatively* undermine the "objectivist" account of knowing,

and

(b) *positively* advance an account of personal knowing.

As noted above, Polanyi is not one for pausing much over alternatives, and although his texts contain a vast array of empirical examples, many on which he was exemplarily well qualified to comment, his interpretations often beg the question at hand. Nevertheless, he does present more formal considerations aimed at impugning "objectivism" (a), the most important of which[4] is hinted at above: a regress argument to the effect that if we accept PC and assume that the subject matter of all inquiries can be fully codified or "intellectualized" (is "capable of being clearly stated"; *TD*: 22) then we will never be able to establish that we know anything. Here's one version, which we will refer to as (I):

(I)   Consider, as part of one's inquiry into how the world is, one's knowledge claim that the Earth is round. If one wishes to explicate this claim one must understand that in making it one is committing oneself to it, asserting it, holding it to be true: "the acceptance of any of our own utterances as true involves our approval of ... a skilful act of our own – the act of knowing" (*PK*: 70–71). Since that commitment or appraisal of our own – our personal – "art of knowing" (*ibid.*: 70) is an act that takes place in the world it is consequently an aspect both of the world and of the knowing that one wishes to explicate. However, to explicate that one must understand that in making it one is committing oneself to it, asserting it ... and so on.

Although the terms in which it is couched are less familiar, this presents us with something akin to the traditional Agrippan argument against evidentialism. If in order for S to be justified in believing that *p* she must be aware that her evidence in favour of *p* has the justificatory force it does one might naturally inquire what justifies S in her conviction that her *evidence* does in fact favour *p*.[5] In other words, if, in order to know that *p*, S must *know* that she knows that *p* then presumably she has to *know* that she knows that she knows that *p* (etc.). Internalist solutions to this sort of threatened regress are traditionally either foundationalist or coherentist. Polanyi's has something of the character of the first: "we always know tacitly that we are holding our explicit knowledge to be true" (*SM*: 12), where such knowledge is understood to be "unformulated knowledge, *such as we have of something we are in the act of doing*" (*ibid.*, emphasis added). Accordingly, we are left in the paradoxical situation with respect to PC that its affirmation presupposes the sort of knowledge it repudiates: "tacit knowing is in fact the dominant principle of all knowledge, and ... its rejection would ... involve the rejection of any knowledge whatever" (*SM*: 13).

In the terms introduced at the beginning of this chapter, it is evident enough that (I) constitutes a transcendental solution to the regress. So the negative and positive phases of the methodical attack on the "objectivist ideal" go together. There is nothing contradictory in believing what can be doubted because doubting, as a reflective action, *presupposes* a structure of *personal* commitments that cannot, on pain of regress, be subjected to recursive scrutiny. We are knowers, then, but we are inescapably *tacit* knowers. Our reflective, "tellable" – for Polanyi, *explicit* – knowledge is possible only on the basis of the sort of "untellable", "unformulated" knowledge that we exemplify when engaged in worldly activities. Moreover, the colloquy between heroic epistemologist and sceptic takes place only (and therefore futilely) against the backdrop of this knowledge "hidden" from doubt. This sounds rather Kantian, of course, but not for nothing is *Personal Knowledge* subtitled *Towards a Post-Critical Philosophy*. Although not judged as culpable as Descartes, then, Kant is nevertheless complicit in the "objectivist ideal" through his insistence that "reason must in all its undertakings subject itself to criticism" (Kant 1996: B766; quoted at *PK*: 271–2). For Polanyi, it is this emphasis on critical reflection that leads to an obsessive insistence on the "objectivity" of explicit knowledge at the cost of remaining insensible to its tacit foundations.

In the light of this anti-Kantian line it is worth presenting another argument derived from Polanyi's work, which we will refer to as (II):

(II)   Imagine one wants to apply a theory T (or, indeed, PC) to an act or object of experience X. To understand X as something to which one might apply *any* theory is an act of tacit knowing. In this sense, the meaning T has as a *theory* (of X) is partly determined by something known prior to and independently of T; but this dependence on the unexplicatable is doubled, for in order for T to be a theory *of X*, one must have "interiorized" T in the sense of having developed a certain mastery in the practical application of T to Xs. So a "theory can be constructed only by relying on prior tacit knowing and can function as a theory only within an act of tacit knowing, which consists in our attending from it to the previously established experience on which it bears" (*TD*: 21).

Crucially, the sort of mastery referred to is taken to be of a kind with the "inarticulate ... art" required to use words denotatively, since that too involves applying "the theory ... implied by our language to the particulars of which we speak" (*PK*: 81).

Now, although (II) is not presented formally as a regress argument, the relation to (I) is clear. Since "deprived of their tacit coefficients, all formulae, all maps and graphs ... mathematical theor(ies) mean(s) nothing" (*KB*: 195), any attempt to construe their meaning on the assumption that they can be made fully explicit/are codified will generate a regress. There is, however, rather more to say about (II), but we will be better prepared to do so having gleaned more details of the positive phase of Polanyi's method. The foregoing considerations seem to suggest that Polanyi would reject not only PC but also PA. Our working hypothesis, then, is that Polanyi subscribes to PI. With that in mind let's turn, then, to what Polanyi has to say about the structure of tacit knowledge (b).

THE TACIT DIMENSION

Since he is aiming at "conceptual reform", Polanyi's empirical examples are on somewhat negotiable terms with the metaphysical claim that tacit knowing is "the dominant principle of all knowledge". He does however recur frequently to two that purport to "show most clearly what is meant by saying that one can know more than one can tell" (*TD*: 8). The first (which captures the basic claim) draws on experiments by McCleary and Lazarus (1949, 1951), which aim to show that tachistoscopic exposures too brief to allow subjects to make conscious (reportable; articulated) perceptual distinctions can result nevertheless in responses that demonstrate the acquisition of non-conscious discriminatory abilities as measured by galvanic skin response (GSR). This level of perceptual discrimination is denominated "subception", and the associated phenomenon came thereafter – appropriately enough – to be called "implicit learning" (learning without awareness).[6] In the example Polanyi chooses, subjects are exposed to a variety of meaningless syllables, some of which are correlated with the administration of an electric shock. After a time, the subject evinces a "subceptive" GSR recognition of the "shock" syllables, although they are unable to identify them consciously.

Polanyi's informal characterization of the process involved here is the "active shaping of experience" (*TD*: 6) that is performed in the discovery of knowledge. This "integrative" principle is deemed at work at all levels: from perception – "its most impoverished form" (*TD*: 7) – and such "extensions" of the perceiving body as are manifest in, say, the use of a stick to help orientate oneself in the world; through skilful performances, such as expert diagnoses and the seeing in the arrangement of pieces on a chess board an opportunity to win; all the way to works of "scientific and artistic genius" (*TD*: 6). Where explicit knowledge is characterized by our ability to reflect critically on our reasons for believing what we do, tacit knowledge, lacking that aspect of discursiveness, is *a*critical and inarticulate, based – crucially – on rules that can be explicated. In each case of the latter we find a triadic relationship involving the two terms of which a subject is aware/knows (Polanyi uses the terms interchangeably) and the subject for whom the connection exists.

In the given example, the subject S has a subsidiary awareness of the particulars that are shock syllables, but only in so far as they are *shock* syllables.

That is to say, to know them tacitly is to "disattend" *from* them *to* something of which one is focally aware; viz., the shocks. The latter are known specifiably. What it is to know something – in the sense of its being an action or object of one's focal awareness – is for it to be the *meaning* of some particulars which are brought together in an integrative act. In this respect, the face recognized *is* the meaning of the particular features that comprise it. What we know, then, when we know something tacitly is the entity constituted by the two terms. But that entity is not their mere juxtaposition; rather, it is the terms *as understood* by a *person*. To know, be aware, or understand that *that* is a face is to "rely on" our awareness of its constituent features for "attending to" their joint meaning (*TD*: 13).

We can make this account of *what* is known tacitly a little clearer – and eliminate a potential misunderstanding – if we return to Polanyi's example. Its illustrative advantage is that it obviates the seeming paradox involved in first-person reports to the effect that one can know more than one can tell since it divides the linguistic labour between experimenter (E, who can tell) and subject (S, who cannot). But this strategy for elucidating the concept is problematic: it implies that what S knows *tacitly*, E knows *explicitly*. What do they both know? Well, perhaps they both know that (say) "'ξ' is a shock syllable". But it seems odd to ascribe that sort of knowledge to S. They might not have any idea what a "shock syllable" is, nor be able to discriminate between "ξ" and some similar but nevertheless distinct symbol untested but identifiable by E. Moreover, if S knows *tacitly* what E knows *explicitly* then there is nothing here to suggest that PC is incorrect.

Despite this, Polanyi is quite clear that S's inculcated anticipation constitutes a form of tacit knowing no different from – to take a favoured example from Gestalt psychology – that manifested in a person's ability to recognize a face or emotion, where what they cannot tell is *how* they know. And as we saw above, tacit knowledge in general is characterized as the "unformulated" knowledge we have of "something we are in the act of doing", which appear subject to PI. The fact that S cannot tell *how* she knows that *that* is John and *that* he is sad ("it *looks* like John"; "he *looks* sad") appear on the face of it to turn on the subsidiary particulars being unspecifiable, and thus something of which she "cannot tell" (*TD*: 8).

One source of confusion here is that Polanyi sometimes talks about subsidiary awareness (of the unspecifiable) *as opposed to* focal awareness (of the specifiable). Since awareness is also used interchangeably with knowledge one might be forgiven for identifying focal awareness with specifiable knowledge (of *things* known specifiably) and for regarding the latter as a discrete state of knowing distinguishable in principle from the (equally) distinct state of knowing the unspecifiable that *is* tacit knowledge. But "all knowledge ... is either tacit or rooted in tacit knowledge" (*KB*: 144); indeed, Polanyi's "solution" to the regress (I) outlined in §"Varieties of objectivity" *requires* that "grounding". Likewise, although Polanyi talks of the particulars subsidiary to, say, an expert diagnosis or act of cotton-classing (or of chick-sexing) as being known "ineffably" (cf. *PK*: 88), the formal definition of tacit knowing is in terms of the *way* something of which we are subsidiarily aware (i.e. know unspecifiably) is presented to us *through* its specifiable meaning (being specifiably known).

Unfortunately, this merely serves to introduce a separate source of confusion because to know something specifiably is related to "identifiable things which can be described in terms of classes of which such things are members" (*PK*: 62). It does not then seem contentious to assimilate "specifiable knowing" to "explicit knowing" and suggest thereby that what one knows but cannot tell are indeed the *un*specifiable particulars involved in an instance of explicit knowing. From the perspective of a contemporary epistemologist, this would serve a particular purpose. Informally, what one might want to say of the chick-sexer or of the Polynesian navigator is that they *in some sense* "know" that *that* chick is male, or that *that* is the right way to head, and that that sense aims at registering their evident success (by explicit standards) in doing what it is that they do. Now, one of the reasons evidentialists have qualms about ascriptions of what we might call *explicit* knowledge in such cases is that nothing adducible – nothing *tellable* – is available to the sorter or navigator that would rationally commit them to believing *this* ("it's male"; "it's *this* way") as opposed to *that* ("it's female"; "it's *that* way"). The specifiable dimension of knowledge, then, is a way of individuating *what* it is *that* someone cannot tell. S cannot tell *how* she is able to recognize John as (specifiably) John, nor John *how* he is able to make a difficult (but specifiable) diagnosis, or ride a bicycle, or sex a chick. On this account, then, S cannot "tell" how they are able to sort the syllables they are presented with.

So what's the confusion? Well, according to Polanyi animals, too, have tacit knowledge. Polanyi's examples range so wide in part because he is at pains to support the view, not only that tacit knowledge is pervasive but that "all human knowledge is ... shaped by the inarticulate mental faculties which we share with animals" (*SM*: 26). Indeed, what Polanyi means by knowledge *simpliciter* is the capacity to learn; in particular to exhibit the sort of "latent learning" that manifests itself as an ability to solve problems in a variety of circumstances (cf. *PK*: 71–7) in what might be called a "skilful" way. It may well take explicit knowledge to *specify* what the term of focal awareness is (and to *theorize* tacit knowing), then, but the role *as* the specified term is functional, and however great our theoretical achievements, they "operate ultimately within the same medium of unformalized intelligence which we share with the animals." (*PK*: 82).

As it turns out, then, unspecifiability is a bit of a McGuffin. Animals know trivially (even if tacitly) more than they can tell because they can tell *nothing*. So Polanyi's position would qualify as PI (as opposed to PC) *on this basis* at least only if the tacit knowing we share with animals was such that the *particulars* known subsidiarily were in principle beyond our ken. This cannot, however, be the case. First, there is no natural order of things known subsidiarily. On the one hand, what is subsidiary can be an object of consciousness. On the other hand, one can, by a shift of attention, make the features attended *from* in seeing a face as a face themselves the objects of focal awareness, or concentrate on the discrete actions that go together to realize a skilful performance. Likewise, although what is known subsidiarily ranges from facial features like noses and sensations to muscular movements and unfelt and involuntary internal processes extending all the way to "neural traces in the cortex of the nervous system" (*TD*: 15), nothing renders any of these things known subsidiarily unspecifiable in principle.

So what is it, then, that is ineffable or untellable? The clue here is what Polanyi calls "weak" or "logical" (*SM*: 44; *PK*: 63) unspecifiability. The phenomenological basis advanced by Polanyi in favour of this is that someone cannot subject their skilled performance to analytic scrutiny (for reasons of improvement, say, or due to paralysing self-consciousness) while undertaking that performance. The tacit knowing exhibited in the skilful action is incompatible with the shift of focal attention towards its (putatively) constituent parts. To put it another way, *what it is* for something to be the demonstration of a skill is for it to involve the active integration of the particulars involved in such a way that one is disattending from them. Although Polanyi does not always make this as clear as he might, this phenomenological feature is a tip-off to the logic of what he sometimes calls "tacit inference" (cf. Polanyi 1966). The relationship between the two terms that constitutes tacit knowing *is* the act of understanding that is exhibited *in practice*: that is the *way* in which the subsidiary particulars, although their "logical" relationship to focal object, are *known*.

We have, moreover, the following: "Since tacit knowing establishes a meaningful relation between the two terms, we may identify it with the understanding of the comprehensive entity which these two terms jointly constitute" (*TD*: 13). That is to say, there is an "*ontological* aspect" of tacit knowing (*ibid.*): "the kind of comprehensive entities exemplified by skillful human performances are real things" (*ibid.*: 33). When S makes an expert diagnosis or *perceives* as supremely accomplished a recital of Liszt's "Petrarch Sonatas", her tacit knowledge is founded on the very relation that constitutes the entity she is perceiving. Tacit knowing is uncodifiable or ineffable, then, because the cognitive integration of the particulars cannot be analytically "reverse engineered" without loss. It is a *personal* act involving the "existential participation of the knower" (*SM*: 32) for which no set of rules can be specified. Equally, when reflection destroys a performance it does so because the entity that is the understanding in practice "disintegrates" under inspection. This does not of course mean that we cannot come up with rules to help instruct the journeyman; but their increasingly skilful judgements are not based on internalizing those rules, merely on using them heuristically.

PLATONISM NATURALIZED

Summarizing the foregoing, tacit knowing is, on Polanyi's account, best characterized as activity-dependent understanding; or as understanding in practice, where practice is expanded to include the conditions required for reflective knowing. In relation to Polanyi's contribution to formulating an account of tacit knowing there are two objectives to evaluate: (a) the *negative* attempt to undermine the "objectivist" account of knowing, and (b) the *positive* construal of an account of *personal* knowing. In relation to (b), the specific challenge is to respect the *personal* basis of all cognition while avoiding lapsing into subjectivism. Polanyi brings forward two sorts of considerations to bear on this challenge, one naturalistic in orientation and the other decidedly rationalist.

The first consideration derives from the repeated claim that even our highest cognitive achievements are, by virtue of their rootedness in the tacit, continuous with the abilities of non-verbal animals. And so, it might be thought, we can achieve the objectivity entailed by a particular sort of "quasi-realism" (cf. Blackburn 1993) by assuming that natural "cognitive" capacities, although rooted in the individual, are nevertheless universal (among the animals that count that is). Whatever its other merits, this would at least support the relevance of experimental psychological data to what are for many (although far from all) philosophers normative issues; and it does not seem entirely alien to versions of a pragmatist conception of inquiry.

Regarding that second consideration, we have the following: "the capacity of our minds to make contact with reality and the intellectual passion which impels us towards this contact will always suffice so to guide our personal judgement that it will achieve the full measure of truth" (*SM*: 27). And again: "discovery of objective truth in science … while using the experience of our senses as clues, transcends this experience by embracing the vision of a reality … which speaks for itself in guiding us to an ever deeper understanding of [it]" (*PK*: 5–6).

According to what Polanyi confesses to be an "out-dated Platonism" (*PK*: 6), the sort of ineffable understanding that we possess when we recognize a problem *as* a problem, or a solution as a solution *to* a problem when no criteria of verification (or, paradigm of normal science) is available is tacit knowing/understanding. Moreover, such knowing is objective (while being personal) because it is (and is *affirmed* as being) based on powers we possess for "recognizing rationality in nature" (*PK*: 13).[7]

Although one can readily sympathize with this hankering after a reconciliation of reason and nature, it is not quite clear how far up the phylogenetic tree one must clamber before one hears the world speak, nor if the bodily nature of our knowledge of it means that no full account of reality can ever be given (or even make sense; cf. Nagel 1986). However, what *is* clear is that on the face of it at least these two considerations – the naturalistic and the Platonic – pull in different directions: the former towards a reductionism that would favour PI and the other towards the sort of intellectualism that supports PC. The question is: can this tension be overcome in such a way that it gives us a satisfactory account of tacit knowledge *qua* personal knowledge?

We can approach this further question by returning to another feature of Polanyi's account of tacit knowledge: *awareness*. As noted, we are said to *rely on* our subsidiary awareness of unspecified particulars *to attend to* (be focally aware of) the thing known specifiably (be it an act or object). But although we can get a phenomenological grip on the idea of *focal* awareness, the idea of awareness in general becomes increasingly elusive as we shift to other "levels". More specifically, as Grene (1977) notes,[8] it seems odd to think of oneself as "aware" of "neural traces in the cortex of the nervous system" (*TD*: 15).[9] Of course, one can see the temptation here. A concept of awareness that is not implicated in the Cartesian metaphysics of mind and traces an intentional arc from neuron to worldly perception would be an admirable way of demonstrating the "bodily roots of all thought" (*ibid.*). Moreover, it may well be the case that awareness here is best thought of as a revisionary concept that aims to capture the findings of relevant scientific research.[10] But that suggestion sits uneasily with the thought that there is no "natural" order of things of which one can be subsidiarily aware.

There are two issues here. The first takes us back to the dust thrown up by Polanyi's temptation to equate awareness with knowledge, thus suggesting that we might talk meaningfully of one's subsidiary awareness in isolation from its focal object/meaning. One possible solution is to think of subsidiary awareness as another name for a subject's (a *person's*) intentional relationship to the world as expressed through her skilful and other doings. As it turns out, that proposal will make a great deal more sense set against the background of a different approach, so we will put it to one side for the time-being. Before considering an alternative solution, let us take up that second issue. Now, we have noted that both states of our physical bodies and theories can serve as the "from" components in tacit knowing; indeed, according to Harré (1977),[11] Polanyi applies his "from ... to" structure to *radically* different sorts of cases. From our perspective two are important: perception/gestalt cases, where we disattend from component parts (noses, elements of the sensory field) to the whole thing, and cases where we attend from a theory to something it applies to. In the first case, Harré takes it that the items disattended from are objects known "by acquaintance", so we cannot tell what we know because such knowledge is non-propositional. In the second case, we cannot tell what we know because, although propositional, we are not attending to it.

Neglecting for the time-being the Russellian assumption about the status of singular thoughts, the mistake Harré makes here – albeit understandably – is to regard the "from …" term as the isolatable component of tacit knowing. That makes more interesting Harré's characterization of the second sort of "attending from":

> revealing the tacit would be revealing the theoretical or cognitive conditions of experience … a contribution to the understanding of the Kantian schematisms by which the categories inform experience … In Polanyian terms we must have a certain theory *from* which we are attending in order to understand or experience whatever … appears in the perceptual field … under a certain category. (*Ibid.*: 173)

We noted above that awareness might have another possible signification – one that captures the personal dimension without sacrificing the knowledge – and here it is: the Kantian suggestion that the "*I think* must be *capable* of accompanying all my presentations" (1996: B132). Let us therefore examine if this gives us a way of thinking about tacit knowledge that overcomes the apparent conflict between intellectualism and naturalism, between what we have and what we share with the beasts.

SCHEMATA

As we have seen, the integration that characterizes tacit knowing is in operation from the most complex employment of theories down to the basic operations of perception. Indeed, the latter, as "the most impoverished form of tacit knowing," forms "the bridge between the higher creative powers of man and the bodily processes" that we "attend from" in our basic dealings with the world (*TD*: 7). Moreover, it will be recalled, many of our basic cognitive abilities (of which perception is the most basic) are shared with (many) animals: they have tacit knowledge because they can learn through interacting with their environment. Although the vocabulary is alien to Polanyi, one way of expressing this is that the tacit knowing of animals is *contentful*; indeed, given its intrinsic "from … to" structure, *intentionally* contentful, although not articulable. And since our explicit knowing is grounded in the tacit, it seems reasonable to conclude that the content of our tacit knowing *qua* tacit knowing is similarly contentful but not articulable. That would in turn lend support to PI. One potentially fruitful way to think about the "integration" that takes place in an act of knowing/understanding is in terms of the *synthesis* of the relevant particulars. In other words, what it is to attend "from ... to" in an act of understanding is to employ the appropriate schema.

In the "Analytic of Principles" Kant (1996) offers a regress argument that should be familiar from the above. Although to understand is to have in one's possession the rule by which a determination (of something) can be made, the actual *use* of a rule requires judgement. When one asks how such judgements are made, however, we find that this could only be made fully explicit if understanding could provide a rule for the *general* application of rules. But, being a rule, this too requires judgement to be used. The only way to escape the threatened regress is to acknowledge that the ability to employ rules correctly is a *personal* matter, which cannot be taught (in the sense of explicit instructions) but only practised (*ibid.*: B172) "through examples and actual tasks" (*ibid.*: B173): "Hence a physician, a judge, or a statesman may have in his mind many fine pathological, juridical, or political rules even to the degree where he can become a thorough teacher of them himself, and will yet easily blunder in applying them" (*ibid.*). Kant then goes on to declare that although "general logic" can say no more here, "transcendental logic" can since it deals with the *a priori* content of cognition; that is to say, with the application of the pure categories of the understanding in experience. As concepts, these are rules that govern the synthetic activity of the subject in thinking as a unity the parts of the manifold given in intuition.[12] The question then becomes: what makes the application of a rule possible? How do the categories determine the manifold by making it intelligible? And the answer is through the intervention of schemata: products of the imagination that constitute rules for "determining our intuition in accordance with such and such a general concept" (*ibid.*: A141/B180). There is no question here of asking what rule governs this rule: it is a "secret art residing in the depths of the human soul" (*ibid.*: A141/B180–81).

One of the peculiarities of this section of the *Critique* is that, while Kant begins by claiming that what we might call empirical rules cannot be made explicit, he introduces the schemata in relation to *a priori* rules which have no bearing on the competencies of judges, physicians and statesmen. One might therefore conclude that schemata have nothing to do with empirical concepts. And yet Kant does discuss them here. In relation to empirical schemata, and to empirical synthesis in general, a relevant debate has emerged about whether Kant should be viewed as a conceptualist or a non-conceptualist (in relation to content). So, for example, on Pendlebury's (1995) "constructionalist"[13] reading,[14] schemata are capacities for synthesis that play an essential role both in the formation and the application of concepts. To flesh this out, he considers intuitions to have (intentional/representational) content by virtue of their being grouped together in certain classes. For an intuition to have the content *green* is for it to be placed in a certain similarity class; and the grouping of intuitions in this way is dispositional. The first point here is that the groupings are not made on the basis of identifying properties in intuitions: the dispositions, capacities and processes involved in their classification is the "secret art" that is *constitutive* of their content. If one is disposed to group {} with the *blues* rather than the *greens* then one determines one's experience as having that content: "the groupings underlying the contents of our intuitions are not found, but made ... they are ... genuine and spontaneous syntheses" (*ibid.*: 786).

The second point is that "schemata and their products" are preconceptual because not "typically accessible to consciousness" and "when exercised ... yield discriminating responses rather than articulable, classificatory judgements" (*ibid.*: 787). On this account, the application of concepts to intuitions is only possible if schemata involve synthesis that delivers up representations with intentional content. But this applies not only to empirical concepts but to the categories themselves: they operate as higher-order meta-dispositions, which order intuitions into kind-classes and in so doing constitute that element of their intentional content.

Pendlebury's account requires that the synthetic work of the imagination is isolatable, not "transcendentally" or conceptually but operationally, from that of the understanding if nonconceptual content is to be forthcoming. This is not merely a question of exegesis, however; the nonconceptualist reading of Kant is intended to buttress the claim that with respect to the synthetic work of the imagination we are dealing with the more primitive, sub-personal aspects of cognition that are shared with animals.[15] To repeat the point: the synthetic work of the imagination, in functional isolation from the understanding (which animals are not deemed to have on this account), is taken to have the plasticity or flexibility ("spontaneity") required to make sense of animals possessing representations with intentional content. If we think about knowledge *per se* as deriving from abilities that are "bolted on" to this shared capacity then we can only be said to *know* more than we can tell in so far as the transition from nonconceptual to conceptual content involves processes that could in some interesting way be regarded as "knowledge" but are not in themselves explicable.

Pendlebury offers no account of how concepts come to be applied to the products – schemata or otherwise – of this nonconceptual synthesis. But this is not a trivial matter, since it bears directly on the question of whether or not "discriminatory responses" should be thought sufficient to deliver up what we might think of as *intentional* content. After all, the point of characterizing the content as intentional is that it represents in their *unity* objects out there in the world – objects that can subsequently be brought under concepts. But it is hard to see how this dispositional account would deliver up representations of objects that populate (in their nonconceptual form) the environment of animals and are at the same time apt to become objects *of* cognition.[16] This introduces a neglected point. As we observed above, one of the reasons given for maintaining that intentional content is nonconceptual is that it is not typically "accessible to consciousness" (cf. Pendlebury 1995: 785), where what's given to consciousness are items "represented in experience" (*ibid.*: 794). In Polanyian terms, this seems to refer to *focal* awareness; but as we have seen, this is not the whole story. Indeed, one might claim that making sense of intentional content necessitates acknowledging the unity that awareness/consciousness brings to the entire process of constitution.

As we have seen, the status of "awareness" is open, but we can get another take on it by looking briefly at a conceptualist approach to content. If nonconceptualism turns on isolating the imagination from understanding, it is perhaps not surprising that conceptualism tends for the most part to assimilate the former to the latter and see the understanding always-already implicated in the synthetic work of the imagination in sensibility. Variations of this approach are offered by, for example, Sellars (1968) and Strawson (1970), its most influential contemporary proponent being McDowell (1994 *passim*). The version we have in mind, however, takes up explicitly the subject of awareness. In a recent piece, Ginsborg (2009) acknowledges that part of the appeal of nonconceptualism is that it "seems to do better justice … to what we might call the primitive character of perception relative to thought and judgement" (*ibid.*: 4). Part of the concern here is that it seems counterintuitive to think that one needs to possess the concept *kudu* in order to have kudu-perceptions; and although it is one of the tricks of the conceptualist's trade to point out that one needs the concept to make *this* point, it is nevertheless the case that one acquires the concept kudu by having perceptions that, while not perhaps being fully fledged kudu-perceptions (lacking the concept), somehow eventuate in one's possession of the concept.[17] Viewed thus, one can see why some spontaneous work on the part of the productive imagination is required; the point is, does it necessitate the "intervention" of the understanding in such a way that content implied is both intentional *and* conceptual? Ginsborg's answer is yes.

According to the sort of naturalistic (one might say Quinean) account given by the nonconceptualist, when a lion perceives a kudu as a potential meal it is through dispositions to associate the perception with evoked past perceptions of kudu, their pursuit, the satisfaction of hunger and so on. On Ginsborg's view, *that* our perceptual experiences have the specific conceptual content they do is due to similar dispositions; but what makes our experiences intentionally contentful in the first place is due to something that the animals do not possess. In our case the "synthesis involves understanding", which is to say that making the associations "involves a consciousness of normativity," of taking oneself to be doing as one ought (Ginsborg 2009: 11). Talk of "consciousness" seems more phenomenologically exacting than "awareness" and Ginsborg does occasionally use the latter term instead so we will stick with that. On this account, then, it is because we, unlike animals, are "aware" that the sorts of associations brought to mind by a present perception are appropriate in relation to it that gives our synthesized perception its object-directedness. One need not possess the concept *kudu* prior to the synthesis that issues in a kudu-perception because in that sense one's response to a kudu is determined by the same sort of natural associative dispositions. But, being *aware*, unlike the lion, of the rightness of our associations in synthesis, perceptual synthesis issues in our case in an intentional representation. That, of course, is only half the story, for the suggestion is that a lion's kudu-perception would have the same conceptual content as ours (assuming identical associative dispositions) *if it had understanding*, and we have yet to see how conceptual content is introduced into the picture. Ginsborg's thought here is a rather Wittgensteinian one: to make the discriminations and associations determined by our natural dispositions, aware that in synthesizing perceptions we do as we ought, *just is* to follow the rule that is the relevant concept:

> The consciousness of normative necessity in these associations is responsible ... for the object-directed character of our perceptions; but insofar as our particular way of associating present with past sense-impressions on any given occasion is sensitive to the object's being of this or that particular kind, it is also responsible for the object's being perceived as belonging to that kind, and thus for the object's being brought under the corresponding concept. (*Ibid.*: 18–19)

TACIT KNOWING SO FAR

Ginsborg is keen to defend the foregoing as a conceptualist account, but it is best characterized as a piece of anti-*non*conceptualist therapy, showing that there is nothing to be gained by digging deep into Kant's modular mind in order to find some level amenable to naturalistic explanation. As such it helps us liberate Polanyi from some of the self-inflicted problems raised in §"Platonism naturalized". As we have seen, awareness is intended to characterize the structure of tacit knowing of all creatures; but if we restrict it in the way suggested by Ginsborg's reading of Kant we can do justice to the complex achievements of other animals – and indeed, to the capacities we share with them – without having to see our skilful copings as directly related to their complex behaviours. On the face of it, this seems entirely reasonable: S's riding a bicycle does not seem commensurate with a chimpanzee's, and the performance of a Beethoven sonata, the delivery of a forehand smash or the diagnosis of a mental illness seem even less productively compared to the abilities of animals. On this view, lacking awareness of the requisite sort, the imaginative synthesis that animals undertake is different from ours, and so we liberate an account of tacit knowledge that is tied to awareness and to the particular competencies of human beings. In doing so we free ourselves from the temptation to take perception[18] as a "primitive" bridge linking us with other animals, and for now at least set-aside this unfortunate contemporary fascination[19] with wrestling something of empirical consequence from the workings of the schematism. It also means that we can return in the appropriate spirit to the argument (II) visited briefly at the end of §"Varieties of objectivity".

As initially presented, the thought was that to use a theory T requires tacit knowing; and that since language is a theory, *all* explicit knowledge "must rely on being tacitly understood and applied" (*TD*: 7). The emphasis here is on the fact that *anything* can serve as the subsidiary term in tacit knowledge, from subliminal processes and objects of perception through to complex theories and – indeed – moral teachings. To understand a theory in terms of the items to which it applies is to "interiorize" it; or, to borrow a term from the hermeneutic tradition (cf. Dilthey), to "indwell" it: "We may be said to live in the particulars which we comprehend, in the same sense as we live in the tools and probes which we use and in the culture in which we are brought up" (Polanyi 1966: 11).

This "indwelling" is intended to connote an extended cognition wherein the "body" as the locus of intentionality "expands" to integrate ever more and more diverse particulars through which it knows the world. Moreover, since the "froms" in the "from ... to" structures constitute no natural class the traditional distinction between the natural- and human-sciences is confuted: we get hermeneutics "all the way".[20] This means that concerning knowledge we cannot invoke "neural" structures in an *explanatory* context, where what it is to introduce something as part of a reductive explanation can be *contrasted* with a use relating to hermeneutic understanding. Likewise, since we are said to understand tacitly *that* a thing is the sort of thing it is (an X, in the sense used in (II)), and therefore an appropriate subject for certain sorts of ascriptions, we understand tacitly that a thing is a *person* prior to any ascription of mental states (cf. Strawson 1959) or to an evaluation of any of their doings: "The recognition of a *person* in the performance of a skill or in the conduct of a game of chess is intrinsic to the understanding of these matters" (*TD*: 30; original emphasis).

This puts us in a position to see that Polanyi can happily acknowledge that Kant's "secret art" of subsuming particulars under a general term is a "tacit art" (*KB*: 191) because (II) amounts to a reconstruction of what Kant's schematism is intended for. Just as for Kant the rule-regress is blocked by the schemata, so for Polanyi it is the practical mastery of concepts manifest in tacit knowing that shows how the reflective judgements constitutive of explicit knowing are possible. Moreover, this picture does not just apply to "theoretical" concepts. S's riding a bicycle and exquisite performance of a piece of music; her diagnosis of a mental illness and appreciation of a well-bowled googly: such skills and abilities as these are forms of tacit knowing that might be regarded as schemata-in-practice. Or, better still, as *personal* schemata.

This may sacrifice (the reductive) part of the "natural" aspect of tacit knowing that Polanyi wished to preserve through the connection with the abilities of animals, and as a consequence render largely irrelevant most of Polanyi's empirical examples. But it gives more traction to the notion that tacit knowing is in some sense *personal* knowing. It also indicates what Polanyi ought to have concluded when he took the following as *evidence* for the claim that "we can know more than we can tell":

- We cannot tell *how* we do something.
- Understanding in practice disintegrates under reflection.

Tacit knowledge might indeed be described as unformulated or untellable. But that is not because we cannot say or tell *how* we do something or *how* we know something, and that holds *even if* we can continue doing it while we are reflecting on it. Rather, it is because the knowledge we have of something when we are doing it is knowledge-how, and *knowing how* is untellable in the limited sense that it cannot be articulated in depersonalized, context-independent terms. Accordingly, the mistake Polanyi makes is to conclude that because something is untellable in the sense that it cannot be codified and is thus not subject to PC it must as a consequence fall under something like PI. That implies that putative untellability gestures towards something hidden, mysterious or ineffable and in turn shapes his particular, unworkable version of naturalized Platonism. But the fact that knowing how is untellable in this restricted sense does not mean that it is inarticulable. If one takes the person and their competences (the *personal*) as part of the context, then there is no reason why the content of knowing how should not be considered fully determinate. Or, rather, knowing how is a form of understanding that can only be appreciated as such when one takes into account the personal as part of the context in which it is manifested.[21] With that in mind, let us turn to a discussion of knowing how.

THE INTELLECTUALIST LEGEND

As we saw in §"Schemata", Kant contrasts the understanding's possession of rules with the ability to apply them to cases *in concreto*. Accordingly, one might be extensively schooled in regulative propositions "to the point of erudition" (1996: B172–3, n.) and yet be precluded from making sound application of them. This observation follows on immediately from the rule-regress argument: it is the very fact that understanding cannot prescribe rules for the application of its own rules that compels us to recognize the role "of so-called mother-wit" (*ibid.*: B172) and to acknowledge that from those who lack it intelligent performances will be in short supply. Indeed, the lack of the appropriate powers of judgement as evidenced in perform-ances (by the judge, the physician, the politician) that misfire "is in fact what we call stupidity, and for such a handicap there is no remedy" (*ibid.*: B172, n.).

Although Kant does not discuss the matter here, just as someone who *can* "tell" the rules might not be able to employ them, another who *cannot* might perform in a skilful, intelligent way. In a favoured example, one can be an intelligent chess player, showing in one's play that it is in accord with the basic rules and tactical principles, without being able to put those rules and principles into words. Equally, even if one can "tell" the rules, it is not the telling that manifests one's skill: that, as we have seen, is held to be what one knows tacitly and what is not *tellable*. And so, although one cannot transmit one's tacit knowledge by *instruction*, one might hope to pass it on by hint, example and criticism. What distinguishes the *expert* (as opposed to the informed but stupid) from the *layman* is not the possession of a body of truths but a diverse set of skills, competencies, dispositions, abilities; what Aristotle, as we saw in the introduction, refers to as *phronesis*. This is what characterizes both the scientific and artistic "explorer" for Polanyi. As we have seen, though, Polanyi's views come with some considerable baggage that we may not wish to check-in. So the question is: is there an alternative? Is there another way of making ready sense of the notion that one might know more than one can tell? The quick answer is yes:

> The fact that mathematics, philosophy, tactics, scientific method and literary style cannot be imparted but only inculcated reveals that these ... are not bodies of information but branches of knowledge-how ... The experts in them cannot tell us what they know, they can only show what they know by operating with cleverness, skill, elegance or taste.   (Ryle 1945–6: 15)

These "disciplines" exemplify in spades a feature common to all intelligent performances, be they practical or theoretical: know-how. We know more than we can tell because knowing how, unlike knowing that, cannot be artic-ulated in depersonalized, context-independent terms.

Ryle's justification of the centrality of knowing how to our cognitive achievements has a familiar structure. A diagnostic concern to show why previous thinkers have been misled on the topic sets the stage for the deploy-ment of versions of a regress argument. The diagnosis – "persuasions of (a) conciliatory kind" (Ryle 1949: 10) – addresses variations on "the Dogma of the Ghost in the Machine" (cf. *ibid.*: 17), the view that Descartes' separation of mind from nature bequeathed us a variety of otherwise dispensable philosophical problems and presuppositions. The Cartesian original sin is founded on, and has consequently given rise to, a category mistake, "the presentation of facts belonging to one category in the idioms of another" (*ibid.*). The *reductio ad absurdum* arguments are intended to expose the categorial misapplications made when the "dogma" or "intellectualist legend" controls one's thinking and open up the possibility of the alternative account of knowledge. We will begin by considering the regress arguments.

INTELLIGENCE IN PRACTICE

According to the "intellectualist legend", intelligent activities are either practical or theoretical. A *theoretical* activity (calculating, inferring, theorizing, etc.) involves the "consideration" of propositions, and in particular the sorts of "regulative propositions" we are accustomed to designate rules;[22] a *practical* activity (an action performed cleverly, skilfully, expertly, etc.) is, in so far as it is seen to manifest intelligence, based on the same activity of consideration, but requires the superaddition of *tertia*: "go-between faculties" (Ryle 1945–6: 1) that ensure that the proposition considered is executed correctly. In his presidential address, Ryle's generalized regress has two complementary lines. First, it is suggested that if we attribute intelligence to any activity on the basis that some rule is being applied "no intelligent act could ever begin" (*ibid.*: 2). The thought here is that to know a rule is not the same as being able to *apply* it, since the latter can be done correctly, *with* intelligence, or stupidly, without. But since to do something intelligently is, by hypothesis, to apply a rule in an appropriate way we open up an endless regress.

The second line applies specifically to practical (intelligent) activities, although not with intelligence per se (as the *intellectualist* views it) so much as with the gap between the consideration of a rule and its translation into action. From the perspective of practice, as it were, one might not see what the appropriate rule was; and from the perspective of intelligence one might fail to see that the rule one was presently contemplating was the correct one to apply in the circumstances. Moreover, even if one did have at one's disposal the correct rule, and even if one did judge that these are the circumstances in which one should apply it, one might still be too stupid to apply the rule correctly. If one did not make the *intellectualist's* distinction between the point of contemplation and the point of application in a practical activity – did not think of the doing bit of a practical activity as something added to the non-doing that is intelligence at work, but regarded them equally as "doings" – then we would be left with the first argument. And indeed, this is the one Ryle offers in *The Concept of Mind*. We have already seen Kant's version of it: if rules, to be applied intelligently (with judgement), required other rules (to be applied intelligently) there would be no application of rules.

This argument has come in for a great deal of attention recently. Since that will be addressed in detail in Chapter 2, it will serve this preliminary survey better to dwell a little on Ryle's positive phase, and the extent to which it supplements or supplants Polanyi's. In the absence of any temptation to locate intelligent happenings in some interior mental space, how should we regard the intelligent doings that constitute both theoretical and practical performances? Clearly, one must be able to disambiguate the skilful performance from the merely accidental occurrence; the artfully timed tumble of the clown, say, from the clumsy stumble of the dyspraxic. In the first instance, then, they are performances of the *person*, for which she is deemed responsible. Attending that attribution of *personal* responsibility is the thought that such performances are normative: in judging that someone has coped skilfully with something, one takes it that their actions were *intended*, that she "applies criteria in … trying to get things right" (1949: 29), and that that involves a critical awareness of and sensitivity to context. The knowledge-how possessed by the intelligent performer is the ability they possess to apply criteria "in the conduct of the performance itself" (*ibid.*: 40).

That sensitivity to context is further exhibited by our willingness to judge performances as clever or adept on the basis of a limited exposure. One would not look much beyond a rally to judge a player at Wimbledon skilful; although one might pause over a game happened upon in a local park. In general, "a modest assemblage of heterogeneous performances generally suffices" (*ibid.*: 45) to establish that someone knows how to do what they are doing. The exhibition of know-how is not exhausted in the performances one witnesses, then. It is part of the recognition of someone's ability that one is warranted in expecting that they will be able to cope skilfully with hitherto unforeseen eventualities. It is for this reason that Ryle is inclined to offer in place of the intellectualist legend an analysis that is broadly Aristotelian; and although he favours the vocabulary of dispositions and semi-dispositions to that, say, of virtues and *phronesis*, the general thought is that the abilities and skills that characterize knowing how are achievements of second nature (cf. *ibid.*: 41, 42). This is not intended to be a phenomenological point: clearly, the intellectualist's consideration and actualization of a rule in practice is not intended to capture the experience of riding one's bicycle, so the opposition to it does not turn in any way on the *failure* of such an account to do justice to such unreflective experience. The thought is just that to become able to do something in a skilful way is a matter not of habit but of intelligent capacities which, while equally unreflective when in operation, exemplify the sort of success-orientated flexibility that habits simply do not possess (cf. *ibid.*:

126–7). Knowing how, unlike habituation, is "not a single-track disposition" (*ibid.*: 46).

One might counter that when one rightly judges a performance skilful one is considering, and as it were imaginatively projecting in one's mind (or having it presented to one in some way), the regulative proposition that the actor is considering and correctly applying in their performance. Notwithstanding the regress employed above, this invites a further *reductio*. To be able to *appreciate* that a performance is clever (or dull-witted or cack-handed) is to grasp in some general sense its performer's intention. But if that implies inferring from their performance to the proposition under consideration, one would have no reason for concluding that one had inferred to the correct rule as opposed to any other rule or set of rules that might be thought to apply to what has happened so far. One would therefore have no good reason to think that one had understood as opposed to *mis*understood their intention. But since understanding *does* take place, the implication is that this is not how it occurs.

So how are we to characterize our *understanding* of skilful performances? Before we can address that question one thing must be made explicit. As we noted above, the distinction in kind made between theoretical and practical exercises of intelligence is not Ryle's (as implied by the simplified version of the regress offered in *The Concept of Mind*). When it comes to reasoning, we find the same sorts of considerations brought to bear. Inspired by Carroll's "Achilles and the Tortoise" problem, Ryle offers a case where a student, presented with a set of premises {P} and conclusion C he understands, cannot see that the latter follows from the former. When it is pointed out to him (call this R) that {P} *entails* C, he readily acknowledges this further premise, but *still* cannot understand the original argument; and the further addition of a premise to the effect that {P} and R jointly entail C (and its endless iterations) does not help. The imputed error is by now familiar: "knowing how to reason was assumed to be analysable into the knowledge or supposal of some propositions" (Ryle 1945–6: 6). Knowing a rule in the sense of being able to apply it is not itself rule-governed and therefore reducible to know-that: "knowing a rule is knowing how" (*ibid.*: 7).

On this account, explicit rules of inference are sedimentations of reasoning practices, and are only possible on the basis of the latter. This does not suggest that statements of regulative and other propositions serve no role. As Ryle readily acknowledges, it would be foolish to deny the importance that knowledge of the rules (and other facts) plays in the development of the skilful performances that become second nature. Ryle denies that the mere "grasp" or "presentation" of those rules eventuates in such skills: they require the development of complex capacities and abilities. But if one were to say of a physician, politician or judge that their performance demonstrated an explicitly stated rule in action, the compliment would be being paid to the knowing how, which is not reducible to the knowing that. The knowing that is "merely" the understanding of the rule may well be an achievement in its own terms but it is not the right sort of achievement for characterizing someone's *doings* as intelligent.

Our understanding of skilled performances applies as much to theoretical as to practical doings; indeed, in many cases no such distinction is very useful. According to Ryle, to understand that someone's performance is skilful is to know something in relation to it: something that the statement "X's advance of their Queen's pawn was a brilliant move" merely symbolizes. "Understanding is a part of knowing *how*" (Ryle 1949: 53). This general claim is quite striking, and we will return to it in due course. Its immediate implication is that one only understands *that* someone's act is skilful in so far as one possesses the sort of knowing how that constitutes "some degree of competence in performances of that kind" (*ibid.*). S understands better than R what makes Djokovic such a great tennis player because he plays tennis, although the more basic understanding of what bodies are and are not easily capable of might suffice to distinguish a Djokovic from a Bloggs. One critical implication of this relates to the transmission of skills. As with Polanyi, this is a matter not of formal instruction (although that may play a role, as noted above), but of imputed authority and discipline. Initially, the neophyte must take on trust the master's competence because they lack the know-how to understand it fully. The second natures that constitute skilful copings are inculcated by appropriate exercises, "corrected by criticisms and inspired by examples and precepts" (Ryle 1945–6: 14). As with Kant, just as the obtuse student might simply lack the wit to follow the argument, there are limits for some on the knowing how that can be acquired. The pupil can exceed the instructor's achievements, no matter how disciplined the latter.[23]

TACIT KNOWING AND KNOWING HOW

On the basis of the foregoing, it would seem that there is sufficient overlap of concern to place Ryle's account of knowing how alongside Polanyi's account of tacit knowledge. As a working hypothesis, then, let us say that tacit knowing is knowing how. But that raises an obvious concern: by virtue of what should knowing how be classified as *knowledge*? Answering or rejecting this question has become a bit of a cottage industry and we will return to it in detail in Chapter 2. Since we are concerned here with the more precise sense in which knowing how might be knowing in the way that *tacit* knowing is we will restrict our attention to what we have picked up from our discussion so far.

Part of the challenge here is the tendency to take as one's paradigm propositional knowledge and then wonder how, given that, anything non-propositional (untellable) could be classed as knowledge. As we saw, Polanyi has two approaches to this problem. The first is to call the abilities to learn that we share with many animals "knowledge". This does little to weaken the tendency to take explicit knowledge as one's paradigm and – perhaps more to the point – it is a line we have chosen to reject in our attempt to present a more svelte and amenable Polanyi. The second approach is to show that explicit knowledge is possible only on the assumption that we have tacit knowledge. Indeed, the point of Polanyi's regress, it will be recalled (§"Varieties of objectivity"), is to demonstrate that tacit knowing is in fact the dominant principle of all knowledge. And this is exactly the line Ryle takes when he declares that "knowledge-how is a concept logically prior to the concept of knowledge-that" (Ryle 1945–6: 15). That Ryle takes this view should be obvious from the foregoing, his "proof" both predictable and familiar.

The demonstration goes in two directions. Right now S knows that it is raining outside. She knows this because she hears the precipitation ricocheting off the tin roof and beating against the glass; observes water running under the door; can see the weather reporter looking forlornly at a map of the area with a big symbolic cloud and dashes superimposed over it. *That* she knows *what* she knows is due to all these other things. Some of these things are further facts; others still the result of "intelligent operations, requiring rules of method, checks, tests, criteria etc." (*ibid.*: 15–16). But since knowing a fact is a discovery that comes about only through the *application* of those rules of method and so on, it is the latter that themselves play the fundamental role. However, the correct application of rules is a matter of knowing how to go about one's business: "A scientist or a historian … is primarily a knower-how and only secondarily a knower-that" (*ibid.*: 16). Running the argument in reverse, the thought is that if S were to be informed that it is raining outside she could only be said to have knowledge of the fact if she could exploit it in some way. We would not attribute knowledge to her if, presented with a bucket and an urgent request for water, she looked at us blankly (*ceteris paribus*). To possess knowledge is to "know how to use" it (*ibid.*).

With this argument in place, a number of further parallels between tacit knowing and knowing how fall into place. Firstly, Polanyi misrepresents Ryle when he insists that his account of tacit knowledge overarches the know-how/know-that distinction (*TD*: 6–7) because for Ryle the primacy of knowing how means that it is always in action. Secondly, there is a clear sense in which knowing how is *personal* knowledge; indeed, it is that feature of it that ensures that it is not *tellable*. And as we have just seen, there is even the common thought that to understand a theory (or fact) requires that one in some sense "inhabits" it; or, rather, that to understand it – to know it tacitly – is to know how to apply it to particulars. Indeed, we are now in a position to relate Ryle's position to the shared structure outlined in §"1976 and all that". While the earlier regress argument operated merely *sceptically* against the intellectualist conception of knowing, the above argument brings out the *transcendental* function of knowing how by blocking the regress argument. That is to say, if one takes it that knowing that is to be characterized in the way Ryle does, one will not find oneself subject to a regress because the application of rules that makes knowledge-that *possible* is a matter not of more question-begging knowledge that but of knowing how. As noted above, then, "knowing a rule is knowing how". And of course, if the schematism is Kant's attempt to block the rule-following regress then Ryle's overall account of knowing how is his answer to the schematism. Perhaps only an Oxonian over-refinement deterred him from remarking its "logical" as opposed to its "transcendental" priority.

This is not to suggest that Polanyi's view of tacit knowledge and Ryle's view of knowing how touch at all points. One obvious contrast is brought out by Polanyi, in one of his other few references to Ryle's work. Contrasting Ryle's view of our grasp of the workings of the mind of another with Tolman's (1932), he notes that the latter mistakenly contrasts "the observation of a mental state with … an observation of its manifestations" (*PK*: 372). Since such an assessment is precisely what Ryle makes, what is the issue? Well, since Ryle "does not have the conception of subsidiary awareness … his identification of the mind with its workings can only mean that the two are identical … as focally observed facts, which is false" (*ibid.*).

Now it is of course true that Ryle has no such contrast and therefore cannot offer an analysis of what's occurring when one understands that a performance manifests intelligence in terms of visual clues attended *from*. The alternative positive account is that knowing tacitly/how is to be cashed out in terms of second nature, but it seems reasonable to assume that that account is more "therapeutic" than constructive. Of course, when one dispenses with the conception of subsidiary awareness one is not, *contra* Polanyi, left with only *his* understanding of focal awareness. And indeed, it seems odd to characterize one's awareness/recognition of a performance as skilful in terms of focal awareness. What one is attending to is the performance, not the body or any part of it.

That might well be taken as support for Polanyi's position. Perhaps the sort of awareness/understanding/knowledge that one brings to bear both in seeing a performance *as* intelligent and in performing intelligently is better seen in the light of some intentional arc than in terms of complex dispositions (even from a therapeutic point of view). With that in mind we must take up something left hanging above, where Ryle was quoted to the effect that "understanding is part of knowing *how*". Ever the sloganeer, this perhaps goes beyond what Ryle intended in his war against Cartesianism. However, it does direct attention to the fact that, for Ryle, knowing how is *essentially* object-involving since it relates to the contextual sensitivity of the abilities and capacities that comprise it. In an obvious sense, then, knowing how does connote a basic structure of intentionality, just like Polanyi's tacit knowing. Nevertheless, there is still the suspicion that on Ryle's account the achievements of second nature that are constitutive of skilful copings and of evaluations of intelligent performances fall short of knowledge. One problem here is that any account of *personal* knowledge must (as Polanyi appreciates) avoid the association with subjectivism; and Ryle's reliance on complex dispositions might be one reason to be tempted by the promised objectivity of the intellectualist legend. So Ryle's logical/transcendental promotion of knowing how suggests that we need some understanding of how this mode of "being" in the world can avoid subjectivism; especially if one's knowing how in some sense constitutes the objects understood thereby.

This says no more than Ryle himself did when, in an early piece, he professed that "the idea of Phenomenology" is a "good" one, but only in so far as it avoids the "progressive trend visible in the philosophy of Husserl and his followers towards a rarified Subjective Idealism or even Solipsism" (Ryle 1929: 362).[24] That directs us towards another way of regarding human being in the world that has a direct bearing on our understanding of tacit knowledge; one where the "alleged cleavage between Consciousness and Being" is subjected to fundamental examination and being "interested in" or "concerned about" is identified as the most "primitive mode of … 'being-an-I'"(*ibid.*: 363, 365; quoting Heidegger 1962). If tacit knowing is to be thought of as knowing how, then, let us see if there are resources in Heidegger for deepening our appreciation of what knowing how is.

BEING IN THE WORLD

Notwithstanding his supposed "turn" and its implications for an understanding of the later essays, Heidegger's early phenomenologically oriented work is complex enough in motivation and design. For the purpose of developing themes already identified in the work of Polanyi and Ryle, however, there is the familiar concern and method. On the one hand, then, we find a negative, diagnostic attitude towards the errors of Cartesianism; and, on the other, in the positive account of personhood (*Dasein*[25]) that develops out of the critique of the former and which it is intended to supplant. More specifically, the negative phase aims to weaken the appeal of exogenous, theoretically motivated distractions from the path "to the things themselves!" (Heidegger 1962: 34; 58);[26] or, more elliptically, from an acknowledgement that the basis of (the only possible) ontology is "to let that which shows itself be seen from itself in the very way in which it shows itself from itself" (*ibid.*). In Heidegger's jargon, things "show" themselves to persons in this more originary or authentic way when they are encountered as *ready-to-hand*: as objects with which we are involved when absorbed in the pursuit of ends comprising complex practices engaged in in ways that imply a variety of competencies and skills. This is contrasted with the way in which an object is encountered as *present-at-hand* when we disengage from some activity and treat it as an item of theoretical reflection. Not surprisingly, then, the principal aim of the negative phase is to associate Cartesianism, and in particular its conception of the person-as-knower, with an inadmissible prioritization of the present-at-hand over the ready-to-hand. Its initial expression takes the form of an argument (of sorts) against Cartesian scepticism; its second a by-now-familiar regress argument against the reducibility of what, as a working hypothesis, we are designating as knowing how to knowledge-that. Let us begin with the first argument.

At some point, any philosophically motivated inquiry into what the world is like will encounter the inquirers themselves. If we are inclined to think that what constitutes them *as* inquirers is something distinct from the world initially inquired into then the question arises as to how as inquirers they are related to that world. From here it is but a short step to wonder if the world as presented to them is as it is in itself, or indeed if such a world exists at all. Both these considerations suggest we need to understand what it is about inquirers that render them capable of knowing the world. Alternatively, we might begin with the assumption that the inquirer is essentially both *of* and *in* the world, in which case it behoves us to undertake an inquiry into what it is about certain sorts of things in the world that allows them (indeed, compels them) to know that world, themselves included. In both cases, then, we are thrown back onto the same question; namely, the Being of the (putatively) "knowing" subject. As Heidegger goes on to suggest (*BT*: 60–62; 86–90), this presents a stark choice: either

(I)   we embrace the challenge to show how our cognitive purchase on the world is possible when we set a knowing subject over and against the world it must somehow represent in some mental *inner*scape;[27]

or

(II)   we presuppose that "knowing is a mode of Being of *Dasein* as Being-in-the-world" (*BT*: 61; 88), and thereby nullify a whole range of epistemological problems.

Heidegger's response, in effect, is to argue that (I) is wholly unmotivated; indeed it *presupposes* a great deal *more* than the view that what it is to be a person is primarily (ontologically) to be *in* the world. Moreover, once we embrace the latter we see the paradoxical nature of the sceptic's concern: "The question of whether there is a world at all ... makes no sense if it is raised by *Dasein* as Being-in-the-world; and who else would raise it?" (*BT*: 202; 246–7).

Taking our "worldliness" as a starting point allows the everyday to reassert itself in its phenomenological positivity and we can begin to see that it involves dealing with entities in a way that is rather different from that characterized by disengaged reflection. Encountered "concernfully" as ready-to-hand, "equipment" like hammers, pens and keys recommend themselves as things with a function or purpose (an "in-order-to"; *BT*: 68; 97) that is intelligible only in the context of particular sorts of practices and of other equipment. Notwithstanding its materiality, a key, for example, *is* what it is through its relations (its "references or assignments"; *BT*: 74; 105) to an "equipmental totality" that includes locks, doors, buildings etc.; and it is only in the midst of this "totality" that a key "shows itself" (*BT*: 68; 98) as what it is. This does not imply that when, absorbed in one's work, one uses a key (to unlock a door, leading to a room, in which we will sit and write …) without the explicit (theoretical; "thematic") awareness that *this is a key* – when the key "is seen from itself" as something ready-to-hand – one is acting "blindly". Rather, one's overall performance is intentional in so far as it is characterized by a different sort of awareness – *Umsicht*, or "circumspection" (*BT*: 69; 98) – which is not levied, as it were, on a single object (the key) but is instantiated in the "totality" with(in) which one is engaged.

The suggestion that it is through our practical coping with things that they show themselves as they really are has a number of important implications. First, it suggests that our "ontological Interpretation" (*BT*: 72; 102) of the constitutive structures of the "Being which belongs to the ready-to-hand" (*BT*: 76; 107), and thus of our worldly being (personhood; *Dasein*) is guided by the "pre-ontological understanding" (*BT*: 72; 102) of the world and of ourselves as part of it that is manifest in such copings.[28] Moreover, just as the readiness-to-hand of a particular object is determined by its relations to the things that make up the appropriate totality, being-in-the-world is itself an ("non-thematic"; tacit; untellable) "absorption in" those relations that constitute the "readiness to hand of a totality of equipment" (*BT*: 76; 107). A second point, then, relates to the world. In so far as our Being and thus our understanding is world*ly*, the world cannot be conceived of as something standing over and against cognizing subjects as an "object" of possible theoretical knowledge. Such a view involves the Cartesian privileging the present-at- over the ready-to-hand. Rather, the world in its structural essence (its "worldness"; *BT*: 72; 102) just is the system of relations as it is understood (as having "significance") in this "pre-ontological" way by beings that are themselves of the world. Such (a) being "is the ontical condition for the possibility of discovering entities which are encountered in a world with involvement (readiness-to-hand) as their kind of Being, and which can make themselves known as they are in themselves" (*BT*: 87; 120).

41

This leads to a third point; namely, that the structures that constitute our concernful dealings with objects are the structures that make those objects the objects they are. To put it more pointedly, the understanding (or "knowledge") manifest in circumspection is (understanding or knowledge) of the things themselves and not *merely* of the subjective conditions for cognition (cf. *BT*: 86; 119). As we have seen, both Ryle and Polanyi are vulnerable to the charge that they deny tacit knowledge/knowing how the objective dimension required for *knowledge*, and Heidegger acknowledges that his approach similarly risks "volatilizing ... the 'substantial Being' of entities ... into 'pure thinking'" (*BT*: 87–8; 121). Crucially, this remark comes amid considerations that bear on the primacy of the ready-to-hand, which, as we will see in §"Regress redux", have been reconstructed by some commentators in terms of a regress argument that seeks to demonstrate the irreducibility of knowing how to knowing that. This parallel between readiness-to-hand and knowing how is clearly important for the purpose of trying to deepen our understanding of the latter, not least because the context of Heidegger's presentation of the regress argument is one in which the risk of subjectivism is in the air; specifically, the sort of subjectivism that arises from an approach that is Kantian in inspiration. To understand more fully what Heidegger can contribute to our understanding of tacit knowing/knowing how we consequently need to delve a little more deeply into this aspect of his work.

A WORLD WELL LOST?

According to what is sometimes called the two-world[29] or two-object reading of Kant's idealism, the objects of knowledge are not things in themselves but only the appearances of things. This appears to be the price paid for making the knower an active participant in the process of cognition – bringing, in that oft-quoted phrase, otherwise "blind" intuitions under otherwise "empty" concepts (Kant 1996: B75; A51) – and rescuing thereby some semblance of a metaphysical project from Humean scepticism. The presuppositions obliging this interpretation appear likewise in recent reconstructions of Kant's thought. With respect to transcendental arguments, for example, there is the charge that they establish not objective necessities (of being) but merely subjective necessities (of thought). And, as we have already seen in outline, there are "constructionalist" (both conceptualist and nonconceptualist) attempts to naturalize Kantian synthesis and demonstrate not how objects themselves but how our *thinking about* or *representation of* them is possible (and therefore as being empirically conditioned).

The suspicion that if we do not assert its metaphysical otherness or acknowledge that in respect of a certain sort of inquiry (philosophical) we are only approaching the *subject* of knowledge then we will "lose" the world is of course what Heidegger is remarking when he observes that his account of the world threatens to collapse being into thought.[30] For Heidegger, that suspicion is sustainable only on the basis of (rejected) assumptions that occasion the privileging of theoretical over practical engagements in the world. And while he acknowledges that Kant's entanglement "in the webs of ancient ontology ... make(s) an unequivocal interpretation almost impossible" (1997b: 69), he is insistent that the two-world interpretation of Kant is wrongheaded:

> Kant never hesitated in his view that the beings that encoun-
> ter us are as such extant. This is expressed in the statement that
> appearances are objects ... appearances are just those things
> themselves that we encounter and discover as extant within the
> world. (*Ibid.*: 69, 68)

For Heidegger, eliminating the two-world view of Kant brings the (proto-Heideggerian) nature of the transcendental project into view (as ontology). Accordingly, when we inquire into how (experience of) objects are possible we are inquiring into – attempting to understand – the Being of those objects. But in doing so we are gaining an at least partial understanding of the being – Dasein – to whom these objects are disclosed or revealed and for whom the "understanding of Being is itself a definite characteristic" (*BT*: 12; 32). Where Kant erred, then, was in allowing his understanding of that which seeks to understand the Being of entities to be determined by an impoverished account of the sorts of entities that are revealed to it; that is to say, to the possible objects of cognition for finite creatures like ourselves. Accordingly, a "true" or authentic understanding of the being to whom entities are given (of the entity for whom "the question of Being arises": our *self*-understanding) remains "hidden", even though it (*qua* "pre-ontological understanding") is what directs us and forms the backdrop to our understanding of "the meaning of entities" (*BT*: 12; 32). In order to understand Being we must therefore understand the entity which phenomena show themselves to as they are or determine the sorts of structures that make such appearances possible. In this regard, the phenomenology of persons exposes the conditions for any possible entity that is not a person and so constitutes "*transcendental* knowledge" (*BT*: 38; 62).

From Heidegger's perspective, Kant promotes both a fundamental error and its essential corrective. As will be apparent from the foregoing, the focus of the error is Kant's account of knowledge. Knowledge *per se* requires that intuitions be brought under concepts (the understanding working on sensibility). But it turns out that the manifold of intuition must first be "gone through, taken up, and combined in a certain manner. This act I call synthesis" (Kant 1996: A77; B102). This synthesis is the work, neither of intuition nor of understanding. Rather, according to Kant, it is "the mere effect produced by the imagination, which is a blind but indispensable function of the soul without which we would have no cognition whatsoever" (A78; B103). The resulting content of this synthesis is not conceptual, but it is a "crude and confused" cognition and therefore has "a certain content" (A77–8; B103).

It is this sort of observation that motivates constructionalist/empiricist reconstructions of Kant's epistemology. For Heidegger it also opens up a basic tension in Kant's thinking: "[I]n all of Kant's subsequent discussions the power of imagination and understanding battle with each other for priority as the basic source of knowledge" (1997b: 198). As Heidegger goes on to note, "pure concepts of understanding are determinations which determine a priori what is extant in its extant character … *which co-constitute the being of beings* and are thus the theme of *ontology*" (*ibid.*: 201; original emphasis). As such the "structure" of objects has the form of that of understanding's judgements: "As constitutive determinations of the *object-character* of objects (categories) are connected to the proposition, to *judgement*, and to *understanding*" (*ibid.*: 201; original emphasis).

On this interpretation, Kant's retreat from the power of the imagination in favour of understanding takes the content of our experience of the world (indeed, the extant *as such*) to be propositionally structured knowledge-*that*. Blindness to the real phenomena of phenomenology and to the world are thus convolved with being "scared away" (*ibid.*: 189) from "the dimension of human *Dasein*" (*ibid.*) that the imagination evinces. And yet it is in relation to one specific aspect of Kant's treatment of the imagination that the corrective lies: the chapter on schematism, for Heidegger "the central piece of the *Critique*" (*ibid.*: 291; cf. *BT*: 23–4, 45).

In §"Schemata" we observed that the schematism of the understanding, whereby intuitions are brought under concepts (as rules), is deemed a "secret art" (a "tacit art" for Polanyi) performed by the imagination, which *as such* blocks the regress argument implied by the repeated exercise of judgement (as the "ability to *subsume* under rules"; Kant 1996: A132; B171). Although emphasizing the extent to which examples of empirical synthesis bear on contemporary debates about non/conceptualism, we noted in passing that the explicit concern of the chapter is with how schemata function in bringing pure ("intellectual") concepts of understanding together with ("sensible") empirical intuitions from which they are heterogeneous. The crucial mediating factor, it turns out, is *time*. Transcendental schemata are rules that can mediate the subsuming of appearances under categories because they are time-determinations, and both appearances and categories have an *essential* relationship to time. Although Kant's account of the role of time in the schematism is far from lucid,[31] as is the temporal nature of empirical schema, it is the hint it provides that is important. As Schaper presents it, "though it is true that we construct, we construct not as minds, or intellects, not by being mind, but by being in time" (Schaper 1964: 281).

The sentiment here is of course Heideggerian. The appeal of the schematism is that in it Kant is regarded as trying to work out "the inner possibility of categories ... the pure transcendental propositions of time" (Heidegger 1997b: 292):

> For Kant schematism is understanding's character as necessarily an enactment by which understanding presents itself in time, that is, working with schemata, shapes, images or views, working with what is purely intuitable, that is, working with purely temporal relations. *(Ibid.)*

If, as Heidegger asserts, imagination is essentially temporal, and it is imagination that makes "understanding possible" (*ibid.*: 225), then time is the "horizon for all understanding of Being" (*BT*: 17; 39) and the structural nature of what is constituted is (like the constituter, *Dasein*) not propositional in the way Kant suggests. In our everyday encounters in which entities "show" themselves as ready-to-hand we encounter likewise the basic temporal structure of our own being; the intentionality in action, as it were, of personhood. If we are to associate knowing how with such worldly copings, then, we must associate with the former some fundamental relationship to temporality. This is not of course to suggest that knowledge *that* is in some straightforward sense "timeless": for Heidegger (cf. *BT*: 18–9; 39–40) that simple bifurcation is part of the legacy of ancient ontology, and since knowing is a way of being for *persons* ("a mode of Being of *Dasein*"), propositional knowledge is implicated in the same structure. But if knowing *that* is to be associated with encounters with things that are present-at-hand there is no escaping the connotations of *presentness*. For entities to become present to us in a way that conduces to their becoming the objects of theoretical knowledge is not to encounter them in a more authentic way (to abjure fully their relationship to temporality). It is rather the case that when a hammer is judged to have mass, for example (as opposed, say, to being *insufficiently* heavy for the task at hand), we make it present in such a way that "its" time and place understood through its "absorbed" employment become irrelevant. It has been "released" from its constituting context (cf. *BT*: 362; 413) for another understanding of Being. When we "thematize" in this way we "free" entities "so that one can interrogate them and determine their character 'Objectively'" (*BT*: 363; 414). These objective characterizations of entities are what are expressed in propositions; but while it makes no sense to "reduce" the truths so expressed to the knowing how that characterizes our worldly being (any more than one could "reduce" a cog to the mechanism from which it has been taken), that everyday involvement with things that are nominated "ready-to-hand" (the "real") is the foundation of knowledge that involves determining the character of something "present-at-hand" and is thus a condition of possibility of knowing truths.[32] The thematizing of entities within-the-world presupposes being-in-the-world as the basic state of *Dasein* (*BT*: 363; 415)

REGRESS REDUX

We noted in §"Being in the world" that some commentators ascribe to Heidegger an argument against the reducibility of the ready-to- to the present-at- that is strikingly similar to Ryle's. Mulhall (1996: 55ff.) follows Dreyfus (1991: 117) in claiming that Heidegger's argument against the primacy of the present-at-hand "amounts to the claim that" (Mulhall 1996: 55) the sort of understanding of the world exhibited in our skilful coping with (say) tools is irreducible to the sort of understanding exemplified when encountering objects as entities fit for theoretical embrace. The reasons brought to bear are twofold. The first, holistic or contextual, consideration is that to confront an entity *as*, say, a cup is to understand its role in a whole range of activities across innumerable contexts and its relationships with a divergent set of other entities. What a cup is made of is significant in some circumstances but not others; the surfaces one can place one on vary in angle, material, and across social context; the importance of "ownership" and entitlements to access are determined by rituals and rites. It is not then *merely* that it is "far from simple" (*ibid.*: 56) to specify these relations. Since every invoked entity (a table; a "social context") *is itself* subject to the same contextual and holistic understanding the task is open-ended. The implication here can be restated in a by now familiar form. *If* the sort of knowing of objects that these everyday skilful dealings constitute has to be reducible to the decontextual sort of knowing associated with the present-at-hand *then* the everyday sort of knowing would imply an infinite regress and thus be impossible. Indeed, this is a feature of Heidegger's argument that both Mulhall and Dreyfus (with similar circumspection) find in Heidegger. Mulhall (1996: 55–9), for example, elucidates Heidegger's strategy by making an explicit link with the Rylean argument for the irreducibility of knowing how to knowing that: if knowing how is to be understood in terms of the application of propositional knowledge in concrete circumstances then either the rules for the application must be propositional in form (inviting a regress) or no such rules are required in which case know-how is a cognitive primitive.

Dreyfus's presentation of the argument is set against his own concern to torment classical AI with his account of the so-called "frame problem". Entities take on specific meaning within contexts. Since contexts themselves are identifiable only on the basis of (further) entities with specific features that are themselves contextually constituted, "the AI worker," striving to codify the know-how immanent in our skilful copings for purposes of computa-tion, "is faced with a regress of contexts" (Dreyfus 1992: 289).[33] Although any specific reference to Ryle's argument is neglected, Dreyfus's conclusion is more emphatic still:

> For Heidegger, who claims our commonsense understanding is a kind of knowing how, not a propositional knowing-that ... our familiarity does not consist in a vast body of rules and facts, but rather consists of dispositions to respond to situations in appro-priate ways. (Dreyfus 1991: 117)

Even with that coy nod towards normativity ("appropriate ways"), talk of dispositions recalls that lurking fear of subjectivism. In response, note that although Heidegger remarks explicitly that the condition of possibility of the form of (theoretical; "functional"; mathematical) understanding of entities that we associate with the present-at-hand is that "ready-to-hand" entities are "discovered as they are 'substantially' 'in themselves'," those entities are themselves only made possible by the "worldhood of the world" (*BT*: 88, 122). This talk of "worldhood" recalls Heidegger's acknowledgement that an understanding of the world as "a system of Relations" (*BT*: 88; 121) risks sub-limating being into thought. So what's the solution? Let's begin by backtrack-ing slightly. As Dreyfus (1993) has it, Heidegger offers us two key insights:

- An understanding of a ("more fundamental") form of intentionality that does not involve "mental intentional content" and which the latter "presupposes". Call this *fundamental intentionality* (FI).
- A conception of our worldly being that in its basic form (i) does not involve intentionality at all, and (ii) is the "condition of possibility" of both contentful/mental and non-mental kinds of intentionality (*ibid.*: 2). Call this *background being* (BB).

Accordingly, we have a transcendental hierarchy running from the (con-templative; mental) intentionality of representative states associated with the present-at-hand (*representational intentionality*, RI); although the (active; non-mental) "primordial" directedness towards the world of the ready-to-hand (FI); to the "originary transcendence" of *Dasein*'s being-in-the-world (BB). For Dreyfus, this "originary transcendence" is the "general skilled grasp of our circumstances" (*ibid.*: 11); the "familiarity with the world" that con-stitutes our "understanding of being" (*BT*: 119); in short, "the non-salient *background*, both for ongoing coping and for deliberately focusing on what is unusual or difficult" (Dreyfus 1993: 10). On this account, then, both know-ing *how* and knowing *that* are founded on a sort of *ur*-knowing how, which comprises the background.

Heidegger's thought, then, is that if one formalizes/mathematicizes involvements with the world – thinks of them as an abstract set of rules, for example, as Kant does with the categories – one will be tempted to think of these as somehow *necessities of thought*,[34] and not as the way the world is in its *world*liness. This in turn introduces various sceptical possibilities: that we might get the world wrong; that our conceptual scheme is just one among many possibilities;[35] that the rules themselves need to be applied. Rejecting that temptation we see that *what it is* to know how things are ("in them-selves") *is* to manifest the sort of understanding exemplified through being able to cope with them in a skilful way, a matter of knowing how to deal with them appropriately. The rules – if we think of them as such – are what they are because of the concernful dealings with the world they articulate, and those involvements are what make the world as a set of entities encountered in themselves (as ready-to-hand) and later as theorizable (present-to-hand) possible. That is to say, the involvements that are manifest in these rules/ norms and which are expressive of our basic understanding of the world ("the intelligibility of Being-in-the-world"; *BT*: 161; 204) are always-already articulated as a discourse that is essentially "worldly" (*ibid.*). Knowing *that* (*asserting* that things are a certain way) is thus made possible by and stands out against the background of the totality of significations that articulate our concernful dealings with the world in the same way that encountering enti-ties as present-at-hand is possible only on the basis of the ready-to-hand.

We can have false beliefs, then; but these are only possible on the assump-tion that we are "already-alongside" the world (*BT*: 61, 88). Equally, no regress threatens because contexts within which objects present themselves as significant/meaningful (as "equipment") are grounded transcendentally in our worldly being. Only if the attempt is made to "intellectualize" or oth-erwise codify the norms constitutive of going about things in the right way (knowing how) by dispossessing them of the "real phenomenal content" (*BT*: 88; 121), which is determined by context, can a concern for their deferred justification arise. And the essential feature of that "phenomenal content" is *time*: the temporal constitution of that which understands (the person) and that which is understood (in knowing how) make the latter irreducible to know-that and the former irreducible to a mere knower of (contextless) propositions. We do not confront this problem because part of what it is to have skills is to be context-sensitive: to be able to determine flexibly the sig-nificance of what we encounter in *dynamic* circumstances.

CONCLUSION

As we have seen, Heidegger presents his account of how we should think of our fundamental way of being in the world as a specific response to Kant's schematism. Unlike Ryle and Polanyi, however, Heidegger is still attempting to make good on Kant's transcendental project by identifying a distinction between the fundamental, *non*-intentional knowing how (BB) that constitutes our understanding of being and the essentially intentional knowing how (FI) that reveals entities as they are in themselves. The transcendental aspiration became an embarrassment to Heidegger, just as it often is to acolytes like Drefyus. We can reject it if we no longer feel compelled either to convict childishly our philosophical opponents of having failed to see that being has concealed its revealing or that the sceptic still needs answering. In doing so we can disenthrall from it much of Heidegger's rich account of the phenomenology of practice, which serves as a useful addition to the description of knowing how offered by Ryle. In this regard his emphasis on the essential temporality of our everyday copings is a corrective to a temptation to regard knowers as acting normatively in response to some rule grasped "in a flash". Indeed, that the regress of rules cannot arise if one acknowledges the temporalized nature of such skills and competencies is one of Heidegger's contributions to our understanding of knowing how, and thus to the development of the notion that tacit knowledge is to be regarded as knowing how. There is a further contribution, which comes in the form of a hint; namely, that BB is "articulated" as a worldly "discourse". If we reject the distinction between BB and FI, can we somehow make sense of the idea that the knowing how that constitutes the level of FI is both worldly and articulated/discursive? If we could, that would support the view ascribed to Ryle (§"Tacit knowing and knowing how"), to the effect that knowing how is object-involving through its relation to the contextual sensitivity of the abilities and capacities that comprise it. In doing so we would simultaneously dispose of the problem that such tacit, qua *personal*, knowing lacks the "objectivity" to be considered knowing proper and thus eliminate the temptation to regard tacit knowing as subject to PI. To that end we will now examine in detail the recent debate concerning Ryle's distinction and show that tacit knowing, as knowing how, satisfies PA.

2. KNOWING HOW AND KNOWING THAT

INTRODUCTION

Chapter 1 introduced tacit knowledge through the work of Polanyi, Ryle and Heidegger. We highlighted an initial connection between Polanyi's slogan that "we can know more than we can tell" and an emphasis both on the personal and practical. One indicator of this connection is a shared *concern* to undermine an overly ("Cartesian") impersonal and intellectual conception of the knower and of their cognitive achievements and a *method* characterized by the deployment of versions of a regress argument. The purpose of the regress arguments can be seen in the light of the three competing principles to which tacit knowledge might be subject:

PC   All knowledge can be fully articulated, or codified, in context-independent terms.

PI   There can be knowledge that cannot be articulated.

PA   All knowledge can be articulated, either in context-independent terms or in context-dependent terms.

The regress arguments target a conception of knowledge constrained by PC. Their purpose is to demonstrate that we are entitled to the concept of explicit knowledge only if we acknowledge that its achievement is grounded in something more fundamental. That leaves open the competing possibilities marked by PI and PA. Rejecting PI, we suggested that tacit knowing, construed in terms of context-dependent knowing how (the sort of activity-dependent understanding that is manifest in practice), resists codification in purely linguistic context-independent terms but can be regarded, nevertheless, as fully determinate (thus satisfying PA) under the appropriate analysis. The task of this chapter is to provide such an analysis by returning to one version of the regress argument outlined in Chapter 1 and examining its role in underpinning the centrality of knowing how and its priority over knowledge-that. Unsurprisingly, its focus is the recent debate about whether Ryle's attack on what he calls the "intellectualist legend" is successful and its consequences for the understanding of know-how we wish to advance; namely, one which makes good on the epithet "personal knowledge" through the connection to the abilities and broader background of know-how of its subject.

As we saw in §"Intelligence in practice", Ryle deploys the regress argument to argue that intelligent action cannot, in general, be explained as the result of prior acts of contemplating propositions. Practical knowledge is not dependent on theoretical knowledge; rather, the priority is reversed and knowledge-that is taken to depend on knowledge-how. But Ryle's views have been attacked in favour of what can, for convenience, be called the "new intellectualism" (see Stanley & Williamson 2001; Snowdon 2004; Stanley 2011a,b). This view centres on three claims:

   (i)   That Ryle's regress argument misfires.
   (ii) That Ryle's constitutive account of knowing how as a complex of abilities is false.
   (iii) That an alternative account of knowing how is available.

Given (i) there would be no reason to deny that knowledge-how is a species of knowledge-that. Given (ii) there would be no reason for maintaining a link between knowledge-how and ability, which would leave space for (iii). On the "new intellectualist" account knowledge-how is a matter of grasping *that* a particular way of acting is a way to act, entertained under a practical mode of presentation: knowledge-how is a species of knowledge-that.

It may seem that a Rylean split between knowledge-how and knowledge-that puts the idea that all knowledge can be articulated under pressure (i.e. PA) and suggests support instead for PI. Against that appearance, we will suggest that there is something agreeable in the "new intellectualist" approach: knowledge-how has a content that can be articulated via demonstratives to ways of going on. Indeed, as we will see in later chapters, this acknowledgment is essential to avoiding PI and the implication that tacit knowledge must be thought of as nonconceptual and ineffable. Even though theoretical knowledge depends on know-how, such practical mastery need not seem mysterious. Notwithstanding this concession, it is equally evident that PA, understood as the principle constraining *personal* knowledge, cannot tolerate the intellectualist split between knowledge-how and ability. To defend as an alternative response to (iii), the suggestion that knowledge-how is *tacit* or *personal* knowing, then, both (i) and (ii) must be rejected. In reply to (i) we will argue that there is a quite natural interpretation of the regress argument that works against an explanation of intelligent action. And in response to (ii) we will claim that once one motivates a distinction between two forms of knowledge-how – theoretical and practical – there is an infrangible connection between knowledge-how and ability. We will begin with (i).

RYLE'S REGRESS ARGUMENT

As we have seen, Ryle's view starts from the claim that knowledge-how cannot be explained through the "intellectualist legend", according to which intelligent action is steered by grasp of a proposition. Ryle argues, instead, that "intelligent practice is not a step-child of theory" (Ryle 1949: 27) through the deployment of a regress argument. Versions of the argument can be found both in "Knowing How and Knowing That" (Ryle 1945–6) and in chapter 2 of his *Concept of Mind*:

> If a deed, to be intelligent, has to be guided by the consideration of a regulative proposition, the gap between that consideration and the practical application of the regulation has to be bridged by some go-between process which cannot by the pre-supposed definition itself be an exercise of intelligence and cannot, by definition, be the resultant deed. This go-between application-process has somehow to marry observance of a contemplated maxim with the enforcement of behaviour. So it has to unite in itself the allegedly incompatible properties of being kith to theory and kin to practice, else it could not be the applying of the one in the other. For, unlike theory, it must be able to influence action, and, unlike impulses, it must be amenable to regulative propositions. Consistency requires, therefore, that this schizophrenic broker must again be subdivided into one bit which contemplates but does not execute, one which executes but does not contemplate and a third which reconciles these irreconcilables. And so on for ever. (Ryle 1945–6: 2–3)

> The crucial objection to the intellectualist legend is this. The consideration of propositions is itself an operation the execution of which can be more or less intelligent, less or more stupid. But if, for any operation to be intelligently executed, a prior theoretical operation had first to be performed and performed intelligently, it would be a logical impossibility for anyone ever to break into the circle. (Ryle 1949: 30)

Recently, there has been a flurry of literature both on the precise nature of this argument and (as a consequence) on whether it amounts to a successful refutation of intellectualism. Complications aside, it involves something like the following regress:

> Suppose all know-how can be articulated (put into words) as a piece of knowledge-that: grasping some proposition that p. Grasping the proposition that p is itself something one can do successfully or unsuccessfully, so it is also a piece of knowledge-how. So, on the theory in question, it will involve grasping another proposition, call this q. But grasping the proposition that q is itself something one can do successfully or unsuccessfully, so it is also a piece of know-how. So, on the theory in question, it will involve grasping another proposition, call this r … etc.

This argument has been questioned by Jason Stanley and Timothy Williamson (Stanley & Williamson 2001; Stanley 2011a, 2011b). They offer the following as a summary of the premises of his argument.

> Ryle's argument has two premises:
>
> (1) If one Fs, one employs knowledge-how to F.
> (2) If one employs knowledge that p, one contemplates the proposition that p …
>
> If knowledge-how is a species of knowledge-that, the content of knowledge-how to F is, for some ϕ, the proposition that $\phi(F)$.
>   So, the assumption for *reductio* is:
>
> RA: knowledge-how to F is knowledge that $\phi(F)$.
>   (Stanley & Williamson 2001: 413–14)

This then leads, apparently, to a regress in the following way (where $C(p)$ stands for the act of contemplating the proposition p):

> Suppose that Hannah Fs. By premise (1), Hannah employs the knowledge-how to F. By RA, Hannah employs the knowledge that $\phi(F)$. So, by premise (2), Hannah $C(\phi(F))$s. Since $C(\phi(F))$ is an act, we can reapply premise (1), to obtain the conclusion that Hannah knows how to $C(\phi(F))$. By RA, it then follows that Hannah employs the knowledge that $\phi(C(\phi(F)))$. By premise (2), it follows that Hannah $C(\phi(C(\phi(F))))$s. And so on.   (*Ibid.*: 414)

However, Stanley and Williamson go on to contest whether there really is a vicious regress to worry about. And if not, then it seems that the intellectualist legend is untarnished. Their own development of a version of intellectualism has two components. First, they argue that there is no important semantic distinction between knowledge-how and knowledge-that. And second, they develop an account of knowledge-how in knowledge-that terms.

We will return to these two further aspects of their view of knowledge-how later in this chapter. This section will concentrate on the regress argument.

Stanley and Williamson contest the claim that there is a stable, consistent way to interpret the premises of the argument. First they dispute the claim that if one Fs, one employs knowledge-how to F. Cases such as digestion undermine this. Thus for example: "'If Hannah digests food, she knows how to digest food' ... is clearly false. Digesting food is not the sort of action that one knows how to do" (*ibid.*: 414). To preserve the truth of the first premise, Stanley and Williamson argue, it has to be restricted to intentional actions. But then this seems to make problems for premise 2. In support of this objection they quote Carl Ginet:

> I exercise (or manifest) my knowledge that one can get the door open by turning the knob and pushing it (as well as my knowledge that there is a door there) by performing that operation quite automatically as I leave the room; and I may do this, of course, without formulating (in my mind or out loud) that proposition or any other relevant proposition. (Ginet 1975: 7)

This example, they contend, shows that instances of knowledge-that are often unaccompanied by distinct acts of contemplating propositions. To preserve the truth of premise 2 in the face of cases such as the one Ginet cites requires construing the "act" of contemplating a proposition as no more an intentional action than digesting food. But if contemplating a proposition is not an intentional action then it does not fit the only plausible interpretation of premise 1. Consequently, there is no consistent interpretation of both the premises, taken together, that can sustain a regress: if the contemplation is not an intentional action then it need not be a case of employing knowledge-how to do something and thus need not itself presuppose the contemplation of any further proposition to encode it.

The first thing to say in response to Stanley and Williamson is that the suggestion they make in defence of the first premise is in precise agreement with Ryle's intended target for the argument: his criticism is levelled at intelligent (intentional) action, not autonomic processes. If a regress argument is to be constructed using their formulation, then, it is the second premise that has to be defended and it has to be done so differently from the way proffered on Ryle's behalf. As it turns out, this is none too difficult, for the attack on premise 2 turns entirely on the strength of an appeal to cases of the sort Ginet describes. Now, as a phenomenological point, it is certainly plausible to say that one can manifest or express knowledge-that without explicitly or consciously "contemplating a proposition". In the seamless cut and thrust of everyday action and conversation, there need be nothing as meditative as that phrase seems to suggest. But since the "contemplative" model is not Ryle's but that of his ("old") intellectualist opponent, convicting Ryle's argument of wrecking itself at this point is to misunderstand the dialectic entirely. Its target need not be a form of intellectualism in which such conscious attention is necessary. Rather it is the idea that knowledge is thought of as encoded in propositional form for the speaker, whether consciously *or* unconsciously. This argument (against PC) is immune to the phenomenological claim.

In his recent restatement of his own views, Jerry Fodor provides a more appropriate account of the debate Ryle is better located within. Fodor takes Ryle to be a spokesperson for the "pragmatists" whom he characterizes in the following way:

> Abilities are prior to theories, they say. Competence is prior to content. In particular, *knowing how* is the paradigm cognitive state and it is prior to *knowing that* in the order of intentional explanation. Therefore, don't think of thinking as being *about* the world; think of thinking as being *in* the world. Do not say that the world is what makes your thoughts true (or false); say that the world is what makes your actions succeed or fail.
>
> (Fodor 2008: 10)

Fodor takes pragmatism to be his main opponent in *LOT 2*:

> From LOT 2's Cartesian point of view, the genius of pragmatism is to get all of its explanatory priorities backward: … Cartesians think that thought is prior to action (because acting requires planning, and planning is a species of reasoning). Pragmatists think the opposite … Cartesians think that action is the externalization of thought. Pragmatists think that thought is the internalization of action. In effect, pragmatism is Cartesianism read from right to left … Thought about the world is prior to thought about how to change the world. Accordingly, *knowing that* is prior to *knowing how*. Descartes was right and Ryle was wrong.   (*Ibid.*: 12–14)

Fodor is broadly correct in his characterization of Ryle as the opponent. Against such an intellectualist account of knowledge (both that and how), however, Stanley and Williamson's appeal to phenomenology has no argumentative force. Hence, contra both them and Fodor, the priority of knowledge-how over theoretical knowledge-that stands.

KNOWING HOW AND KNOWING THAT

Taking themselves to have undermined the regress argument (i) and as a consequence Ryle's positive account of knowledge-how (linking it with ability), Stanley and Williamson undertake the task of offering an alternative. Their aim is to show that it is a form of knowledge-that. In this section we will examine two arguments for assimilating knowledge-how to knowledge-that which form part of the new intellectualist backlash against Ryle. The first, negative, argument is that since there is no significant semantic distinction between the two forms of knowledge, there is no reason to mark out knowledge-how as a particular contrast to the rest of knowledge. The second, positive, argument is that knowledge-how can be expressed in specific knowledge-that terms once one accepts that knowledge-that is not restricted to cases which can be conceptualized in general and non-context-specific terms. We will concede the first argument subject to a distinction between what we will call theoretical and practical knowledge-how. Since the aim is to defend the claim that knowledge-how is subject to PA we will also accept a strategy akin to the second argument to suggest that knowledge-how is conceptually structured. It should be noted, however, that since on the proposed account the regress argument to show the priority of knowledge-how is still in force, the dialectical role of this strategy is quite different.

The idea that there is a distinction between practical knowledge, or knowledge-how, and theoretical knowledge(-that) seems to be encoded in a semantic distinction which complements Ryle's regress argument and others like it. Recent work in an analytic or linguistic philosophical tradition has, however, called any such semantic distinction into question. As Adrian Moore points out, ascriptions of knowledge-how are answers to an implicit question of how something was done. But just as there can be such "how" questions, there can also be questions as to when, where, whether and why something was done:

> The familiar use of "knows" alongside an interrogative arises because states of knowledge, by their very nature, can be pressed into service in addressing questions, whether formulated or unformulated, whether theoretical or practical. Hence "knows when", "knows where", "knows whether", "knows why". "Knows how" is just another member of this list".   (Moore 1997: 167)

But if one knows *when* something happened, for example, there is no need to have a special non-propositional knowledge (knowledge-when, perhaps) rather than simply knowledge that it happened at such and such a time. Such knowledge-when *is* simply knowledge-that. Similarly, to know how something was done can simply be to know *that* it was done in such and such a way so that such knowledge-how is an instance of knowledge-that.

Knowledge-how is no more distinct than knowledge-when, -where, -whether or -why: all are answers to implicit questions, and all can be instances of knowledge-that.

A more promising semantic marker of a practical mode of knowledge is the use of the infinitive. It is one thing to know how something was done, another to know how to *do* it. However:

> The important difference between its use [i.e. the use of "knows how"] in "knows how the getaway was made" and "knows how to charm people" is not the difference between two senses of the phrase, as it were a "propositional" sense and a "practical" sense. It is rather the ensuing difference between the finite verb and the infinitive. (Moore 1997: 168)

Just the same kind of difference – between infinitive and finite verbs – occurs in cases of knowledge-when. The difference between finite verb and infinitive is between corresponding implicit questions about how things are and what to do rather than between distinct kinds of knowledge.

In addition to the lack of a characteristic semantic marker, there are instances of knowledge of how to do something that seem, simply, to be cases of having knowledge-that. To know how to escape might be to know *that* a way to escape is via the laundry. Such cases blur the apparent boundary between knowledge-how and knowledge-that. To know how to spell "comma", for example, is nothing other "than knowledge that it is spelt 'c', 'o', double 'm', 'a'" (Moore 1997: 171). As Paul Snowdon argues:

> It seems to me that there are clear enough cases where "knowing how to" fairly obviously does reduce to, or consists in, "knowing that". For example, I am thinking about a chess puzzle and, as we say, it dawned on me how to achieve mate in three. Surely, the onset of this knowledge consisted in my realizing *that* moving the queen to D3, followed by moving the knight to ... etc., will lead to mate in three ... Again, S knows how to get from London to Swansea by train before midday. S's knowing how to do that surely consists in knowing *that* one first catches the 7.30 a.m. train to Reading from Paddington, and then one ... etc. Finally, if someone knows how to insert footnotes using Word then they know *that* the way to insert footnotes is to click on Insert and then on Reference, and so on. (2004: 12)

Thus, to summarize these points, there is no neat semantic marker for a practical mode of knowledge and some instances of knowledge-how are not practical but consist merely in knowledge-that.

We concede both these points. That there is no general context-independent semantic marker of a distinction does not imply that there is no such distinction. It simply suggests that it has to be drawn or understood in context. That *some* answers to the question of how to do something consist in knowledge of facts does not imply that others are not essentially practical. In what follows, when it is necessary to distinguish between these two senses of knowledge-how, we will refer to them as *practical* knowledge-how, or know-how, and *theoretical* knowledge-how. So far, nothing has been said which undermines the distinct status of the former.

The second strand of argument concerns the positive account of know-how in knowledge-that terms. There is agreement among supporters of intellectualism that part of the attraction of a separation of knowledge-how and knowledge-that is the assumption that knowledge-that can always be expressed in context free general terms. If that were so, then given that knowledge-how seems sometimes to resist such expression, that would be an argument for their separation. However, such a distinction ignores the resources for the articulation of knowledge-that as well as knowledge-how. Some of what one can know to be the case can be expressed in general terms. One may know that all swans are white, or that all forces, masses and accelerations are governed by the equation $F = ma$. But even knowledge of some apparently singular cases may in fact be general. This is the underlying idea of Bertrand Russell's theory of description. Some claims, which seem to be of the form subject-predicate, are really disguised quantified general claims. Thus, for example, "The present king of France is bald" is analysed as a conjunction of three general quantified sentences:

1. There is at least one present king of France.
2. There is at most one present king of France.
3. Every present king of France is bald.

As Russell argued, however, there are in addition genuine instances of singular thought: thought whose constitution – as well as truth or falsity – depends on contextual relations – acquaintance – between a subject and a particular object. Propositions that connect to objects through the epistemic relation of acquaintance are those that contain "genuinely referring expressions" or "logically proper names". The key difference between propositions which link to the world through descriptions and those that contain genuinely referring expressions is that the latter are vulnerable to the vicissitudes of the empirical world in the following way: logically proper names combine with predicates to express propositions which would not be available to be expressed at all if the objects referred to did not exist.

Of course, Russell places a severe restriction on the application of acquaintance in such a way that this possibility is ruled out. He argues that one can *only* be acquainted with one's sense data and (perhaps) oneself. Thus the only logically proper names are uses of "this" and "that" for sense data and "I" for oneself. In these cases, there is no possibility of entertaining a singular proposition and merely being under an illusion that the logically proper name has a bearer. It is because this restriction is placed on singular propositions that the Theory of Descriptions is required to analyse such sentences as "Homer was bald", which even more so than the present king of France, appear to contain direct referring devices but which might be subject to error. These are also analysed as implicitly containing general quantified claims.

More recently, however, Gareth Evans and John McDowell have argued that Russell's idea of singular, or object-dependent, propositions can be widened by giving up Russell's restriction on the objects available for acquaintance. If instead of placing philosophically motivated limits on this, one accepts at face value the idea that perception provides a form of acquaintance with everyday objects, a different conception of singular propositions (or, to use Fregean terminology, *thoughts*) emerges:

> A typical visual experience of, say, a cat situates its object for the perceiver: in the first instance egocentrically, but, granting the perceiver a general capacity to locate himself, and the objects he can locate egocentrically, in a non-egocentrically conceived world, we can see how the experience's placing of the cat equips the perceiver with knowledge of where in the world it is (even if the only answer he can give to the question where it is is "There"). In view of the kind of object a cat is, there is nothing epistemologically problematic in suggesting that this locating perceptual knowledge of it suffices for knowledge of which object it is (again, even if the only answer the perceiver can give to the question is "That one"). So those visual experiences of objects that situate their objects can be made out to fit the account I suggested of the notion of acquaintance: abandoning Russell's sense-datum epistemology, we can say that such objects are immediately present to the mind.   (McDowell 1998a: 231)

The idea that knowledge can be of *particular* objects in context-dependent thoughts expands the range of knowledge-that from what can be given context-independent articulation to cases that are context-dependent. Object dependent singular thoughts thus provide the resources for *one* way to augment the articulation of knowledge, thereby undermining a false contrast between knowledge-that and knowledge-how.

A *second* way relates to the idea that acquaintance can not only underpin the referential aspect of context-dependent thought or knowledge where the subject already possesses a linguistically expressible concept but also underpin *concepts* that are not fully linguistically expressible. In recent years, this idea has been promoted by McDowell as part of a defence that experience itself is conceptually structured but – crucially – the idea itself need not be linked to that further claim. McDowell's target is the assumption that experience must have a content which is not itself conceptually structured because experience seems to be more fine grained than the concepts that speakers typically possess. Evans, for example, offers the example of colour experience. He suggests that our experience can outstrip our conceptual repertoire because, even if we master labels such as "red", "green" or even "burnt sienna", our experience can present us with detail as fine as individual lines on the spectrum. Thus it seems that experience can contain more detail than can be linguistically codified. McDowell's response is to suggest that experience itself can equip a subject with concepts.

> But why should we accept that a person's ability to embrace colour within her conceptual thinking is restricted to concepts expressible by words like "red" or "green" and phrases like "burnt sienna"? It is possible to acquire the concept of a shade of colour, and most of us have done so. Why not say that one is thereby equipped to embrace shades of colour within one's conceptual thinking with the very same determinateness with which they are presented in one's visual experience, so that one's concepts can capture colours no less sharply than one's experiences presents them? (McDowell 1994: 56)

When presented with a colour experience, a subject with the general concept of "shade of colour" can acquire a particular concept expressed with the demonstrative phrase "That colour!" or "That shade!". Such a concept is not linguistically codified, but that need not preclude its being conceptual. Some further conditions have to be met, however, for it to count as conceptual. One such plausible condition is what Gareth Evans calls the "generality constraint" (Evans 1982: 100–105). Conceptually structured thoughts are combinable. Thus to be able to think that that a is F, one must be able to think that a is G, H or I and that b, c or d is F (although one need not think they actually are). In this case, the recognitional capacity on which the concept depends needs to last longer than the experience that gives rise to it itself even if it is short lived.

> It is the conceptual content of such a recognitional capacity that can be made explicit with the help of a sample, something that is guaranteed to be available at the time of the experience with which the capacity sets in. Later in the life of the capacity it can be given linguistic expression again, if the course of experience is

favourable; that is, if experience again, or still, presents one with a suitable sample. But even in the absence of a sample, the capacity goes on being exploitable as long as it lasts, in thoughts based on memory: thoughts that are not necessarily capable of receiving an overt expression that fully determines their content.

(Ibid.: 57–8)

As long as the capacity has some duration it can allow a particular experienced shade of colour to play a role in reasoning – via inferences, for example – and thus count as genuinely conceptual. While a full evaluation of other arguments for nonconceptual content, such as those based on the explanation of conceptual abilities, is beyond the scope of this book, the idea of demonstrative concepts can at least counter the most obvious phenomenological objection to the idea that experience is conceptual (see Ch. 5 for an objection to this strategy).

Just as recognition can play a role in constituting a demonstrative thought which can underpin knowledge-that, so it can underpin knowledge-how. A first step is to consider a demonstrative to a way of acting – "that! way", for example – as a way to ride a bike.[1]

> If we are seeking a candidate piece of information that is known to be the case in such examples as knowing how to ride a bike, it is that this sequence of actions – present to the agent and knower in the course of actions and accessed by knower as his or her actions – is a way to ride a bike. The aim of this rather rough formulation is not to slot the proposal into some standard account of knowledge, but rather, in a relatively theoretically neutral way, to indicate a candidate for what might count as the kind of information in question in such cases. The agent need not be riding a bike to have the sample actions available to him or her, because, in principle, there might be simulation devices in the context of which the agent performs the actions without actually riding a bike. (Snowdon 2004: 28)

The idea is that a demonstrative indication of a *way* of riding can carry the content that is known in such a case. Just as such demonstratives have become familiar in the context of knowledge-that so they can also serve to articulate the content that is known in practical know-how. We will approach this idea in stages.

As noted above, there are cases of (theoretical) knowledge-how which are instances of knowledge-that because they comprise merely knowledge of facts as to how something was or is to be done *carrying no implication of ability*. In the examples given earlier, the facts known were all fully linguistically codified (how to spell "comma"; how to get to Swansea by train). But there are also cases of theoretical knowledge-how which are context-dependent: for example, knowledge of how to leave a building which consists in the non-practical knowledge that that! way is the exit. A demonstrative element enables thoughts that rely on contextual links and hence both knowledge-that and theoretical knowledge-how.

But in the case of practical knowledge-how to ride a bicycle, there seems to be something yet further, beyond even the demonstrative element: an essentially practical or personal form of knowledge. To clarify this, consider the case of a child being taught how to ride a bicycle by an adult, at a stage in the learning process in which the child still has the common – if inexplicable – habit of taking his feet off the pedals, leading to instability and collision. His teacher gives a demonstration of proficient cycling, with steady pedalling, steering and gradual braking and says: "That! is the way to ride." Both adult and child can entertain the thought that that! way is the way to ride. Both can acquire a piece of knowledge-that because both can acquire the knowledge-that that! is the way to ride. And thus, in one sense, both can have knowledge-how to ride a bike. They both know how to ride a bike in that they both know that that! way is one way to ride a bike. Only one of them, however, has practical knowledge-how to ride a bicycle. So in the sense of knowledge-how which is connected to ability (know-how), only one has it.

In the quotation from Snowdon above, this distinction can be captured in the idea that the way to ride a bike is "present to the agent and knower in the course of actions and accessed by knower as his or her actions". In other words, the action is not merely available to the knower as a demonstrative thought: that! way of riding is a way to ride a bike. Rather, it is specifically available to the rider as *her* way of riding. Stanley and Williamson address this distinction more explicitly in their account of knowledge-how which builds on the aforementioned notion of demonstrative content but augments it so as to distinguish the cases of agent and spectator.

> Suppose that Hannah does not know-how to ride a bicycle. Susan points to John, who is riding a bicycle, and says, "That is a way for you to ride a bicycle". Suppose that the way in which John is riding his bicycle is in fact a way for Hannah to ride a bicycle. So, where the demonstrative "that way" denotes John's way of riding a bicycle, (28) seems true:

> (28) Hannah knows that that way is a way for her to ride a bicycle.

> Relative to this context, however:

> (29) Hannah, knows (how PRO, to ride a bicycle).

> seems false ... Where the demonstrated way is the only contextually salient way of riding a bicycle, (28) and (29) ascribe knowledge of the same proposition to Hannah. But this proposition is ascribed under different guises. In (28), knowledge of the proposition is ascribed to Hannah under a demonstrative mode of presentation. In (29), Knowledge of that proposition is ascribed to Hannah under a different mode of presentation, what we call a *practical* mode of presentation.
>
> (2001: 428–9)

("PRO" is a kind of pronoun to mark the subject of the infinitive. It means either the subject of the main clause or something like "one" in English.)

> So, here is our complete account of knowing how. Suppose modes of presentation are semantically relevant. Then (29) is true relative to a context if and only if there is some contextually relevant way $\dot{\omega}$ such that Hannah stands in the knowledge-that relation to the Russellian proposition that $\dot{\omega}$ is a way for Hannah to ride a bicycle, and Hannah entertains this proposition under a practical mode of presentation.
>
> (*Ibid.*: 430)

On this account, know-how is a species of knowledge-that. It is not only in those cases where the answer to the implicit question of how something is to be done turns out to be expressible in straight forwardly knowledge-that terms, but also in cases of *practical* know-how. The content of the knowledge is captured through the demonstrative thought; its (separable) *practicality* or *personal* nature is captured by the idea that the content is entertained under a "practical mode of presentation".

This account is put forward by Stanley and Williamson as part of their intellectualism. It is a rival to the Rylean account that knowledge-how consists in a complex of abilities and propensities. One reason for needing it – and for the specific shape it takes – is that they take the regress argument to have been disposed of. We have of course demonstrated that that is not in fact the case under a plausible interpretation of it. But there is another and independent line of thought which is simply that there is no connection between know-how and ability. Before returning to reassess the role of expressing know-how in demonstrative terms in our own account, we will examine that further line of thought. Does know-how imply ability?

KNOWING HOW AND ABILITY

As outlined in Chapter 1, Ryle's response to his regress argument is to flesh out some account of how the "exercise of intelligence in practice" is not a twofold operation of considering a prescription and then executing it but rather one thing. His account stresses action and ability. Considering a boy learning to play chess, Ryle suggests that this may begin through explicitly learning the rules. But eventually his making only correct moves need not be the result of citing any such rules to himself. He may even forget how to articulate the explicit rules. Equally, however, one can learn how to play chess just by watching moves made or corrected and withdrawn, without ever acquiring a theory of correct play.

> The boy is not said to know how to play, if all that he can do is to recite the rules accurately. He must be able to make the required moves. But he is said to know how to play if, although he cannot cite the rules, he normally does make the permitted moves, avoid the forbidden moves and protest if his opponent makes forbidden moves. His knowledge-how is exercised primarily in the moves that he makes, or concedes, and in the moves that he avoids or vetoes. (Ryle 1949: 41)

Over the course of the *Concept of Mind*, Ryle develops a number of distinctions between capacities and mere habits and between task verbs and achievements which contribute to his positive characterization of know-how. But the basic idea is that there is an essential connection between such knowledge and ability. This connection is, however, contested by the new intellectualists.

> It is simply false, however, that ascriptions of knowledge-how ascribe abilities. As Ginet and others have pointed out, ascriptions of knowledge-how do not even entail ascriptions of the corresponding abilities. For example, a ski instructor may know how to perform a certain complex stunt, without being able to perform it herself. Similarly, a master pianist who loses both of her arms in a tragic car accident still knows how to play the piano. But she has lost her ability to do so. It follows that Ryle's own positive account of knowledge-how is demonstrably false. (Stanley & Williamson 2001: 416)

The converse implication from ability to know-how is also questioned.

> A man is in a room, which, because he has not explored it in the least, he does, as yet, not know how to get out of. In fact there is an obvious exit which he can easily open. He is perfectly able to get out, he can get out, but does not know how to (as yet) … Martin is someone who can do fifty consecutive press ups. Let us

suppose that none of us here can do that. It would be, I suggest, quite counterintuitive to say that Martin knows how to do something we do not know how to do. Rather, he is, simply, stronger then we are. He is stronger, but not more knowledgeable.

(Snowdon 2004: 11)

If the putative connection that Ryle stresses between knowledge-how and ability can be questioned, then that undermines Ryle's positive account of such knowledge and thus provides a further, and independent, line of argument for intellectualism.

Why might knowledge-how not imply ability? Recalling the distinction drawn earlier between varieties of knowledge-how, one form can be ascribed correctly to someone who has *theoretical* knowledge (of) how something can be or is to be done. To repeat an earlier example, one knows *how* to get from London to Swansea by train before midday by knowing *that* one first catches the 7.30 a.m. train to Reading from Paddington, and then one from there onwards and so on. In at least some such cases of theoretical knowledge-how, there need be no implication from knowledge to ability. Thus is the ski instructor's knowledge of how to perform the stunt comprises knowledge-that it consists of five steps, there is no implication for ability. In general, theoretical knowledge-how seems to carry no implications for (the most readily associated) ability.

The Rylean can concede that when the knowledge-how is of this sort there is no connection with an ability; but there are some cases of theoretical knowledge-how which do at least raise the expectation of its presence. John Bengson and Marc Moffett contrast two examples (Bengson & Moffett 2007). Consider:

Irina knows how to do a quintuple salchow.

Like the example of the ski instructor it seems that the following claim does not follow.

Irina is able to do a quintuple salchow.

It is thus possible that Irina knows how to do a quintuple salchow, but she is unable to do one. By contrast, if

Irina knows how to add.

then it seems that

Irina is able to add.

And it would be odd, at the very least, to say that Irina knows how to add, but she is unable to do so.[2] In the former case, the knowledge ascribed might be theoretical knowledge-how. She knows that in order to do a quintuple Salchow, one must take off from the back inside edge of one foot and land on the back outside edge of the opposite foot after five complete rotations in the air. Such knowledge carries no implication for an ability actually to make that jump.

Even if what is ascribed in the second case is also ascribed on the basis of a similar theoretical consideration there does seem a connection to ability. A theoretical ascription might be made on the basis of knowledge of the axioms of Peano arithmetic and the definition of addition. Thus to know how to add might be to know that ... But even so, this case does seem to carry some expectation of an ability. In the absence of particular defeating conditions, such as an abysmally short memory or an inability to focus on figures, an inability to add would undermine even the ascription of the theoretical knowledge. A failure to be able to add would suggest, in the absence of further explanation, a failure to understand the truths ascribed. Such cases complicate the idea that theoretical knowledge-how carries no implications for ability: in some cases it seems that it does.

In any event, this does not appear to be the concern in Stanley and Williamson's other example: the pianist who loses both of her arms in a car accident. Stanley and Williamson claim that while she has lost her ability to play, she has not lost her knowledge-how to play. Hence the Rylean connection between know-how and ability is threatened even in a case that looks to be practical rather than theoretical knowledge-how. But it is not clear that this is so. A defence of the connection could be made in one of two ways. One could either argue that she no longer knows how to play the piano or one could argue that she still knows how to play and she is still able. Alva Noë argues for the latter:

> I agree that there would be no contradiction in supposing that Maestra knows how to play (the) piano, even though she cannot now play. But this doesn't show that knowing how to play the piano is not the same as having the ability to play. For there are (uncontroversially) at least two different ways one can be unable to play the piano (or exercise a skill). One might be unable to play because one doesn't know how; because, that is, one *lacks* the ability. Or one might be unable to play because, even though one does know how, conditions whose satisfaction is necessary for one to exercise one's ability are not satisfied. For example, no matter how good a piano player I am, I won't be able to play piano if there is no piano ready to hand. Lacking access to a piano would mean I would be unable to play, even though I

> would not, for that reason, lack the relevant know-how. This explains, I think, our shared judgement about Maestra. We judge she knows how to play even though she is now unable to play, because we think of the loss of her arms as comparable (in the relevant sense) to the loss of her piano.   (Noë 2005: 283)

This line of argument requires thinking that the lack of arms is akin to a lack of a piano on which to exercise one's ability. That may seem hard to swallow, but it can be complemented by thinking about the former option.

It is important to keep in mind that for this example to be distinct from the interpretation offered above of the ski instructor – in order, that is, to offer the broadest argument against Ryle – the kind of knowledge ascribed is not merely *theoretical* knowledge-how. It is not merely knowledge *that* notes are struck with fingers in such and such order. Rather, it is knowledge that such and such a way is a way to play the piano where the way is picked out through a demonstrative thought and also as her actions or under a practical mode of presentation. So one way to think of her remaining knowledge is as knowledge "from within" of how and where her fingers would need to be moved, if she still had any, to strike the notes, and thus to play the piano. But now, lacking the arms, hands and fingers to locate a space of possible movement, it is not clear that she still can have *this* knowledge and, consequently, that she has either the ability or the practical know-how.

The injured pianist is thus not a knock down objection to the connection between practical knowledge-how and ability. If we concede that she does retain her knowledge, we can also argue that she retains her standing ability to play. It is just that it can no more be exercised without arms than it can without a piano. On the other hand, if it seems strange still to say that she retains that standing ability, that may be because without relevant body-parts through which to locate a space of possible action, she no longer has practical knowledge either. What seems likely is that the pianist slips from one case to other as the plausibility of an ascription of relevant fine-grained spatial and personal demonstrative knowledge weakens over time.

So a Rylean can concede that knowledge-how is ascribed in two ways, which are blurred by relevant semantic markers (such as the use of the phrase "knowledge-how" or the infinitive of the verb which follows) and have to be picked out in context. One of them is an answer to an implicit question of how something is to be done which, in the context, requires merely theoretical knowledge with no implication for ability. The other marks a practical capacity for which the Rylean connection to ability holds. Counter examples to the Rylean connection seem to turn on an interpretation of the former theoretical sort. There is no reason to think that they work for the latter sort.

PRACTICAL MODES OF PRESENTATION

Although Stanley and Williamson reject the connection between knowledge-how and ability, their analysis of knowledge-how includes the idea of a *practical mode of presentation*. This enables them to distinguish between the case of the proficient cyclist and the learner, both of whom are able to recognize that a particular way of acting (that! way) is a way to ride a bicycle. The learner may have theoretical knowledge-how. He may be able to answer questions as to how to ride a bicycle by saying that one needs to keep the feet on the pedals, that one not actively steer the bike so much as lean, that braking should be smooth. Such answers are general and fully linguistically codified. But he may also, in the presence of his teacher's graceful performance, be able to add to those answers a context-dependent demonstrative: "In fact, one should ride like that!" Still, that is merely theoretical practical knowledge.

The teacher, by contrast, is able to entertain the thought that a *particular* way is the way to ride a bike in a different way: under a practical mode of presentation. Stanley and Williamson introduce the practical mode of presentation by analogy with a first-person mode of presentation.

> Suppose that John is looking in a mirror, which he mistakenly believes to be a window. Seeing a man whose pants are on fire, and not recognizing that man as himself, John forms the demonstrative belief that that man is on fire. Intuitively, however, John does not believe that his own pants are on fire. That is, relative to the envisaged context, (26) is true and (27) is false:
>
> (26) John believes that that man has burning pants.
>
> (27) John believes that he himself has burning pants
>
> Given that "that man" refers to John, however, the complement clauses of (26) and (27) express the same proposition, namely, the singular proposition containing John. To distinguish between (26) and (27), contemporary advocates of Russellian propositions appeal to different modes of presentation under which that proposition is entertained. In the envisaged context, (26) is associated with a demonstrative mode of presentation (or guise) of the relevant proposition, whereas (27) is associated with a first-personal mode of presentation of that very same proposition.
>
> (Stanley & Williamson 2001: 428)

John does not believe that his own pants are on fire but he does believe that someone's pants are: the man whom he can see. So he believes, of that man, that his pants are on fire. Since that man is himself, he believes, of himself, that his pants are on fire. His belief is true (as in fact it is) if and only if his own pants are on fire. That is also what would have made true the belief that he does not (yet!) have: namely, that is own pants are on fire. Despite that similarity (what would make the beliefs true, both the actual belief he has and the one he might have had and will surely come to have), these are different beliefs. Crucially, the different beliefs lead to different actions. In the actual case, he might move forward to try to open a window and warn someone else of their predicament. In the counterfactual case in which he realizes that that man is actually himself, he will attend to his own clothes.

One way to accommodate the sameness and difference in play is to think that there is a common state of affairs (John's pants being on fire), which can be thought of in two ways: either as that! man's or as mine. The two ways of thinking motivate or rationalize different further beliefs and actions. One is a demonstrative belief; the other is a first-person belief. The thoughts are thus differently presented to, or entertained by, the thinker. The different properties of these different ways of holding thoughts that are related to the same state of affairs is widely taken to justify philosophers postulating such distinct "modes of presentation".

Stanley and Williamson argue that the same sort of argument justifies the postulation of practical modes of presentation (in addition to first-person modes and demonstrative modes). Just as there is a difference between:

(26) John believes that that man has burning pants; and
(27) John believes that he himself has burning pants

so there is a difference between the learner/spectator and the proficient cyclist, both of whom are able to think, of a way of cycling, that that! is a way to ride a bike:

(28) Hannah knows that that way is a way for her to ride a bicycle; and
(29) Hannah, knows (how PRO, to ride a bicycle).

Where the difference in the former case turns on how thoughts that are related to the same state of affairs can be differently entertained, in the latter it relates to how a state of affairs – that a particular contextually indicated way is a way to ride a bicycle – is thought about.

Little further detail is given regarding the nature of practical modes of presentation over and above pointing out that it is (also) very difficult to characterize the nature of first-person modes of presentation. But this does not, it is argued, show that practical knowledge is not propositional or a species of knowledge-that. There are, however, some complications with this approach:

1. There is a disanalogy between first-person modes of presentation and practical modes. The former stand in *justificatory* relations to other thoughts and actions. But the latter is enabling rather than justificatory.

Realizing that one's own trousers are on fire is a *reason* to direct one's attentions to oneself rather than anyone else. It justifies thoughts and action with a different focus to the thought that that! man's trousers are burning. But entertaining the thought that that! way is a way to ride a bike under a practical mode of presentation does not seem to play the same justificatory role. Of course, if one *believes* that one knows how to ride a bicycle then, like any belief, that belief stands in justificatory relations to other beliefs and actions. So, similarly, if one believes that one entertains thoughts about ways to ride under practical modes of presentation, that belief will justify others. But it seems unlikely that the practical mode of presentation itself can be nominated through its distinctive justificatory relations.

2. The analysis suggests that Stanley and Williamson's criticism of the Rylean connection between practical knowledge-how and ability is surprising. Given the lack of independent characterization of the practical mode of presentation, it is characterized instead through the difference between the cases summarized as 28 and 29 above. That is the difference between having and not having practical knowledge-how. But given that Stanley and Williamson are aiming to shed light on that distinction, they cannot rest content simply with an unanalysed appeal to its existence. So the distinction seems instead to depend on the fact that a proficient cyclist knows how to ride a bicycle not just in the sense that she can answer questions about in what that consists but in the practical sense that she is able to do it as an intelligent action. That in turn suggests that what the practical mode of presentation is designed to capture is the connection between practical knowledge-how and ability: a Rylean connection they reject.

Since they think that the injured pianist retains knowledge of how to play the piano even though she has lost the ability to play it, she must be able to entertain thoughts about relevant actions under practical modes. But without some broader account of why she retains this ability (to entertain such thoughts), a brute appeal to the example does not help shed light on such practical modes and on how they can serve as a rival to the Rylean conception of what practical knowledge-how comprises.

It is worth keeping in mind the role of this form of analysis for intellectualism. Since it takes the regress argument to be unsuccessful and denies the link between know-how and ability, the full weight of a constitutive account falls on the account given in knowledge-that terms. But it is not clear that one aspect of that – the practical mode of presentation – can be clarified in the absence of the connection to ability.

This suggests a dilemma for Stanley and Williamson's account. It might be that, having initially severed the connection between practical know-how and ability, they still want, sometimes at least, to earn the right to some such connection. Perhaps in some key central cases practical knowledge and ability do go hand in hand. But if so, something like Ryle's regress argument threatens since practical ability would be explained using intellectualist materials. If on the other there is no *a priori* connection between the practical mode of presentation and ability, in what sense is it practical? However, if one takes the Rylean view of the priority of know-how to be an insight, and the regress argument to be broadly successful, those views can be combined with the idea of demonstrative concepts to show how know-how can be put, relative to a context, into words. What it is to entertain a demonstrative thought under a practical mode of presentation is to have relevant practical know-how.

INTELLECTUALISM, KNOWING HOW AND GETTIER CASES

If intellectualism were correct and know-how were a species of knowledge-that then one would expect features of knowledge-that to have equivalences in the case of knowledge-how. One such possibility is that of Gettier cases. These have been familiar in debates about knowledge since the 1960s to criticize the justified true belief analysis of knowledge-that. In such cases, a subject has a true belief for which they also have a justification but, intuitively, this still does not amount to knowledge. Gettier's own examples include this one:

> Suppose that Smith and Jones have applied for a certain job. And suppose that Smith has strong evidence for the following conjunctive proposition:
>
> (d) Jones is the man who will get the job, and Jones has ten coins in his pocket.
>
> Smith's evidence for (d) might be that the president of the company assured him that Jones would in the end be selected, and that he, Smith, had counted the coins in Jones's pocket ten minutes ago. Proposition (d) entails:
>
> (e) The man who will get the job has ten coins in his pocket.
>
> Let us suppose that Smith sees the entailment from (d) to (e), and accepts (e) on the grounds of (d), for which he has strong evidence. In this case, Smith is clearly justified in believing that (e) is true.

But imagine, further, that unknown to Smith, he himself, not Jones, will get the job. And, also, unknown to Smith, he himself has ten coins in his pocket. Proposition (e) is then true, though proposition (d), from which Smith inferred (e), is false. In our example, then, all of the following are true: *(i)* (e) is true, *(ii)* Smith believes that (e) is true, and *(iii)* Smith is justified in believing that (e) is true. But it is equally clear that Smith does not *know* that (e) is true; for (e) is true in virtue of the number of coins in Smith's pocket, while Smith does not know how many coins are in Smith's pocket, and bases his belief in (e) on a count of the coins in Jones's pocket, whom he falsely believes to be the man who will get the job.   (Gettier 1963: 122)

Whatever the appropriate philosophical response to such an example – whatever its consequences for a justified, true belief analysis of knowledge, and whatever might need to be added to that analysis to rule them out – it seems that our intuitions about the nature of knowledge allow for the construction of cases like this where the three conditions at least appear to be met and yet this still does not amount to a case of knowledge. So it would be evidence that know-how really is a species of knowledge-that if similar cases could be derived for it.

While Stanley and Williamson report that they doubt "that every kind of knowledge-that is susceptible to Gettier cases" they still suggest that although "one might think it is difficult to conceive of Gettier-cases for knowledge-how. But if knowledge-how is really a kind of knowledge-that, there should be such cases." They go on to sketch such a case:

Bob wants to learn how to fly in a flight simulator. He is instructed by Henry. Unknown to Bob, Henry is a malicious imposter who has inserted a randomizing device in the simulator's controls and intends to give all kinds of incorrect advice. Fortunately, by sheer chance the randomizing device causes exactly the same results in the simulator as would have occurred without it, and by incompetence Henry gives exactly the same advice as a proper instructor would have done. Bob passes the course with flying colors. He has still not flown a real plane. Bob has a justified true belief about how to fly. But there is a good sense in which he does not *know* how to fly.   (Stanley & Williamson 2001: 435)

In the case of theoretical knowledge-how, Gettierization is straightforward precisely because you can *tell* how to do something. From the earlier case of knowing how to get from London to Swansea by train before midday by knowing that one first catches the 7.30 a.m. train to Reading from Paddington one could construct a Gettier case in which one's apparent knowledge of the 7.30 a.m. train to Reading from Paddington were in fact merely a true belief justified in an appropriately flawed manner (for example, via a false lemma). But the example given by Stanley and Williamson looks instead to be of practical knowledge-how. Even in this case, they suggest, an ability to fly a plane arrived at in an appropriately wrong way will fail to count as knowledge of how to fly the plane. This, however, puts intuitions about know-how under some strain. As Ted Poston argues, there is a conflict between the necessary requirement for something to count as a Gettier case of know-how and for it to count – contra to its Gettier status – as knowledge.

> The first premise of the argument states that Gettier cases for know-how, if they exist, require that the subject intelligently and successfully φ, where φ ranges over actions. In general, Gettier cases for know-how, if they exist, would require that the intelligence condition and the success condition are satisfied. These conditions are analogous to the justified belief condition and the truth condition in Gettier cases of knowledge-that. In a Gettier case for know-that justified belief comes apart from the truth in a way that is incompatible with knowledge-that. So also, in a purported Gettier case for knowledge-how the intelligence base the subject uses doesn't connect to success in the right way to yield knowledge-how … The second premise of the argument is that one knows how to φ, if one can intelligently and successfully φ. If, for instance, Sally intelligently moves this way and that way with the goal of riding a bike and she succeeds then Sally knows how to ride a bike. So given the first premise, the sufficient condition for knowing how laid down in the second premise is satisfied. Therefore any alleged Gettier case for knowing how will turn out *not* to be a Gettier case, for it will be a genuine case of knowing how. (Poston 2009: 744)

The significant step of this argument is the second. It would not help intellectualists to challenge Poston's specific suggestion for how Gettier cases of know-how are to be constructed. The key claim is that successful action (of the right intelligent sort) implies possession of know-how. Poston proceeds to argue that there is an underlying disanalogy between knowledge-that and knowledge-how: "Knowledge-how isn't constrained by the same anti-luck intuitions as propositional knowledge" (*ibid.*: 746). Acquiring the right sort of skill through luck does not, he contends, undermine the status of the know-how ascribed on the basis of that (right sort of) skill. Now it is important to note that this is not an acceptable conclusion respecting PA. Since the principle asserts that nothing cognitive cannot be explicated in context-dependent terms (where the *personal* is an irreducible part of the context) then in so far as luck effects knowing it must effect knowing how. There is however a possibility that Poston overlooks; namely, that luck affects know-how differently to knowledge-that and as a consequence affects the nature of relevant Gettier cases.

Take the case of someone who has practised bowling googlies and can reliably bowl them under most conditions, although sometimes his skill lets him down. When all goes well, a successful bowl can be ascribed to his know-how, which as a general and standing ability explains its instances. But, contra Poston, it does seem that a Gettier case can be generated even for a successful instance. Suppose that, unknown to the bowler, his ability is systematically fallible and would break down under particular wind conditions. He cannot bowl googlies in a specific but unusual combination of wind speeds and directions. But on a particular occasion, distracted, he moves his arm non-standardly but in such a way that combines with the wind conditions to yield a perfect googly. This is a case where a generally reliable piece of know-how lets the subject down but, by luck, yields successful action. It is a practical analogue of a Gettier case but distinct from the form suggested by Stanley and Williamson (see also Stanley 2011a: 175–81).

This suggests that Gettier examples can be helpful in our analysis. The distinction between theoretical and practical forms of knowledge-how was introduced to distinguish between cases where the ascription of knowledge-how as an implicit answer to the question of how to do something carries no general expectation of an ability from cases where it does. That is our *first* diagnostic test.

The distinction itself has two immediate difficulties, however. First: how can it avoid a dormitive-virtue-like vacuity? Since the idea of the distinction between theoretical and practical forms of knowledge-how was set out as it was, how can the claim that only the latter supports a Rylean connection to ability be informative? Equally, how can the concession to intellectualism that theoretical forms do not in general (*modulo* the conceptual examples mentioned above) support that connection be constrained so as not to concede the game?

The second difficulty is this: how can one frame the distinction? If demonstratives can be used to construe context-dependent thoughts in propositional or theoretical terms and practical knowledge-how is a species of knowledge-that, then even practical knowledge-how is an answer to an implicit question of how something is to be done (even if the thought involves a practical mode of presentation). After all, the prima facie appeal of "mode of presentation" talk is that it allows one to factor out the complicating talk of cognitively relevant abilities and specify (*tell*) the content of a piece of know-how.

The possibility of constructing Gettier examples serves as a *second* diagnostic test. Where knowledge-how supports Gettier examples of the standard sort, there it is theoretical. Where it supports a mere analogue form, there it is practical. In other words, we can distinguish (practical) knowledge-how to φ from (theoretical) knowledge-how to φ because the former and not the latter imply ability, the mark of which is that luck comes into play at a different level: specifically, at the level where ability is already presupposed and which gives us some insight into the *content* of the know-how in question. So the point at which luck affects knowing how reveals the sort of knowledge it is: that is to say, *personal*. For the bulk of this book, we are concerned with practical (personal) knowledge-how.

INTELLECTUALISM AND RYLEANISM

As we saw at the start of this chapter, the "new intellectualist" backlash against Ryleanism centres on three claims:

(i) That Ryle's regress argument misfires.
(ii) That Ryle's constitutive account of knowing how as a complex of abilities is false.
(iii) That an alternative account of knowing how is available.

We have attempted to argue against the first and the second of these claims. Something like Ryle's regress argument sheds light on the relation of theoretical and practical knowledge. As Ryle says, "intelligent practice is not a step-child of theory". And once one distinguishes between theoretical and practical forms of knowledge-how, recognizing that there are no general context-independent semantic markers, the second claim can be disputed. There *is* a connection between practical knowledge-how and ability.

What then of the third aspect? Earlier we argued that, having rejected the connection between know-how and ability, intellectualists were unable to give a satisfactory account of what they meant by a practical mode of presentation, which is a key element of their constitutive account of know-how. By contrast, although it has been traditionally put forward as part of an *opposition* to a Rylean view, if it were added to a Rylean account, it would not face that same difficulty. Further such a combination has the virtue of shedding light on what is known in know-how and hence rendering tacit knowledge less mysterious.

Recall the principles of *codifiability* and *articulacy*:

PC   All knowledge can be fully articulated, or codified, in context-independent terms.

PA   All knowledge can be articulated, either in context-independent
     terms or in context-dependent terms.

The recognition that knowledge-that need not be expressible in context-independent and general terms – that is, rejecting PC – undermines an important unfortunate assumed contrast between it and knowledge-how. On that assumption, knowledge-how is distinct in part because it resists codification in fully linguistic, context-independent terms. But further, with no model for an alternative to that form of articulation for knowledge-that, this assumption can put under strain the idea that knowledge-how is really a form of knowledge at all. Rejecting PA puts the status of know-how as tacit *knowledge* under strain. The reason for this is that it can seem to lack any kind of conceptual articulation and thus any kind of content. Outside conceptual articulation, it is not clear what grasp we have of any notion of a content to be grasped by a knowing subject. But if there is no content to the subject's "attitude" to the world, how can this be a form of knowledge at all?

While some philosophers whose work is associated with tacit knowledge (such as Hubert Dreyfus, although he takes himself to be articulating something deeper and less intellectual than tacit knowledge) embrace this idea, we do not, and we will return to our disagreement with Dreyfus in Chapter 5. But it is useful here to summarize our agreement with intellectualism.

Like intellectualism, we agree that demonstrative thoughts serve as a model for the articulation of the content of both theoretical and practical knowledge-how.[3] Demonstrative elements can underpin thoughts that could not be articulated using linguistic tokens only. Such thoughts can underpin knowledge-that. So knowledge-that can be articulated using demonstratives. The same applies to knowledge-how. There is thus no reason to take the fact that the content of such practical knowledge cannot be fully linguistically codified (that is, put in context-independent terms) to suggest that it is in any sense ineffable. PC can be rejected without rejecting PA. Practical knowledge can be expressed through suitable demonstrations in which actions themselves serve to convey what it is that is known.

This line of thought may prompt three immediate worries. First, even though the failure of full linguistic codification need not imply that knowledge-how is not conceptually articulated (any more than it implies that theoretical knowledge is not conceptually articulated), there may, still, be reason to think that some forms of practical knowledge-how, especially those relevant to tacit knowledge, are *not* conceptually articulated. One reason for thinking this has already been suggested in the previous chapter by the various versions of the regress argument. If these show that theoretical knowledge presupposes practical knowledge, might that not show that such practical knowledge is somehow pre- or nonconceptual? We will return to this question in Chapter 5.

Second, even though the failure of full linguistic codification need not imply that knowledge-how is not conceptually articulated, there may still be reasons to think that some forms of practical knowledge-how, especially those relevant to tacit knowledge, are *ineffable*. One reason for thinking this is that while practical knowledge might be expressible piecemeal, its full expression may seem impossible. We will return to this question in the discussion of Adrian Moore's reading of Wittgenstein in Chapter 3.

Third, as has already been discussed in this chapter, while a demonstrative indication of a way of riding a bike makes available the thought that that! way is a way to ride, there remains a difference between the thoughts that a spectator and a proficient teacher can thus have. In an account of knowhow, this appeal to a demonstrative element does not capture what seems, against a Rylean background, to be the key thing: the difference between having and not having the ability to ride in that way. And thus it might seem that that key aspect is, precisely, *not* expressed or articulated in the way so far indicated.

Our aim is not to undermine the Rylean emphasis on the priority of practice. It follows from the regress argument. There is no need to think that, in accordance with what Ryle calls the "intellectualist legend", one can explain skilful practice through prior grasp of propositions. Thus there is no reason to think that the difference between the learner and the teacher can be first explained and then crossed by the marshalling of propositions. But what the teacher can do, which the learner cannot yet do, can be expressed by saying that it is doing this! And that demonstrative element can bring a practice into the realm of thought.

But let us probe the gap between the teacher and learner a little more. Suppose that the lesson takes place near a circus and one of the clowns rides by. Both pupil and teacher can agree that despite the clown's manifest skill, that! is not a way for the pupil to attempt to ride by contrast with the teacher's staid and modest approach thus!. But agreement at that level may mask aspects of the teacher's way of riding that the learner has simply not grasped. He has, perhaps, not noticed the placing of the balls rather than the instep of the teacher's feet, nor the way she concentrates on turning circles, rather than simply pressing down on the pedals with her feet. For the teacher, these are all aspects of her performance which can be gestured towards and recognized in others' performance. The pupil's lack may thus, in part, be an intellectual one. With this contrast, the teacher's ability does seem to approach meriting the label "knowledge". It is a fitting together of articulable subsidiary elements.

But perhaps the pupil is an old cycle lesson hand. He knows that he should do all those things. He can spot particularly fine examples among his fellow learners. It is simply that he cannot attune his body to the simultaneous demands he understands and how one does that, how one learns to do everything together, might be something about which the teacher has no views.

Does such knowledge explain the expert's greater expertise or does it merely result from it? Is the difference of ability a matter of underlying pre-epistemic substrate? Here is an analogy. The congenitally blind lack the capacity for practical colour discrimination. They thus lack full colour concept mastery. Thus they lack some knowledge of colour including, for example, practical knowledge concerning paint matching, bird recognition, pictorial aesthetics and so on. Is the difference between the congenitally blind and people with full colour vision, and thus greater conceptual mastery, one of *knowledge* of colour – both theoretical and practical – or underlying pre-epistemic substrate? The question is surely mistaken. The causes of blindness and sight may not be the result of the subject's knowledge or lack. The clearest explanatory cause may be physiological. Still, the difference between those who can and those who cannot recognize birds by the colours of their plumage, or select matching or interestingly complementary paint colours is one of knowledge. In situations where they can be exercised, ability and practical knowledge-how go hand in hand.

Ryle's regress argument has provided the basis in this chapter for a suggestion for an analysis of tacit knowledge as personal and context-dependent knowing how. It balances the idea that it is practical knowledge with the idea that can be articulated. Even though the articulation is context-dependent and practical, that avoids the threat that tacit knowledge might fail to be any kind of knowledge at all.

The next chapter will begin an analysis of Wittgenstein's regress argument, based on an analysis of rule-following. Although there are clear similarities between it and Ryle's regress argument, it has been used to defend a different view of the role of tacit knowledge, one which, we will argue, plays up its tacit status only by risking its status as knowledge. Wittgenstein's regress argument has been thought (i) to undermine the idea that there is anything properly graspable when one grasps a rule, or (ii) to make to make it ineffable, or (iii) to make it dependent on a deep background of tacit understanding. By providing a distinct response to Wittgenstein's argument over the course of the next two chapters, we aim further to defend the conception outlined in the first two chapters.

3. WITTGENSTEIN'S REGRESS ARGUMENT AND PERSONAL KNOWLEDGE

INTRODUCTION

In Chapter 1, we examined three historical resources for an account of tacit knowledge: the work of Polanyi, Ryle and Heidegger. We argued that through a shared opposition to a Cartesian approach to knowledge they also share an emphasis on the priority of both practical knowledge over theoretical knowledge and the importance of the person and the personal. All three also deploy a regress argument against a view of theoretical knowledge. Taken together, this suggested a clue for thinking about tacit knowledge. Tacit knowledge is practical knowledge or know-how. But this left the nature of what is known and the precise sense in which it is tacit undetermined.

In Chapter 2, we examined Ryle's regress argument and his account of know-how in more detail. We defended the regress argument against recent criticism by defenders of "intellectualism". But we conceded to them two important points. First, there is no general semantic marker for practical knowledge: practical knowledge-how has to be distinguished from theoretical knowledge-how in context. But that does not threaten the distinction. Second, practical knowledge has a conceptually structured content that can be articulated "from within". To that extent, practical knowledge is more like theoretical knowledge or knowledge-that than might at first be thought. So if tacit knowledge is construed as practical knowledge there is, nevertheless, a content known. But unlike theoretical knowledge (and contra the new intellectualists view), there is, as Ryle asserts, a close connection between practical knowledge and ability.

To what extent is the resultant view of tacit knowledge really tacit? We ended Chapter 2 with the claim that it merits that label because it cannot be put into words independently of a context. It cannot be fully linguistically articulated or "codified". That is the sense in which our view of tacit knowledge fits the first of Polanyi's clues: that we can know more than we can tell.

We know more than we can tell using purely linguistic resources. So tacit knowledge violates PC, but not PA.

PC   All knowledge can be fully articulated, or codified, in context-independent terms.

PA   All knowledge can be articulated, either in context-independent terms or in context-dependent terms.

As this summary highlights, this approach to tacit knowledge rests in part on a regress argument to establish the priority of the practical. But it might be thought that a related regress argument drawing on Wittgenstein's work supports a stronger conception of tacit knowledge; one which violates not just PC but also PA. This chapter will examine an argument that seems to support the idea that some of what we understand resists expression or is ineffable. In accord with the principles introduced in the introduction, that looks like support of what we called the *principle of inarticulacy*:

PI   There can be knowledge that cannot be articulated.

The understanding in question is of rules or concepts, and the argument is contained in discussion in Ludwig Wittgenstein's *Philosophical Investigations* often referred to as the "rule-following considerations". On an initial reading of the regress argument it seems to show that nothing could possibly come to mind, and nothing could be put into words, which contains the knowledge we have when we understand a rule such as, for example, the rule governing the use of a word or the continuation of a mathematical series.

To examine whether this really is the case and to explore the extent to which Wittgenstein's rule-following considerations do support tacit knowledge, this chapter will first set out a summary of his regress argument and then examine two responses to it.

First, according to Kripke's contested (but nevertheless influential) interpretation, Wittgenstein's argument is a sceptical argument aimed to show that the very idea that one can know the meaning of a word or grasp a rule rests on a mistake. Properly speaking, every use of a word is a leap in the dark. But something like a normative notion of the correct usage can be extracted from the relation of individuals to their surrounding communities. An individual can be deemed to be "correct" in so far as they have not diverged from communal judgements. But that suggests that individual knowledge of rules is essentially tacit: there is nothing for an individual to make explicit.

Second, Adrian Moore offers a novel interpretation of Wittgenstein, which suggests that while knowledge of the rules governing word use might be *tacit* because, answering to nothing, it is ineffable,[1] it is nevertheless still a form of *knowledge* because it shares three key marks of knowledge.

We will argue, however, that neither of these views is correct. Despite initial appearance, Wittgenstein's regress argument does not support an account of tacit knowledge that rejects PA as well as PC. But our positive view of Wittgenstein's regress argument will be postponed until Chapter 4, where we will first examine the idea that rule-following is based on a tacit Background.

WITTGENSTEIN'S REGRESS ARGUMENT AS SUPPORT FOR A TACIT DIMENSION

Like Ryle, Heidegger and Polanyi, Wittgenstein also deploys a regress argument against a form of intellectualism. This section will set out Wittgenstein's argument, which complements the discussion of Ryle's regress argument in the previous chapter.

Wittgenstein's argument uses a number of different examples, including understanding the meaning of a word, grasping what a picture depicts and following a mathematical sequence. But these different examples have one thing in common. They are all normative. In each case, there is a difference between a correct and incorrect move or application. All are instances of following a rule. The regress argument concerns in what rule-following can consist.

The first hint of the nature of the regress occurs when Wittgenstein considers the case of understanding the meaning of a word and an explanation of it (with echoes of seventeenth-century philosophy) that involves having a mental picture. The problem, and the possible solution, are introduced in this set of passages.

> When someone says the word "cube" to me, for example, I know what it means. But can the whole use of the word come before my mind, when I *understand* it in this way?
>
> Well, but on the other hand isn't the meaning of the word also determined by this use ? And can these ways of determining meaning conflict? Can what we grasp *in a flash* accord with a use, fit or fail to fit it? And how can what is present to us in an instant, what comes before our mind in an instant, fit a *use*?
>
> What really comes before our mind when we *understand* a word? – Isn't it something like a picture? Can't it be a picture?
>
> Well, suppose that a picture does come before your mind when you hear the word "cube", say the drawing of a cube. In what sense can this picture fit or fail to fit a use of the word "cube"? – Perhaps you say: "It's quite simple; – if that picture occurs to me

and I point to a triangular prism for instance, and say it is a cube, then this use of the word doesn't fit the picture." – But doesn't it fit? I have purposely so chosen the example that it is quite easy to imagine a *method of projection* according to which the picture does fit after all.

The picture of the cube did indeed *suggest* a certain use to us, but it was possible for me to use it differently ...

Then what sort of mistake did I make; was it what we should like to express by saying: I should have thought the picture forced a particular use on me? How could I think that? What *did* I think? Is there such a thing as a picture, or something like a picture, that forces a particular application on us; so that my mistake lay in confusing one picture with another? – For we might also be inclined to express ourselves like this: we are at most under a psychological, not a logical, compulsion. And now it looks quite as if we knew of two kinds of case ...

Suppose, however, that not merely the picture of the cube, but also the method of projection comes before our mind? – How am I to imagine this? – Perhaps I see before me a schema shewing the method of projection: say a picture of two cubes connected by lines of projection. – But does this really get me any further? Can't I now imagine different applications of this schema too? – Well, yes, but then can't an *application come before my mind*? – It can: only we need to get clearer about our application of this expression. Suppose I explain various methods of projection to someone so that he may go on to apply them; let us ask ourselves when we should say that *the* method that I intend comes before his mind.

(Wittgenstein 1953: §§139–41)

The way the example is introduced emphasizes two aspects of understanding word meaning. First, if one understands the meaning of a word then one has an extended ability to use it. But second, it is possible to grasp the meaning of a word at a particular moment or in a flash. The challenge is to reconcile these two aspects. Can the whole of a potentially unlimited number of ways of correctly using a word come before the mind in a flash? That seems implausible. How could one, somehow, survey all possible correct applications in an instant? If not, however, then one seems to be faced with the challenge of postulating something that can come before the mind at a particular time but which has the right normative properties to determine – through action at a distance – the correct applications over time. What would such an item be like?

The difficulty of this challenge can be brought out by considering an example that makes vivid just how constraining the grasp of a rule can be

and just how miraculous it can seem. Building on an example from an earlier paragraph (*ibid.*: §143) of a pupil being taught to count up the natural
numbers in ones, Wittgenstein considers understanding a mathematical rule
such as the rule for counting in twos.

> Let us return to our example (§143). Now – judged by the usual
> criteria – the pupil has mastered the series of natural numbers.
> Next we teach him to write down other series of cardinal num-
> bers and get him to the point of writing down series of the form
>
> 0, n, 2n, 3n, etc.
>
> at an order of the form "+ n"; so at the order "+ 1" he writes down
> the series of natural numbers. – Let us suppose we have done
> exercises and given him tests up to 1000.
> Now we get the pupil to continue a series (say + 2) beyond
> 1000 – and he writes 1000, 1004, 1008, 1012.
> We say to him: "Look what you've done!" – He doesn't under-
> stand. We say: "You were meant to add *two*: look how you began
> the series!" – He answers: "Yes, isn't it right? I thought that was
> how I was *meant* to do it." – Or suppose he pointed to the series
> and said: "But I went on in the same way." – It would now be no
> use to say: "But can't you see … .?" – and repeat the old exam-
> ples and explanations. – In such a case we might say, perhaps: It
> comes natural to this person to understand our order with our
> explanations as we should understand the order: "Add 2 up to
> 1000, 4 up to 2000, 6 up to 3000 and so on."
>
> (Wittgenstein 1953: §185)

The example may seem to present the problem as though it is one of third-
person epistemology: both of us determining whether the pupil has grasped
the series and of the pupil understanding what is intended. That is indeed
part of the problem. But the more fundamental issue is not just the epistemology but rather what understanding the series can consist in, given that
a proper understanding has to rule out divergences of the sort suggested.

Suppose that the mathematical rule (or, by analogy, the meaning of a
word) is taught by examples, by the first few numbers of the series (or some
paradigm examples of word use). The hypothetical example of the deviant
pupil suggests the following worry. Since finite examples underdetermine
the correct later applications (of a word or series) they can only determine
the correct rule under a specific interpretation. They must be interpreted as
indicating a particular continuation, for example. If so, however, this leads
to a problem.

> "But how can a rule shew me what I have to do at *this* point?
> Whatever I do is, on some interpretation, in accord with the
> rule." – That is not what we ought to say, but rather: any inter-
> pretation still hangs in the air along with what it interprets, and
> cannot give it any support. Interpretations by themselves do not
> determine meaning.   (Wittgenstein 1953: §198)

The problem is not simply that the selection of an interpretation to single
out a particular set of applications is so far unjustified. That does seem to
be a problem in so far as the first few numbers are consistent with an infinite number of interpretations (we shall return to this). But there is a more
fundamental problem, which is that the meaning of the interpretation itself
has somehow to be specified and the original dilemma is still in play for any
account along the same lines of how that is possible.

If possessing the right interpretation (of the initial numbers in the mathematical series or of finite examples of the use of a word) simply consists in
having a potentially unlimited number of correct applications come before
the mind, how is that possible? That seems to be an absurd idea. But if possessing the right interpretation is having a mental item, or image, or mental
talisman, before the mind's eye, how does it determine subsequent correct
moves? Surely, it can only do that under a particular interpretation? Such an
item seems no more to determine what would accord with it, and what not,
than the finite examples of word use, or the first numbers in the series, with
which we began. But if such an interpretation only determines what accords
with it under a further interpretation then it "still hangs in the air along with
what it interprets, and cannot give it any support. Interpretations by themselves do not determine meaning".

One example, repeatedly used by Wittgenstein, serves both to explain the
problem and point towards his suggested solution:

> A rule stands there like a sign-post. – Does the sign-post leave
> no doubt open about the way I have to go? Does it shew which
> direction I am to take when I have passed it; whether along
> the road or the footpath or cross-country? But where is it said
> which way I am to follow it; whether in the direction of its finger
> or (e.g.) in the opposite one? – And if there were, not a single
> sign-post, but a chain of adjacent ones or of chalk marks on the
> ground – is there only *one* way of interpreting them?
>   (Wittgenstein 1953: §85)

If one understands which way a signpost points then one knows it points in
the direction of the "finger", not the other way. But one might have taken it
to point the other way. The signpost does not take a viewer by the throat as

Achilles suggests that logic will take the Tortoise by the throat (Carroll 1905). So it can seem that the signpost points, again, only *under an interpretation*. But what would grasp of such an interpretation consist in? Again we can frame a dilemma. It either consists – impossibly – in grasping all the potential places to which signposts might point (the way out, the pub, the lecture-room). Or it consists in entertaining a mental item which determines all those places relative to a given signpost. In this case, the most obvious candidate would be an inner image of a signpost with an indication of which way it points. How? By another signpost, perhaps. And so a regress begins.

This case makes the problem very clear. In this key respect (which way it points), the inner signpost is no different from the outer one. If the outer signpost needs an interpretation then so will the inner one. And that threatens a vicious infinite regress, stopping short of completing which will leave the subject with *no* understanding of which way any of the – inner or outer – signpost-posts point. It will leave *no* understanding short of impossibly completing the infinite series of signposts because for any signpost all one knows is that *if* the next higher order sign post points left then so does this one and *if* it points right then so does this one, but as yet, one does not know which way that higher order sign points. For it, an equivalent conditional applies with respect to the yet higher signpost.

After asking "is there only *one* way of interpreting them?", Wittgenstein continues: "So I can say, the sign-post does after all leave no room for doubt. Or rather: it sometimes leaves room for doubt and sometimes not. And now this is no longer a philosophical proposition, but an empirical one" (Wittgenstein 1953: §85). But that reassurance prompts the question of the connection between the signpost and understanding which way it points given the logical problem highlighted by the regress argument. Wittgenstein returns to the example of the signpost in the way that the later paragraph we have been discussing, §198, continues:

> "Then can whatever I do be brought into accord with the rule?"
> – Let me ask this: what has the expression of a rule – say a signpost – got to do with my actions? What sort of connexion is there here? – Well, perhaps this one: I have been trained to react to this sign in a particular way, and now I do so react to it.
>
> But that is only to give a causal connexion; to tell how it has come about that we now go by the sign-post; not what this going-by-the sign really consists in. On the contrary; I have further indicated that a person goes by a sign-post only in so far as there exists a regular use of sign-posts, a custom.   (*Ibid.*: §198)

Wittgenstein suggests that in the face of the regress of interpretations that rule-following is a regular use, or custom of practice. He continues:

This was our paradox: no course of action could be determined by a rule, because every course of action can be made out to accord with the rule. The answer was: if everything can be made out to accord with the rule, then it can also be made out to conflict with it. And so there would be neither accord nor conflict here.

It can be seen that there is a misunderstanding here from the mere fact that in the course of our argument we give one interpretation after another; as if each one contented us at least for a moment, until we thought of yet another standing behind it. What this shews is that there is a way of grasping a rule which is *not* an *interpretation*, but which is exhibited in what we call "obeying the rule" and "going against it" in actual cases.

Hence there is an inclination to say: every action according to the rule is an interpretation. But we ought to restrict the term "interpretation" to the substitution of one expression of the rule for another.

And hence also "obeying a rule" is a practice. (*Ibid.*: §§201–2)

We can now return to the earlier worry of whether finite examples of word use or a mathematical series or signpost following can determine the correct use. Suppose that the answer to this question is "not without an interpretation", then we are faced with Wittgenstein's regress. The only prospect of halting it would be finding an interpretation which somehow logically compelled how it was itself to be understood: a kind of self-interpreting sign. Wittgenstein spends some time discussing and rejecting such latent Platonism. But the very idea smacks of desperation and we will not pursue it further here.

Instead of attempting to block the regress once started, Wittgenstein invokes the idea of a custom or practice. If there is a regular practice of signpost use then, practically, a signpost may leave no doubt as to where it points. (In some circumstances, it may leave doubt but that is, as he says, an empirical rather than a philosophical matter.)

This suggests the following broad outline of the connection between the regress argument and tacit knowledge. The argument threatens the idea that grasp of a rule, or the meaning of a word, can be anything explicit because anything explicit just stands there like a signpost in need of a further interpretation which can itself only be made explicit by similar means and thus subject to the same problem. Short of a self-interpreting sign, whatever that would be, once started, the regress of interpretations is vicious. The alternative is to invoke implicit and practical knowledge: "and hence also 'obeying a rule' is a practice". The gap between an explicit statement or explanation of a rule – which, short of, impossibly, completing the regress, underdetermines the rule – and the rule itself is filled or bridged by implicit or tacit knowledge.

This line of thought is explicit in an early work by the sociologist Harry Collins, which explores the role of tacit knowledge in scientific practice. In the introduction to his book *Changing Order* he attempts to shed some light on the nature of tacit knowledge by connecting it to Wittgenstein's regress argument. He argues that continuing the series the "2, 4, 6, 8" sequence with "10, 12, 14, 16" cannot be a matter of following the rule "go on in the same way" because "this rule allows for a number of possibilities" (Collins 1985: 13). Nor, assuming that that rule is merely insufficiently specific, does further codification that one sequentially adds 2 help, he argues, because that might result in the continuation "82, 822, 8222 …" or other typographic variants, each of which amounts to adding 2 in some sense.

He argues that the regress argument establishes a number of points which include that the notion of "sameness" is ambiguous and that it is not possible fully to specify a rule (unless a limited range of response is defined in advance). Further "since in spite of this we all know the correct way to go on, there must be something more to a rule than its specifiability" (*ibid*.: 14) something which explains the "*mysterious abilities* that enable us to know when to continue '2, 4, 6, 8' with '10, 12, 14, 16' and when with 'who do we appreciate?'" (*ibid*.: 22, emphasis added). The answer is that social entrenchment underpins tacit knowledge of rules:

> Tacit knowledge usually finds its application in practical settings such as bike riding or other "skilled" occupations. However, it is equally applicable to mental activity. Thus, to return to an earlier example, the member of a social group who has the ability to continue the sequence "2, 4, 6, 8" with "10, 12, 14, 16" as a matter of course, without even thinking about it, also possesses something that the stranger to our culture and the newborn do not. This is sometimes referred to as a "social skill" but we can call it tacit knowledge without doing too much violence to the term. It forms the foundation upon which formal learning rests. If I am taught some new algebraic manipulation in school, and the teacher tells me to do it the same way next time, I can say that it is my tacit knowledge which tells me what counts as the next instance of the same problem as well as what is meant by proceeding in the same way. (*Ibid*.: 56–7)

On Collins's picture, the gap between what can be made explicit in explanations of rules and what is in fact grasped is bridged by tacit knowledge. So following a rule depends on tacit knowledge.

There is something right about this line of thought, but it needs more careful handling including, to anticipate our argument, critical attention to whether there really is a gap to be bridged. The next two sections of this chapter will further explore two ways in which one can construe the regress argument to undermine the idea that understanding a rule can be a matter of explicit knowledge and thus support a form of tacit knowledge. Neither approach, however, is satisfactory. Our own positive account of the argument will be outlined in the next chapter but only after we have examined the often supposed role of the Background to underpin the conceptual order.

THE TACIT DIMENSION IN KRIPKE'S RESPONSE TO WITTGENSTEIN

The picture that emerges from a first reading of Wittgenstein's regress argument is that it puts under pressure any explicit account of what is understood or known (nothing here turns on the difference) when one grasps a rule. If the meaning of a word, or the rule that governs a mathematical series, is knowable at all then it can only be known tacitly. To examine whether this is really so it will be useful to begin by outlining Kripke's famous interpretation.

Since our aim is to head off a particular understanding of the connection between Wittgenstein's regress argument and tacit knowledge, we will present a brief and traditional view of Kripke's argument. That is, we will ignore recent defences of Kripke by Kusch and Hattiangadi (Kusch 2006, Hattiangadi 2007). One key difference is that we take Kripke to agree with Wittgenstein that rule-following (and grasp of meaning) is properly understood to be normative. The normativity of meaning is both an element in Kripke's sceptical argument and something he attempts to recover in his positive account, according to the traditional view of him that we share.

Kripke presents his summary of Wittgenstein's critical argument using a more focused example than Wittgenstein's actual text. He focuses on the question: what justifies the claim that answering "125" is the correct response to the question "what does 68 + 57 equal?", building in two simplifying assumptions. The first assumption is that "correct" means simply in accordance with the standards of one's previous usage of the signs involved. The second is that one has never calculated that particular sum before.

Normally if called upon to justify the answer "125" one might give two sorts of response. Arithmetically, one might ensure that one has carried out the computation correctly. Metalinguistically, one might assert: "that 'plus', as I intended to use that word in the past, denoted a function which, when applied to the numbers I call '68' and '57', yields the value 125" (Kripke 1982: 8). Kripke now introduces the sceptical hypothesis that in the past one might have followed a different mathematical function: the *quus* function. This is defined to agree with the plus function for all pairs of numbers smaller than 57. For numbers greater than or equal to 57 the output is 5. Kripke now presses the question: what facts about one's past performance show that one was calculating in accordance with the plus function rather than the quus function?

There is a further condition on any satisfactory answer to the question. It must show why it is *correct* to respond 125 rather than 5. It must have the right *normative* properties. This precludes citing facts about one's education or training which now *dispose* one to answer 125. It may be true that one has such a disposition, but that will not show that one is *correct* to answer 125. One may equally be disposed to make mistakes when adding large columns of figures. Mere dispositions are not a solution to Kripke's challenge.[2]

Kripke then deploys broadly Wittgensteinian arguments to show, apparently, that no facts about one's past actions, utterances or dispositions can justify an answer (Kripke 1982: 7–54). Anything one did or said in the past could be interpreted as following the quus rule. It appears that nothing that one said or did or thought to oneself can justify the claim that answering "125" is going on in the same way. Consider two initially attractive lines of thought. While it seems that the problem is set up so that one's past *actions* might equally be interpreted as according with the plus or quus function, one might still settle the issue if one previously said or thought to oneself "now I'll *add* these numbers". But this would only answer the sceptic if there were an independent way to settle the correct *interpretation* of these words. Perhaps they meant *quad*. Suppose, now, that one had explicitly added, *sotto voce*, "And by add I mean a function based on *counting* in the following normal way ..." Whatever follows would also depend on the interpretation given to the word "count". Perhaps it meant *quount*, defined as the same as counting except in the case of the combination of numbers 57, 68.

By such means, Kripke argues that there are no facts about one's past behaviour nor one's past mental history that allow one to read off the further fact that one has, in the past, followed the addition rule and meant addition by the word "addition". Thus nothing makes it correct to answer 125 today. Generalizing from this, he argues that there are no facts about meaning anything by any word.

Kripke's interpretation of Wittgenstein's critical arguments differs from the brief summary in the previous section in three respects, two of which are minor, but the third of which is significant. First, instead of concentrating on the future directed link between the understanding of a rule that one may have in a flash and the applications that one must make subsequently, Kripke questions how one can *now* know what rule one was following in making *previous* applications. But despite this difference of tense, the focus of the investigation remains what feature of my previous state could prescribe the responses that one *ought* to make rather than merely did make.

Second, Kripke's interpretation of Wittgenstein is explicitly sceptical. It may therefore appear to have an epistemological rather than a constitutive or ontological focus. That is, it appears that Kripke is concerned with the question of how one can *know* which rule one followed in the past rather than the nature of rules themselves. The emphasis on epistemology rather than metaphysics is, however, more apparent than real. An ontological point is made by epistemological considerations. This will become clear in the context of the analogy, described below, which Kripke suggests between his investigation of rule-following and Hume's investigation of causation.[3]

Finally, and most significantly, Kripke interprets Wittgenstein not as merely rejecting particular explanations of what grasp of a rule comprises, or raising a puzzle about it, but as rejecting the very idea that rules have determinate content. This claim, which we will call Kripke's "non-factualism", will be developed at some length below.

The analogy that Kripke suggests with Hume (mentioned above) is threefold:

- Kripke's Wittgenstein, like Hume, deploys epistemological scepticism to raise a constitutive or ontological question.
- They both offer sceptical solutions to their sceptical problems.
- Their sceptical solutions are forms of projectivism.

The first analogy is the use of scepticism to raise a constitutive or ontological question. For Hume, the subject matter is the relation between cause and effect. For Kripke, it is the relation between a rule and its correct applications. After investigating possible sources of knowledge of the link, both conclude (according to Kripke) that there is no factual link. Hume argues, on the basis of an investigation of how we could come to know about such a connection, that there cannot be a necessitating connection between cause and effect of the sort supposed pre-philosophically. The sorts of considerations deployed by Hume are that we cannot observe any such connection when we observe paradigmatic cases of cause and effect. Neither can we arrive at such an idea from other experiences we have, such as the experience of the workings of the will.

The fact that he draws a metaphysical conclusion from merely epistemological considerations may seem startling. Surely, it is tempting to argue, the most that could justifiably be concluded is that we cannot *know* that any necessitating connection exists.[4] Nevertheless, whether or not his reading is exegetically correct, Kripke argues that Hume draws the yet stronger conclusion, that "even if God were to look at the events, he would discern nothing relating them other than that one succeeds the other" (Kripke 1982: 67). Likewise, the conclusion Kripke draws for understanding rules is that there is no fact of the matter as to which rule I followed in previous behaviour. Furthermore, since the same argument could be given for my current behaviour, there is no fact of the matter about which rule I *ever* follow.

How can Kripke draw such a substantive conclusion from epistemological considerations? The answer is that an important assumption is built into the sceptical approach. If there were some fact that constituted the relation between a rule and its applications, it would be independently identifiable by the idealized subject that Kripke postulates. Kripke supposes, for the purpose of argument, that one may have all possible information about one's past experiences, mental states and inclinations. He then asks whether any of these would be sufficient to determine the rule that one were following. His conclusion, based on his interpretation of Wittgenstein's arguments, is that none would be. Given the idealizations involved, and the assumption that had any fact constituted the rule one were following one would have known it, then there is no such fact of the matter.

This sceptical interpretation of Wittgenstein is reinforced by Kripke's reading of §201. Wittgenstein writes there:

> This was our paradox: no course of action could be determined by a rule, because every course of action can be made out to accord with the rule. The answer was: if everything can be made out to accord with the rule, then it can also be made out to conflict with it. And so there would be neither accord nor conflict here.
>
> (1953: §201)

Wittgenstein continues that there is a quite different way of grasping a rule which is not an interpretation. Neglecting this different conclusion (to which we will return), Kripke interprets this as a sceptical problem generated by the arguments that have preceded it. Kripke writes:

> The sceptical argument, then, remains unanswered. There can be no such thing as meaning anything by any word. Each new application we make is a leap in the dark; any present intention could be interpreted so as to accord with anything we may choose to do. So there can be neither accord, nor conflict.   (Kripke 1982: 55)

The second analogy between Kripke and Hume is their response to the scepticism they articulate. Kripke distinguishes between "straight" and "sceptical" solutions to sceptical problems (*ibid.*: 56). *Straight* solutions are those which show that scepticism about a certain matter is, on investigation, unwarranted. Scepticism is, so to speak, disproved. A *sceptical* solution, by contrast, accepts that the sceptic has proved her point and attempts to suggest some other kind of justification for the matter in question. According to Kripke, Hume offers a sceptical solution to the problem of the link between cause and effect. Kripke, likewise, suggests a sceptical solution to the normative link between rule and applications.

Hume's account accepts that there is no necessitating relation between cause and effect and offers a different kind of explanation of our pre-philosophical beliefs about them. On experiencing the constant conjunction of events of some first type with events of a second we have a natural propensity to expect the "effect" having observed the "cause". As a result of projecting this natural habit into the fabric of the world, we mistakenly postulate a necessitating relation to explain our expectation. Kripke suggests that a similar solution can be given to his sceptical problem.

The third similarity between Kripke and Hume is thus the use of projectivism in their sceptical solutions. Hume's account of causation is not based on finding a worldly necessitating relation, which would run counter to the sceptical argument. Rather, our expectation that events of one sort are always followed by events of a second sort are "projected" onto the world. We are "led astray ... when we transfer the determination of the thought to external objects, and suppose any real intelligible connexion betwixt them; that being a quality, which can only belong to the mind that considers them" (Hume 1967: 168).

Kripke offers a similar projectivist account when he outlines his own sceptical solution. The heart of his positive account of concept mastery consists in replacing any idea that understanding is captured or summarized in some sort of mental state or process with something much thinner.

> It is essential to our concept of a rule that we maintain some such conditional as "If Jones means addition by '+', then if he is asked for '68 + 57', he will reply '125'" ... (T)he conditional as stated makes it appear that some mental state obtains in Jones that guarantees his performance of particular additions such as "68 + 57" – just what the sceptical argument denies. Wittgenstein's picture of the true situation concentrates on the contrapositive, and on justification conditions. If Jones does *not* come out with "125" when asked about "68 + 57", we cannot assert that he means addition by "+". (Kripke 1982: 94–5)

Whether one person is "following a rule" depends on their being so dignified as a rule-follower.

This in turn depends on the individual standing in a relation to a community. We speak as though there were an individual factual relation occurring between the individual's understanding and his or her action or practice, but this is not so. Really, for an individual to be considered a rule-follower, she must be considered as part of a community.[5]

> If our considerations are so far correct ... if one person is considered in isolation, the notion of a rule as guiding the person who

adopts it can have *no* substantive content. There are, we have
seen, no truth conditions or facts in virtue of which it can be
the case that he accords with his past intentions or not. As long
as we regard him as following a rule "privately", so that we pay
attention to *his* justification conditions alone, all we can say is
that he is licensed to follow the rule as it strikes him ... The situation is very different if we widen our gaze from consideration
of the rule follower alone and allow ourselves to consider him
as interacting with a wider community. Others will then have
justification conditions for attributing correct or incorrect rule
following to the subject, and these will not be simply that the
subject's own authority is unconditionally to be accepted.

(Kripke 1982: 89)

But this invocation of the community is not supposed to amount to an explicit
account of grasp of the content of rules or concepts.

It is important to realise that we are not looking for necessary
and sufficient conditions (truth conditions), or an analysis of
what such rule-following (or meaning) "consists in". Indeed such
conditions would constitute a "straight" solution to the sceptical
problem, and have been rejected. (*Ibid.*: 87)

So it is not simply that the content of the rule emerges in the actual practice of the community. That would be an account of what grasp of a rule
consists in. But such actual practice, being finite, is, according to Kripke,
subject to the same kind of sceptical argument and thus cannot be used
(by him at least) as a direct response. Further, a counter-factual reading of
what the community would say under certain circumstances, such as being
asked, would fail to capture the normativity of rule-following which Kripke,
correctly in our view, stresses. The content of the rule transcends actual
practice. But it is still connected to the ongoing corrective practice of the
community through the interpretation of the conditional – If Jones means
addition by "+", then if he is asked for "68 + 57", he will reply "125" – that
Kripke puts forward.

Kripke's reading of Wittgenstein's argument suggests the following central
role of a tacit dimension underpinning the conceptual order. The content of
a rule cannot be made explicit. It cannot be reduced to any finite examples,
nor to the grasping of any symbols. Nor does it consist in the dispositions
of individuals or communities to make particular judgements. Nevertheless,
individuals whose judgements or actions do not diverge from that of a community can be deemed to have mastery of a rule or to have gasped a concept.
But such mastery or grasp is not guided by anything that is explicit to them.

It is not encoded in their mental states, for example. Thus such understanding seems clearly tacit. Of necessity, it transcends anything that can be made explicit. It is essentially implicit.

Now, one reason for thinking that such mastery is tacit seems to be the role that the community plays in Kripke's exegesis. An individual's grasp does not consist in anything dependent on him or herself. Rather, it depends in part on what they say and do but also their relation to the community. Given that the community's reaction lies outside their ken, it seems that there is no subject for whom conceptual mastery might be explicit. It is not, in other words, personal knowledge in any sense. The individual cannot, for example, grasp the pattern of reaction that the community will exhibit. That is just the sort of thing that Kripke's sceptical argument undermines. Still, the community's correction of the individual is a central aspect of the positive account of rule-following or meaning that Kripke attempts to sketch.

But given that the individual does not grasp the pattern of likely community reaction, it puts under considerable stress the idea that the individual has knowledge – personal knowledge – of how to go on and thus that this merits the label "tacit *knowledge*". In other words, on Kripke's interpretation, Wittgenstein might provide support for the idea that rule-following involves something which could not be explicit and is thus tacit, in some sense, but undermines its status as possible knowledge and hence tacit knowledge.

This is not just a problem for a communitarian account of rule-following of this – projectivist – nature, however. To establish this, we will examine one criticism of Kripke. In "The individual strikes back", Simon Blackburn argues that the community cannot be an essential part of a sceptical account of conceptual mastery because the presence of a community does not make a decisive difference. The argument turns on examining the role that the community is supposed to take. It is invoked after Kripke's version of the regress argument has undermined any personal or individualistic facts that might be thought to constitute grasp of a rule.

> The individual couldn't make the sceptic appreciate the kind of fact it was, that he was being faithful to a principle, or rule or previous intention, when he gave some answer. The sceptic charges that there is no fact of the matter whether the bent rule or the natural rule was the one intended, or whether one principle of application or another was in force yesterday. And if there is no fact of the matter of this sort, then there is really no fact of the matter that any principle at all was in force. Any answer to the new sum can be regarded as equally "right" and that just means that we cannot talk about right. Faced with this impasse the individual thankfully turns to the community. He can point to his inculcation in a public practice, his gradual conformity to

patterns of behaviour accepted by others, and his acceptance as a
competent operator with "+".   (Blackburn 1984: 291–2)

That is Blackburn's summary of Kripke's positive account: the sceptical solution. But he goes on to cast doubt on how invoking communal resources can
help turn aside the sceptical argument.

> The sceptic might allow all this to make the difference. But he
> has suddenly gone very soft if he does. He can easily specify bent
> principles, with points of singularity where neither I nor anybody
> else used the terms yesterday. If such points worried the individ-
> ual, then they should equally worry the community. So how does
> mention of the community give us the determinate rule?
>
> (*Ibid.*: 292)

In other words, the same arguments that served to show that nothing about
the finite past practice of an individual nor features of his or her mental life
could have the right normative properties to underpin rule-following can be
applied to an aggregate of individuals in a community.

But, as we emphasized above, Kripke is explicit that his sceptical solution is not supposed to be a constitutive analysis of the content of a rule or
concept. That would amount to a straight solution to the sceptical argument
hope of which, he has given up. Blackburn is aware of this. He concedes:

> [Kripke's] answer is that in a sense it doesn't ... The community
> is as much at a loss to identify the fugitive fact as the individual
> was. The position is supposed to be no different metaphysically.
> The difference is that the community endorses or accepts the
> competent operator. They or "we" *allow* him to be using "+" to
> mean addition. He is "seen" or *dignified* as a rule-follower.
>
> (*Ibid.*)

But, and this is the key point, if a communal form of a projectivist solution
is allowed, then the same move can be made in the individual case. There
seems to be no difference in principle between the two cases.

> It may be helpful to think of it like this. The members of a com-
> munity stand to each other as the momentary time-slices of an
> individual do. So just as the original sceptic queries what it is
> for one person-time to be faithful to a rule adopted by a previ-
> ous person-time, so the public sceptic queries what it is for one
> person to be faithful to the same rule as that adopted by another.
> Now if the public sceptic can be by-passed by, in effect, saying

> that this is what we do – we see each other as mutually under-
> standing the same rule, or dignify or compliment each other as
> so doing, provided the exposed practice agrees well enough, then
> the private sceptic can be by-passed in the same way. His doubts
> admit of the same projective solution. When LW denies that "we
> have a model of this superlative fact" (§192) we can, as far as
> the metaphysics goes, shrug and say that this is how we see our-
> selves.   (*Ibid.*: 294)

Blackburn's articulation of Kripke's dialectic suggests that any support for a
sceptical interpretation of Wittgenstein's regress argument does not depend
on the fact that rule-following is a communal matter. Rather, it depends on
the fact that no constitutive account can be given and that nothing explicit is
sufficient to encode what is understood when a rule is understood.

Blackburn's argument suggests that there is no principled difference
between Kripke's communitarian projectivist account of rule-following and
Blackburn's individualist projectivist account. To the extent to which the first
is a satisfactory response to Kripke's version of the regress argument, a version
that stresses its sceptical powers, then so is the second. That suggests that it
cannot be used to justify a communitarian account over an individualist rival.

But the comparison helps clarify a second similarity. Just as the communitarian account suggests something tacit but at the cost of undermining
tacit *knowledge*, so does the second. On Blackburn's account, the individual
is merely dignified a rule follower because of his or her relation to earlier and
later time slices. But those are no more part of his or her cognition of the
demands of a rule than the actions of the rest of the community in Kripke's
account. Blackburn's account might seem to defend the personal but it does
not defend a notion of personal knowledge.

This helps reinforce a moral for a defence of tacit knowledge invoking
Wittgenstein's discussion of rule-following. No merely sceptical or projectivist account will do. It will have instead to support the idea that in grasping a
rule, or the meaning of a word, there is something to be grasped. Only so can
it support a notion of personal or tacit knowledge. In the next section, we
will turn to a distinct response to Wittgenstein, which meets this constraint.

ADRIAN MOORE ON INEFFABLE KNOWLEDGE

A different connection between Wittgenstein's regress argument and tacit
knowledge can be drawn from Adrian Moore's book *Points of View* by
charting his arguments for ineffable knowledge. (Moore himself retains the
phrase "tacit knowledge" for something else, something for whose existence
he offers no explicit argument.) While, in one paper, Moore argues directly

that conceptual mastery is a form of ineffable knowledge, in his book, this is placed in a broader context of responding to Wittgenstein (Moore 1997, 2003). We will follow that latter route first.

Moore suggests that, in his discussion of understanding a rule or grasping a concept, one of Wittgenstein's targets is the idea that our concepts answer to a "super-physical landscape". Discussing the idea that there is a necessary connection between the concept of aunt and being female, for example, he suggests that Wittgenstein rejects the idea that such concepts "were things we just stumbled across, the one an inseparable part of the other". But instead of charting such an independent super-physical or Platonic realm, Wittgenstein's discussion makes it clear instead that "it is on our own contingent practices that we are focusing" (Moore 1997: 128).

The connection between meaning and contingency is this. Recall the summary of Wittgenstein's regress argument (§"Wittgenstein's regress argument as support for a tacit dimension") and Kripke's reconstruction of it (§"The tacit dimension in Kripke's response to Wittgenstein"). According to both, it seems that nothing that can come before the mind's eye, nor anything that can be put into words, nor any finite examples of past practice, can determine a rule or a concept. What then explains our ability to go on in the same way?

Moore quotes, approvingly, a famous passage from Stanley Cavell:

> That on the whole we ... [make, and understand, the same projections of words into further contexts] is a matter of our sharing routes of interest and feeling, modes of response, sense of humour and of significance and of fulfilment, of what is outrageous, of what is similar to what else, what a rebuke, what forgiveness, of when an utterance is an assertion, when an appeal, when an explanation – all the whirl of organism Wittgenstein calls "forms of life".   (1976: 52, quoted in Moore 1997: 128–9; text in square brackets is by Moore)

Because of this shared background, he argues, we react in similar ways to explanations of rules and concepts and make the same projections of word use into the future. Lacking something like a Platonic landscape to chart, or a signpost that needs no further interpretation, it is a shared whirl of organism that underpins the conceptual order. But if so, then this suggests that what seem to be necessary features of our concepts themselves depend on a background of contingencies. The contingencies do not merely concern the fact that, for linguistic historical reasons, the word for aunt is "aunt" and female is "female". Rather, the very idea that aunts are female seems to depend on the whirl of organism. Similarly the truths of mathematics and logic.

> On a Wittgensteinian view, not only does 2 + 2 equal 4, but 2 + 2
> must equal 4. "2 + 2 = 4" is a rule. And yet − it is a rule only
> because of our contingent linguistic practices (and not just in the
> sense that we might have used different sounds or inscriptions to
> express it).   (Moore 1997: 132)

But that idea seems simply false. As Bernard Williams puts it: "if our talk of
numbers has been determined by our decisions, then one result of our decisions is that it must be nonsense to say that anything about a number has
been determined by our decisions" (Williams 1981: 163).

One response to this, which Moore considers but rejects, is to attempt to
distinguish between an empirical and transcendental interpretation of the
role of contingency. While within the empirical realm it seems simply false
to say that the truths of mathematics or the greenness of grass, for example,
depend on our whirl of organism, perhaps there is a way to advance such a
claim at a transcendental level, off stage. On this approach, conditionals such
as "had our language been different then grass would not have been green"
do not express empirical possibilities or point to alternatives that are alternatives *for* us. Located as we are in the empirical realm, we can make no sense
of them. But, Moore argues, this leaves the thoughts that have apparently
been expressed in the words of the conditionals still incoherent, as pure and
utter nonsense. Like so-called "resolute interpretations" of Wittgenstein's
Tractatus, Moore argues that nonsense really is nonsense: a lack of sense.[6]

Moore's own response to the tension is nuanced and lies mainly outside
the scope of this book. But one element connects to his claim that conceptual understanding is ineffable. In the face of the tension outlined, we
are inclined to ask: "'But what, ultimately, does somebody's being an aunt
consist in? What does something's being green consist in?' We cannot help
asking these questions because we cannot help wondering about the basic
form of that to which our representations answer" (Moore 1997: 134). Such
questions presuppose that our concepts answer to something: the underlying form of the world, its necessary background logical structure. Given the
apparent insight from Wittgenstein's regress argument that necessary features of our concepts themselves depend on a background of contingencies,
answering these questions in their own terms leads inevitably, Moore says,
to transcendental idealism, which is nonsense. Moore suggests that, instead,
the questions should be rejected. But this is not *just* in order to try to escape
the tension. Rather, it is because grasp of concepts or rules does not *answer*
to anything.

> Focusing self-consciously on our understanding, we recognize
> the deep contingencies that sustain it ... [But] Our understand-
> ing has nothing to answer to. It is part of how we receive the

> world ... If we do achieve such clarity, then what we actually get into focus is an arrangement of interlocking, mutually supporting practices that are grounded in one another's contingency, a complex knotted structure that might easily have been different.
>
> (*Ibid.*: 162)

So part of Moore's response to the regress argument and the tension it seems to set up between necessity and contingency is to deny that conceptual mastery answers to anything. It is not representational knowledge. For that reason, he claims, it is ineffable.

> My understanding of English is a prime example. I would certainly count that as ineffable, even though it includes large tracts of effable knowledge such as ... that the word "green" denotes green things.
>
> Understanding, of the sort that I have in mind, has nothing to answer to. Of course, I may think that I know what a particular word in English means and be wrong: I may think that the word "rabbit" denotes hares as well as rabbits. If that is the case, then what I understand is strictly speaking an idiolect distinct from English. But I do still have my understanding ... a mode of reception. It is not itself a reception. It includes my knowing how to exercise the concept green, for instance, which in turn includes my knowing what it is for something to be green. But this is not the same as my having an answer to any question. (Still less is it the same as my having an answer to the pseudo-question, "what is it for something to be green".) (*Ibid.*: 184)

Elsewhere – the direct argument mentioned above – Moore advances a similar line of argument more directly but which also more clearly connects back to the regress argument and the role of Platonism. As reported in Chapter 2, Moore criticizes the view that there is any neat semantic marker for a distinction between knowledge-how and knowledge-that and he argues that in many cases know-how can be put into words. This might suggest that the know-how involved in knowing how to use words or follow rules could also be put into words. But Moore argues that it is ineffable: it cannot be expressed.

> Consider my knowledge of what it is for an object to be green. On [Stanley and Williamson's] view this is knowledge, concerning something, that that thing is what it is for an object to be green. But concerning what? A simple reply would be: "What it is for an object to be green." But what kind of thing is that? If I

> try to express my knowledge by indicating a green object and saying, "This is what it is for an object to be green," what can I be referring to by "this"? There does not seem to be any good answer. Nothing short of an unacceptable Platonism, it seems to me, can subserve the extension of their account to this case. I do not think that my knowledge of what it is for an object to be green is knowledge that anything is the case. Nor, crucially, do I think that it is effable. (Moore 2003: 177)

In the case of grasp of a concept such as green, Moore argues that the demonstrative approach fails to work. It could only work if something like the whole use of the word were available for demonstrative singling out. But, failing Platonism of that form, that cannot be the case. He goes on to suggest that where knowledge is ineffable, the attempt to put it into words can only result in nonsense. Further such nonsense really is nonsense. There can be no "suggestion that there is nonsense that captures in some more or less obscure way *how things are*" (Moore 1997: 201). Nevertheless, that attempt can produce something that has a role in showing even while it cannot say anything. Showing, however, is not merely shorthand for saying in some more or less obscure way how things are. Rather: "To say of some piece of nonsense that it is the result of attempting to express the inexpressible is something like making an aesthetic evaluation" (*ibid.*: 202).

We will not follow Moore's thought further along this trajectory of using nonsense to show something about our grasp of rules but rather examine the stage-setting already in play. Two elements inter-mingle in the claim that grasp of concepts is ineffable. One is the failure of a demonstration to express what one grasps when one grasps the concept of greenness. The other is the diagnosis of this that it is because that concept does not answer to or represent anything independent of it. Understanding the meaning of a word is not an instance of representing something as the case but rather a general precondition of any such representation.

> My understanding is knowledge of how to acquire knowledge., then. But it is not itself true representation of how things are. It is not a representation at all ...
>
> My understanding is not true, nor true of anything, nor yet true to anything. But the fact that other people communicate with me as they do is reason for my having an understanding that will enable me to make good sense of them (as mine does). More generally, the fact that the world is the way it is is a reason for my having an understanding that will enable me to make good sense of it. And as for what "good" means here: it means, not "right", but ... something more like useful. This is not to say that, granted

> the concepts I have, there is no right or wrong in how I use them to arrive at my interpretations. The point is rather that there is no right or wrong in the concepts I have. (*Ibid.*: 185–6)

The claim that grasping a rule does not answer to anything suggests a worry that such understanding cannot be a form of knowledge. Moore considers what he calls "the effability argument" to the effect that answering to something independent is an essential feature of knowledge. Thus for example, strength is a capacity that enables one to do particular things in particular circumstances. But its success conditions are "simply the conditions in which the subject is in that state". It is more or less useful but does not get anything right. Strength is thus not knowledge. By contrast, practical knowledge of how to make an omelette answers to facts about eggs and temperature. Had those been different, a given state of practical knowledge would fail. Thus, the latter is a form of representational knowledge. It is thus effable, according to Moore, because it can be articulated through suitable demonstratives.

How, then, can something, which does not answer to anything independent of it, count as knowledge? Moore aims to earn the right to call understanding a concept a form of *knowledge* by identifying three general marks or indicators of knowledge:

- *Versatility* – there is no relevant foreclosing of the possibilities it affords a subject.
- *Performance transcendence* – evidence for its possession must be more than someone simply "bringing something off".
- *Rationality* – it stands in logical relations to other cognitive states.

Now, while states that answer to something independent of them can meet these three conditions, so also can ineffable knowledge, because, roughly, by being the right sort of precondition of representational knowledge, it can inherit these three marks.

Moore is free to define "ineffable" knowledge the way he wishes: as practical knowledge that is non-representational because it does not answer to anything independent of it. But it is not meant to be a purely stipulative definition. It is tied to a pre-philosophical sense of "ineffable" because, for example, the meaning of "green" cannot, he argues, be expressed in words. This in turn is reinforced by something like Wittgenstein's regress argument. Only if Platonism were true could one use a Platonic conception of the real underlying extension of our concepts both to explain to what they answer but also to be the object of a demonstrative to express conceptual mastery in words (as "green is *that*!"). Lacking Platonism, the regress argument shows that no other attempt to capture one's understanding in words will succeed. Any utterance will stand in need of an appropriate interpretation.

This is not Moore's own account of tacit knowledge. He reserves the phrase "tacit knowledge" for something of whose existence he is agnostic (Moore 1997: 192–3). Nevertheless, it serves to locate a possible response to the regress argument that could be used to support a role for tacit knowledge. Concentrating on the negative moral of the regress argument, it seems that grasp of a rule, or a meaning, cannot be made explicit because any utterance stands in need of interpretation and that initiates a regress. Equally, it cannot consist in any mental talisman akin to a signpost because that will also stand in need of interpretation. Kripke's response to this accepts that, properly speaking, nothing is grasped in the way originally assumed. Understanding meaning is indeed tacit, although not in any clear sense knowledge, because it is a matter of projection based on not being out of step with a community. Blackburn suggests that a similar account could be given for an individual, in a sketch of what is in some sense personal but not personal knowledge.

Moore's response also accepts the negative thrust about what can be put into words (although in other cases of practical knowledge, such as omelette making, he happily endorses demonstrative expression). It is ineffable. We might say: tacit. But he nevertheless wishes to preserve the idea that it is knowledge even though this puts under strain the idea that it has content because it does not answer to anything and is thus (unlike omelette making) not representational knowledge.

At the end of the next chapter we will attempt to outline more directly how an account of tacit knowledge can be drawn from Wittgenstein which rejects to Moore's account as summarized here that grasp of a rule is ineffable but still, somehow, knowledge. Two claims will be key. The first is that Wittgenstein's discussion allows more to be expressed than either Kripke or Moore accepts and that helps undercut Moore's claim that conceptual understanding cannot be expressed. The second is that part of the attraction of a substantive "ineffabilist" account of tacit knowledge stems from an only partial rejection of Platonism. A more thorough going rejection of Platonism removes this spurious support. But it will be helpful here to mention a further point of disagreement specifically with Moore's account.

We said above that Moore mingles the claim that conceptual grasp cannot be expressed with the idea that it is non-representational. He says: "This is not to say that, granted the concepts I have, there is no right or wrong in how I use them to arrive at my interpretations. The point is rather that there is no right or wrong in the concepts I have" (Moore 1997: 186). This latter claim reflects a central theme in Wittgenstein's later work referred to by commentators as the "autonomy of grammar" (cf. Hacker 1972: 159–61). It expresses the view that an explanation of conceptual connections in independent terms is impossible. They do not, for example, track independent Platonic extensions. Following a rule is not a matter of going over in bolder pencil moves already somehow made.

One can, however, concede that claim while insisting that understanding a concept *does* answer to something: a normative pattern of use which prescribes correct instances which is reflected in the first part of the quotation above: This is not to say that, granted the concepts I have, there is no right or wrong in how I use them. That is the content of the substantive knowledge one has when one knows the meaning of a word or a rule. There is no link from the autonomy of grammar as a whole – the fact that it does not *represent* an underlying Platonic structure – to the inexpressibility of what one understands when one understands a concept.

We can now summarize the view of Wittgenstein's regress argument that we oppose. According to it, the regress argument highlights a gap between what is expressed in explanations of a rule and what is understood as "correct" by someone who has been appropriately encultured.[7] The gap is filled in some way by tacit knowledge. But if so then at best what is communicated in successful explanations appears to be invisible in those explanations. At worst, there can be nothing communicated and rule-following is tacit but not knowledge. In the middle, there is an account that gestures at some substantive understanding but renders it ineffable and thus mysterious. Our own account of the regress argument will reject the premise that drives all three versions of this version.

THE APPEAL OF THE BACKGROUND?

One response to Wittgenstein's regress argument starts with Cavell's appeal to the "whirl of organism" Wittgenstein calls "forms of life". If what is explicit cannot determine a rule or the meaning of a word in itself, perhaps it can when set against an appropriate contingent background of animal instincts and dispositions. The challenge of such an approach is to retain the sense that rules really can exert normative commands, that there can be a difference between correct and incorrect applications, in the face of the idea that they can only do this against a contingent background which is pre- or nonconceptual.

Taking the idea that the background to rule-following activity is a shared set of "routes of interest, perceptions of salience, feelings of naturalness", the Wittgensteinian philosopher Jonathan Lear expresses the tension in the idea of grounding our grasp of rules in such a background. He suggests that reading Wittgenstein's regress argument produces two, interchanging and unstable responses or gestalt views of our rules:

> In one gestalt, one becomes aware that there is nothing to guarantee one's continued correct language use beyond the fact that one happens to share with one's fellow man routes of interest,

> perceptions of salience, feelings of naturalness etc. From this per-
> spective, one's continued hold on the world appears the merest
> contingency ... As the gestalt shifts, one comes to see that there
> is no genuine possibility of having fundamentally different routes
> of interest and perceptions of salience, for that is the spurious
> possibility of becoming other minded. The illusion of possibil-
> ity is engendered by considering our form of life as one among
> others.   (Lear 1982: 386)

The problem, which we will discuss at some length in the next chapter, is how to relate the explicit normativity of rule-following to the apparently non- or pre-normative background which, on one reading of the regress argument, makes such understanding possible. But if that problem can be solved, it suggests a further way of taking the rule-following considerations to support a conception of tacit knowledge. Not, as in their various ways, Kripke, Blackburn and Moore suggest, as a direct response to the regress of interpretations but rather playing a role in the background which makes explicit knowledge possible. But while philosophers such as Cavell and Lear begin to sketch this possibility, it has received much fuller expression else-where. For that reason we will begin the next chapter with an account of Searle's version of the regress argument and his appeal to the "Background" before outlining our own response to the regress.

4. BEING IN THE BACKGROUND

INTRODUCTION

In Chapter 1 we introduced three thinkers whose accounts of human nature and knowing have a bearing on our understanding of tacit knowledge. Having dealt at length with the debate that has arisen around Ryle's distinction between knowing that and knowing how, we turn now to considerations that give succour to the idea that in so far as tacit knowledge is associated with the latter it characterizes a distinct mode of being of creatures like ourselves. The key idea was introduced in §"Regress redux" in relation to Heidegger. It is that the "familiarity with the world" that is our "understanding of being" forms what Hubert Dreyfus characterizes as the non-intentional "background" (BB) to both the *fundamental intentionality* (FI) of the know-how that comprises our ongoing coping practices, and the *representational intentionality* (RI) of the states characterized by having disengaged reflectively from our practices and associated with the knowledge-that of what is present-at-hand.

At the time we noted that Heidegger's distinction between the "ur" know-how of the background and the more intramundane know-how of our practices was not something we wished to uphold. It is also, of course, a source of embarrassment to phenomenologists of a Dreyfusean persuasion. Like Polanyi, for example, they want to argue that the knowledge-how that exhibits the "naturalness" of our natures should be understood to denote a mode of being shared with other animals (and consequently illuminated by the sort of experimental finding Polanyi was so fond of). But this is prima facie in tension with the idea that the background-as-understanding-of-being (BB) is the transcendental condition of possibility of such skilled coping, and attempting to demystify the background by characterizing it in terms of (yet more) "skilful coping" does not appear to help matters. Indeed, this is, we maintain, *potentially* misleading. Perhaps surprisingly, given our subsequent support for a reformed analysis of knowing how – and hence of tacit knowing – in terms that respect the *principle of articulacy* (PA), we support Heidegger's anthropocentrism; although we lack sympathy with the way he chooses to realize his project of transcendental phenomenology.

We will return to the phenomenological attempt to ground our worldly being in skilful coping in Chapter 5. But as Dreyfus himself observes, his account of the background is not the only one available; indeed, he concedes, it sounds similar (albeit "deceptively"; Dreyfus 2003: 11) to one John Searle introduces as an essential ingredient of his own account of intentionality. Since this is both naturalistically orientated and can be seen usefully as a response to the Kripkean account of rule-following outlined in §"The tacit dimension in Kripke's response to Wittgenstein", it suggests that there might be an alternative way of thinking about the relationship between knowledge-how and knowledge-that. More specifically, it suggests that, in so far as we associate tacit knowledge with knowledge-how, it is somehow "hidden" from view, forming the background to our conceptually articulated achievements. Since this potentially runs counter to the analysis we have offered in terms of PA, the topic of this chapter is whether Searle gives us good reasons for thinking that tacit knowledge or knowledge-how must be thought of as comprising a distinct *background*. As we will go on to see, evaluating this indicates a way in which, suitably modified, one might elaborate on the understanding of tacit knowledge presented hitherto; one according to which there is nothing *hidden* going on in the background. To make the connection with Chapters 1 and 3 more perspicuous, then, our contention is twofold:

1. Invoking some version of a background in order to block the rule-regress issues from a misunderstanding of the nature of the challenge rule-following considerations present.
2. The background serves no explanatory purpose.

We will conclude that, with the correct interpretation of the rule-following considerations in mind, no invocation of a background is required. Either it is nonconceptual, in which case it is "mere" neurology, or it is (tacit) knowledge, in which case it is open to view to those who have the ability (understanding) to see. To recall a theme from Chapter 1, if the account of background knowing how takes on the role of the schematism in blocking the rule-following regress, the work of the schematism is manifest in our practices not *hidden* behind them.

INTO THE BACKGROUND

Searle's conception of the Background is of central importance to his related accounts of both intentionality (1983) and the ontology of social reality

(1995; 2010). Beginning with the earlier work, Searle's discursive strategy has a by-now-familiar structure: first, a negative phase aims to demonstrate the incoherence of a specific explanatory framework; second, a positive phase advances the alternative conception and introduces the "hypothesis" of the Background (*sic.*). With respect to the movement between these two modes, Searle likewise entertains diagnostic-cum-therapeutic ambitions: "Many philosophical problems," he suggests, "arise from the failure to understand the nature and operation of the Background" (1983: 158). Although the only "problem" discussed in detail relates to what he later designates "External Realism" (cf. 1995 passim), he does make one more general observation which, as we will see, counts against his own position.

Turning first to the negative phase, we find that it again takes the form of one or more regress arguments, although their status is uncharacteristically equivocal. As Stroud, for example, observes, it is difficult to determine "where the negative thesis leaves off and Searle's positive "hypothesis" begins" (Stroud 1991: 247); and Searle confesses that he finds the "considerations" advanced in favour of his (positive) conception of the Background "more convincing than … the traditional sounding argument for it" that they are said to suggest (Searle 1983: 152). Now, in general, a ("traditional sounding") regress argument (against, say, X) is dialectically insulated from any "positive" recommendation a theorist may hope to advance, and so (formally at least) would not constitute an argument "for" it. However, Searle contends that his "hypothesis" is the "converse" (*ibid.*) of the view opposed (X) and so, one might assume, anticipates that since any negative argument will have implications for the plausibility of the alternative, the regress might be thought to have a more broadly positive function. Moreover, since the regress is still in essence a *negative* argument, one might infer further that the "considerations" upon which it is putatively based are more convincing still in their "positive" setting. This rests a great deal of weight on the status or nature of the considerations raised, and in particular on the extent to which they can be articulated independently of the opposed view (X). It does not, however, militate against the strictly *negative* effectiveness of the regress argument; and we will understand better the "nature and operation" of Searle's conception of the Background if we look at how the argument works against that "converse" view.

Imagine that a theorist holds that an account of intentional phenomena can be given in terms of a mind populated by representations with specific content. If we are to capture something of the phenomenology of thought and action, it seems we must introduce the idea that these representations are grasped or understood or in some other way "used" by a thinker/doer. If, on the one hand, we focus attention on the thinker/doer, the implication is that such an entity must itself possess some intentionality; but since it is intentionality that we are aiming to explicate such a strategy implies an

109

infinite regress of such "homunculi". On the other hand, if we attend to the grasping itself then we introduce another mental activity that is either immediately unanalysable or must itself be understood in terms of further representations and more (perhaps increasingly "primitive") instances of grasping which either bottom out at something unanalysable or introduce another regress. If we think of "graspings" in terms of understanding, or interpreting, or know-how – the loci of the agent's fidelity to norms – then what we have here in a more generalized form is something familiar: either a rule-regress or "a way of grasping a rule which is *not* an *interpretation*" (Wittgenstein 1953: §201). We will return to this in §"Rule-following redux".

Searle introduces the "homuncular" strand of this argument in the context of his own representationalist account of intentional content (1983: 21–2). Since the regress requires a formal separation of representation and intender, "the way to its dissolution" (*ibid*.: 22) is to construe the content of an intentional state as *intrinsic* rather than being due to any *use* to which it may be put. What gives S's belief that she is in bed the *content* it has is that it represents as pertaining particular states of affairs in the world, conditions of satisfaction which, in the case of conscious belief, are accessible to the believer (and which in this slightly complicated instance will include the notion that the being-in-bed perception is caused by what would satisfy it). In the parallel, active case, the *intention* to be in bed is likewise a representation of the conditions that would satisfy it, including the notion that the intention is the cause of the appropriate actions. Since one advantage of the homunculus-as-intender is the possibility that "it" might already be (as it were) *in* the world, the price paid for this "dissolution" is that intentional states are not *de re*. From a methodological point of view, at least, states have the content they do irrespective of one's epistemological environment, although as we will see things are not quite as clear-cut as this.

Regarding the second strand of the regress, one might think that since intentional states have intrinsic content the whole "grasping" issue falls by the wayside; and, indeed, that is how Searle represents the situation in his response to Stroud (Searle 1991: 291–2). The regress as *he* sees it addresses not the graspings of otherwise free-standing intentional contents but the "interpretation" or "application" of otherwise grasped meanings. The central idea here is presented in the first two of his three "considerations" in favour of the Background in *Intentionality* (*ibid*.: 145–9); namely, that the *literal meaning* of words underdetermines the full understanding of (both ordinary and metaphorical) sentences. Presented in this way, the *real* difference in argument might seem obscure: if we integrate the "grasping" of meaning into the conditions for semantic content and call the "understand(ing that) goes beyond meaning" (*ibid*.: 146) *U*-grasping (of *U*-meaning), then the regress can be presented in terms of the rules for the interpretation/understanding/ *U*-grasp of sentences. But of course the point at which the argument gets going is important: after all, one might attempt to block the original regress in the spirit of Searle's response to the "homunculi" argument and argue that *what it is* for an intentional state to have the content it has – and, crucially, to be *understood* as having that content – is for the *full situation* to be "grasped" by the thinker. That would make content *de re*, of course, and as such violate the strictures of Searle's methodological solipsism. To maintain the latter one needs precisely the difference between intrinsically determined intentional contents and the "knowledge" of "what to *do* with them" that together constitute "full" understanding/*U*-grasping (Searle 1983: 152).

In so far as Searle's first two considerations amount to no more than a theoretical commitment (or, for Searle, "the logical nature of Intentionality"; *ibid.*: 15) to a distinction between (intrinsic) semantic content and "full" understanding, they do not appear to support the "hypothesis" of the background; rather, they function to constrain a response to the rule-regress by requiring an understanding of how we "follow a rule" (for applying a semantic content) without "any further rules for interpreting" it (*ibid.*: 153). Before discussing the third consideration, it is worth noting at this point that Searle embraces but ultimately restricts the scope of one traditional solution to "regress" arguments: the "virtuous circularity" of the coherentist. As we have noted, the content of an intentional state is held to determine its conditions of satisfaction. But it possesses the conditions of satisfaction it does – and thus *is* the state it is – "only in relation to numerous other Intentional states" (*ibid.*: 141). This holistic nexus Searle capitalizes as the "Network". Notionally, then, one does not "grasp" meaning or form an intention in isolation. One grasps the (or at least *a*) "whole", although since intentional states are not in this sense to be regarded as individuable the concept of whole here is necessarily obscure. Although one might be tempted to view the Network as part of a solution to the threatened regress, when Searle comes to formulating his "traditional sounding argument" it becomes clear that although an intentional state's position in the Network makes it *in some sense* the state it is,[1] it (the position) does *not* give the rule specifying how it is to be applied. In other words, since no set of suitably related contents constitute good reasons for applying or interpreting a particular meaning in the right way, no explicit semantic content – no knowledge *that* (cf. *ibid.*: 143) – can give a rule that does not invite (regressive) interpretation. Whatever the grasp of the whole or part-whole amounts to, it does not amount to the required knowledge of what to *do*. The "knowledge" that constitutes full understanding and which explains *how* we can follow a rule without interpreting it lies outside or beyond the Network, constituting part of what Searle calls the Background. Indeed, it transpires that we cannot *really* talk about a state having the content it does in relation to the Network alone, because "Intentional states only have their conditions of satisfaction ... against a Background of" (Searle 1983: 20) "nonintentional or preintentional" (Searle 1995:

129) "mental capacities" (Searle 1983: 20). These include the "abilities, dispo-sitions, tendencies, and ... know-how" (Searle 1995: 130) that "enable inten-tional states of function" (*ibid.*: 129).

The characterization of the Background in terms of abilities and know-how returns us to that third consideration. Even if (codified) rules play a role in the development of physical skills, subsequent performances should not be thought of in terms of the "internalization" of those rules (as "unconscious Intentional contents"). Instead, the skilful "body takes over"; which is to say, the "rules ... recede into the Background" (Searle 1983: 151, 150). Now, the idea that rules are still in some sense "there" in the Background will turn out to be important, although if they are "there" their correct application cannot be a matter of interpretation. Putting that to one side, the greater mystery is what the positive consideration is meant to be. First, it has already been asserted that *qua* interpreted contents, verbalized instructions require a/the Background. Moreover, since Searle is tempted towards, but ultimately shies away from, phenomenological evidence,[2] he cannot invoke the comparative *experiences* of a stumbling neophyte and an expert immersed in a consum-mate performance (for more on this see See §"Dreyfus and McDowell"). If, as Searle suggests, embodied-norm talk is far more plausible than the intel-lectualistic alternative, it is because that *relative* plausibility is underwritten by the threat to the latter of a rule-regress. That, however, does nothing to lend *independent* support to the view that the abilities in question are non-/pre-intentional, and there's no "consideration" from the "logical nature" of intentionality that is of direct relevance.

The point of highlighting the elusiveness of Searle's "considerations" is that it is in the character of an *explicans* to tip us off to the nature of the *expli-candum*, and in the present case we are left with only a vague sense of what the Background is. We can therefore sympathize fully with the observation that "there is real difficulty in finding ordinary language terms to describe the Background" (Searle 1983: 156). Despite the fact that one is intentional and the other its non-/pre-intentional "bedrock" (*ibid.*: 143), for example, the Network is said to "shade off" into the Background, the latter to lay "not on the *periphery* of Intentionality but (to) *permeate(s)* the entire Network of Intentional states" (*ibid.*: 151). Likewise, although in earlier work Searle sometimes implies that the relationship between the two is otherwise, the "capacities" that make the states the states they are (that "enable" them) are held to be "*causal structures*" not "logical conditions of possibility" (Searle 1995: 130); as, indeed, must be the case if the regress of rules is to be avoided (*unless* cast in the form of a transcendental response). But this point is hard to keep in view when, for example, he says that there is a "Background pre-sumption of general regularities" which stands as "a condition of possibil-ity ... (of) applying the notion of making something happen" (Searle 1983: 133) and talks of the Background as "the embodiment of my commitment to

realism", which "preintentional realism ... gives representations the character of 'representing something'" (*ibid.*: 159) and functions as a "condition of
intelligibility on having certain sorts of theses" (Searle 1995: 182).

Searle offers two thoughts that might be of use in reconciling these ten-
sions, although they pull in different directions. As part of the "diagnostic"
element, he suggests that one of the reasons that the Background is easy to
misconstrue is that "when it comes to examining the conditions of possibility of the functioning of the mind" (Searle 1983: 157) we are condemned to
fall back on the only descriptive resources available to us: the language of
first-order intentional states. This is part of his general dissatisfaction with
"the traditional vocabulary of 'mental' and 'physical'" (Searle 1991: 291), and
one can feel his pain: if we had an idiom for talking about non-intentional
mentation then that would indeed ease the transition from physical-state
to intentional descriptions. But then, if Descartes had been able to make
sense of the operation of the Pineal gland we would not have worried about
the mind–body problem for the past few centuries. The second thought is
that when we are talking about (what we find it difficult to talk about) the
capacities, abilities and know-how that make up the Background, what we
are *really* talking about are neurophysiologically causative structures, albeit
at a "much higher level" (Searle 1995: 129). Although this is "forced" upon
us by our ignorance of the neurophysiology, the compulsion does not render
our descriptions "disreputable" (*ibid.*); indeed, the mind generally is regarded
as "a set of higher-level features of the brain ... that are at once 'mental'
and 'physical'" (Searle 1983: 9). But if we can make sense of this identity of
mental/physical features, and of an unimpeachable hierarchy of levels, why
should we not conclude that the "intentionalization" of the Background is
legitimate?

This fancy to intentionalize is tickled by two further aspects of Searle's
position. The first is that "Intentionality is ... a ground floor property of the
mind" (Searle 1983: 26), which is to say, of the brain. As such, the intentionality of propositionally contentful states is founded on the more "biologically primary" or "primordial experiences" of "perceiving and doing" (*ibid.*:
36) that are shared with non-linguistic "infants and many animals" (*ibid.*:
5). Oddly enough, one of the reasons given for attributing intentionality
to such creatures is the desire to explain their actions, and Searle makes
it clear that in such circumstances they "literally" have the desires and
beliefs ascribed to them (*ibid.*). Putting that to one side, it is not clear why
we should therefore "insulate" this physical property of the brain from the
ultimately equally physical know-how that makes up the Background. One
reason for resistance on this point is that it would "pull" the Background
out of the domain of the mental. Whatever discomfort Searle feels about
the mental/physical distinction, that between the *subjective* and the objective remains crucial:

> Without my biological constitution, and without the set of
> social relations in which I'm embedded, I could not have the
> Background that I have. But all ... this embeddedness, is only rel-
> evant to the production of the Background because of the effects
> that it has on me.   (Searle 1983: 154)

Although strictly physical, then, calling something *mental* is a way of characterizing whatever is important for understanding the *subject*. But Searle's
internalism/solipsism logically requires some "outside" against which to
trace the contours of a subject whose Background (since it determines conditions of satisfaction) makes it the subject it is. One might be willing to
indulge the view that the fantasy of a merely envatted brain has a "logical"
use, and thus acknowledge that content is fundamentally object-insensitive
in this way. But we are still left with the conclusion that all that pertains
to our interest in the *person* is at the "higher level", and that an integrated
account of the personal would be more likely if we acknowledged that the
know-how and cognate abilities that characterize the Background are intentional. Indeed, the principal reason we have to resist that conclusion, it
seems, is the threat of a regress that takes the quasi-positive form it does
only because of Searle's account of the "logic" of intentionality.

The second aspect to be noted here is the developing richness of Searle's
account of the Background. Notwithstanding the temptation to indulge in a
little philosophical therapy, the conception of the Background in *Intentionality* is relatively austere, although it does, crucially, include linguistic skills
(Searle 1983: 54). In later work, however, the account of the "sort of knowledge about how the world works" (Searle 1995: 131) required to account
for intentional phenomena becomes more expansive. So, for example, we
find that the Background "*structures*" experience by manifesting the ability to apply categories of classification that are both "episodic" (*ibid.*: 134)
and "dramatic" (*ibid.*: 135) in character. Martha's seeing something in a field
as a rabbit and the "scenarios of expectation" (*ibid.*: 135) that lend cosmi-
cally greater shape and significance to her experience are likewise regarded
as due to categorical operations of the Background. The contingencies that
comprise our basic and oftentimes idiosyncratic preferences; the expectations that determine the horizon of possibilities in experience; the basic
ways in which I physically and culturally comport myself: all are ways in
which "Background abilities manifest themselves in actual occurrent forms
of intentionality" (*ibid.*: 137).

Described thus, one thing becomes immediately evident: Searle's Background takes on (in notionally naturalistic form) *the function of the schematism* (described in Chapter 1). Of course, with the move from static to
dynamic categories and the *back*grounding of what in another idiom might
be called "facticity" we have the appearance of a more existential, and in

particular Heideggerian, view of our condition and thus of what schema-tism is supposed to achieve. However, one must remember that this is still all higher-level talk of *causal structures*. Given the above observations, the obvious concern is with how this talk of causation can be squared in an enlightening way with the construal of the Background as the locus of the *subjective*. Dealing with this point will suggest why Searle's conception of the Background might be put to good (dialectical) use in our attempt to eluci-date the structure of know-how and tacit knowledge; but before we can take it up we need to say a little more about Searle's project in *The Construction of Social Reality* (1995).

ONTOLOGICAL RELATIVITY

The task Searle sets himself in *The Construction of Social Reality* (1995) is to explain how, given certain ontological commitments, we can account for the objectivity of judgements appertaining to facts that would not obtain if certain sorts of animals did not exist. Reference is made to "animals" rather than humans because although *institutional facts* (IFs) like "the Swiss franc is stronger than the US dollar" require the complicity of linguistic animals, the broader class to which these belong – *social facts* – do not. Social facts, then, contrast with *brute facts* (BFs). Where the latter are ontologically *objective*, picking out features the world possesses non-relationally/intrinsi-cally, SFs are ontologically *subjective*, relating to features that are in essence non-intrinsic; which is to say, "relative to the intentionality of observers, users, etc." (Searle 1995: 9). Given that social reality supervenes in this way on brute reality, the challenge is to show how the ontologically subjective can be construed as sufficiently independent of observers, users and so on to figure epistemologically. The fast and, from our perspective, unsanitary answer to this is that the "features of the observers that enable them to create ... observer-relative features of the world" (*ibid.*: 11) are not them-selves observer-relative, since as we have already observed "mental states ... are intrinsic features of reality" (*ibid.*: 12). It is the Background that is of interest, then: the "standpoint of beings who are ... inside the world that includes us as active agents" (*ibid.*: 12). In addition to his basic set of dual-isms, however, Searle introduces three key concepts that have a bearing on the Background and which it is worth quickly describing: collective inten-tionality, assignment of function, and constitutive rules.

Social reality begins to emerge when, as a feature of their intentional-ity, creatures impose on (brute) things certain uses in accordance with their needs, interests, values and so on. Whether it is humans using bits of paper as money or chimpanzees a stick as an insect-lure, these assignments of "agentive" function institute conditions of normative evaluation "outside" or "beyond" the brute facts of the matter (including the causal facts). The basic form of such assignments is: "The function of X is to Y", where it is understood that X is *supposed* to (norm) cause Y. Now, one assumes that the intentionality that plays a part in the function-assignment can be individualistic at the most primitive level. At the level of IFs, however, language is "essentially constitutive" (Searle 1995: 59) and language is *itself* institutional; and, although social facts per se do not require language, they do "presuppose all sorts of cooperative behaviour" (*ibid.*). The basis of that behaviour, and thence of social and indeed institutional reality is *collective* (C) intentionality. Although Searle does not reflect on the appeal of an analysis of "I" intentionality in terms of C-intentionality, he is adamant that no reduction of the latter to the former will work: we cannot spin a collective notion out of complex iterations of "I" intentions. Like intentionality, then (by which one assumes he means "I" intentionality), C-intentionality is "a biologically primitive phenomenon" (*ibid.*: 24), although this leaves obscure the relationship between the two "primitive" phenomena that nevertheless belong to the same genus.[3]

Cavils aside, it is with the concept of C-intentionality in play that we get to the meat and potatoes of the normative issue. A *status* function takes the form of a *linguistic* rule that is *constitutive* for the institutional phenomenon in question (say, Y) only if it is intended *collectively* that X is to serve that function (as Y). If the non-linguistic have a "thinner" social ontology, however, it is not because they do not answer to social facts. Along with C-intentionality, an animal's "language-independent thoughts", or "intentional states with full intentional content" (*ibid.*: 62), appear to provide sufficient normative grip to allow them to "impose functions on natural phenomena" (*ibid.*: 40), which can even be "transmitted".[4] But these do not amount to *status* functions, which have an essentially linguistic form ("X counts as Y in C") and "are almost entirely positive and negative deontic powers: rights, duties, obligations, entitlements, authority, penalties, hierarchies and institutional power generally" (Searle 2001–2: 277).

Although it is clear that in these terms many – indeed, most – stretches of social reality are regulated by a naturalistic/evolutionary process rather than by fiat (and natural language itself would be the most significant of these "institutions"), that does not derogate from the fact that "someone must be capable of understanding" or "must understand, consciously or unconsciously" the use to which something is being put (Searle 1995: 22). If one imagines some aspect of social reality having degenerated into vacuous ritual (or a "purely decorative activity on a level with a kind of dancing"; McDowell 2000: 118) no one either does or *can* understand the relevant functions because, in point of fact, the interests, values and what have you that would constitute the capability are simply absent. Likewise, although this in-principle understanding is essential to keep things as it were "real", agentive functions do not require the constant ("occasionalistic") intentional consciousness of agents (nor of a Berkeleian deity). In the absence of intenders and of their collective ability to transmute lead into normative gold there would be nothing here to flatter with the epithet "ontology"; but at the same time, the entities constituted through their industriousness cannot be so subject-dependent that all that is solid might so easily melt into air and bring about the collapse of the social–epistemological superstructure.

With these elements introduced, we can begin to give general shape to Searle's problem: how do we *explain* the fact that when people are initiated into normative structures – structures involving, for the greater part, entities constituted through that most complex of human institutions, natural language – they are not only customarily ignorant of the relevant rules, but often entertain explicit beliefs that appear to belie their apparent mastery of them? Or as Searle would prefer it: given naturalistic constraints on admissible forms of explanation, how do we account for the fact that ontologically active rules "play ... a causal role ... in the actual behaviour of those who are participating in ... institutions" (Searle 1995: 127)?

The clue here takes us back to the second consideration, and the rather infelicitously phrased suggestion that in the development of skills "rules recede into the Background". In the context of social facts, the gloss put on that transition is that neither mental causation nor "brute physical causation" (*ibid.*: 139) will suffice for an account.[5] Since it operates over intentional/contentful states, the rejection of the former is unsurprising as it eliminates the need for any Background and is therefore inconsistent with the basic analysis of intentionality. Given that we are supposedly talking about neurophysiology, however, the rejection of the latter is more revealing. It demonstrates the difficulty of squaring the need for some understanding of how the Background might have a sufficiently "rational structure" (*ibid.*: 141) to operate normatively with the requirement that an adequate (naturalistic) explanation must be causal. The key, he tells us, is "to see that the Background can be causally sensitive to the specific forms of the constitutive rules of the institutions without actually containing any beliefs or desires or representations of those rules" (*ibid.*)

To return to the skills example, when Tom is instructed in an activity – perhaps through the use of explicit rules – his increasing competence is not due to an internalization of the rules (which would invite the regress) or to their metaphorical withdrawal from the (intentional) Foreground; rather, it is an indication that he has developed skills, abilities and know-how "functionally equivalent" (*ibid.*: 142) to the rules. Equally, when he learns to navigate his way amid the shoals of social reality, it is because he is now disposed to behave in a way that is in accordance with the standards of correctness dictated by the specific content of the rules that constitute it.

Above, we argued that Searle's headline "considerations" do little to advance a *positive* conception of the Background. The truly effectual matter, it now appears, is the requirement to account for the objectivity of the puta-tively *subjective*. This in turn inspires Searle to enrich his account of the Background to incorporate structural features of experience that, notwith-standing their ultimately causal analysis, would shame no existential phe-nomenologist. What we have in place, then, is an enhanced account of the Background that, in fulfilling the work of schematism, constitutes a solu-tion to the rule-regress. With that in mind let's return to our principle con-cern, which was raised at the end of §"Into the background": the extent to which Searle's conception of the Background can make a contribution to our understanding of personal (tacit) knowledge-how. More specifically, the question at this juncture is to whether or not Searle's account of the relation-ship between a broad class of facts and the Background can be amended to shed some light on the recognition that the *tacit* feature of tacit knowledge – or the *ability/capacity* aspect of knowledge-how – introduces a subjective/personal dimension to such cognitions that is prima facie in tension with the requirement for objectivity.

Now, *understood in a particular way*, the "tacit" dimension of tacit knowl-edge appears to require a lack of transparency or awareness or access (of "tellability") on the part of the knower without impugning their cognitive standing. On Searle's account, we have good reasons for thinking that, while the rules that ultimately conduce to the mastery of a particular stretch of social reality might be "hidden" from a particular subject, the rule-sensitivity of their dispositions ensures that they *act* appropriately. Moreover, since standards of correctness are determined by linguistic rules instituted through collective intentionality, these rules are sufficiently external to the subject to underpin claims to knowledge. We might therefore hazard that what Tom *knows* when he knows tacitly are those rules; and since the complex rights and obligations that characterize the deontic powers enshrined in those rules are subject to in-principle "explicit codification" (Searle 1995: 88) there is nothing subjective about the facts such rules constitute. Similarly, such knowledge is *tacit* because it registers the fact that Tom's knowing results from his dispositions (and *not* his reflective – "tellable" – capacities). Finally, one might then add that what it *is* to have the appropriate dispositions is to have know-how, which seems appropriate since the rules themselves, even when codified, are not self-interpreting, but require such Background capac-ities. In this sense, knowledge-how transcends mere ability-to-do precisely because of its isomorphic relationship with what is *known* (albeit tacitly).

This suggests a (Searle-inspired) naturalistic competitor to the analysis of tacit knowledge outlined in Chapter 1 and detailed in Chapter 2. It is a position that has a *reductively* Rylean resonance in so far as it grounds tacit knowledge in a Background of non-intentional know-how and does not – as we propose – assimilate the latter (as *personal* knowledge-how) to the former. On our account, nothing is "hidden" from view in the Background:

it is Foreground all the way. Consequently, the task for what remains of this chapter is to show what's wrong both with this alternative view and with that "certain way" in which the tacit dimension of tacit knowledge is understood. That will in turn return us to the correct interpretation of the rule-following consideration and more dialectically nuanced understanding of what our proposal amounts to.

INTO THE FOREGROUND

Searle's account of the crucial role the Background plays in our individual and collective lives appears to offer a naturalistic model for the intersecting concepts of tacit knowledge and knowing how. To be a credible alternative to the claim that tacit knowledge is personal knowledge-how, however, some concerns must be addressed, the most immediately obvious of which is that it applies only to social/institutional facts. That appears unproblematic if one endeavours to illuminate the concept of tacit knowledge through some of the paradigm cases of know-how. Without "agentive functions" of a sort there would be no sensitive interpretations of the *Grosse Fuge* or well-timed sprints to the finishing line; no googlies bowled or faces recognized. But while it seems odd to think that someone might know tacitly that $E = mc^2$, intuitions are less clear when it comes to the cognitive achievements of chick-sexers, Polynesian navigators and medical diagnosticians. If one knows tacitly that John has some particular disease one presumably (for Searle) knows a fact of a different variety to that grasped by the googly-identifier, *even if* one cannot tell how it is that one has arrived at one's conclusion. We might of course choose to bite the bullet; but before doing so we will consider the basic problems with Searle's account, and any improvements that might as a result suggest themselves.

The key assumption driving Searle's ontological reform is the distinction between the brute, intrinsic, brain-independent facts and social, relational, brain-dependent facts. Indeed, Searle's commitment to "external realism" (ER) has the air of a moral crusade, since it is taken that the "common" attempt "both to deny the existence of a reality independent of human representation and to deny that true statements correspond to facts" (Searle 1995: 149–50) must be resisted. The defence of ER is a little confusing, however. Since realism is not a belief or hypothesis, but something presupposed by "any *showing* or *demonstrating*" (Searle 1983: 159); and since, moreover, such activity "presupposes the Background, and the Background is the embodiment of my commitment to realism" (*ibid.*); then this suggests that the only way to reject realism would be to fail to do any showing or demonstrating. The implication here is made explicit in later work; namely, that since ER "functions as a taken-for-granted part of the Background" that functions as a "condition of intelligibility on having certain sorts of theses" (Searle 1995: 182) it can only be demonstrated *transcendentally* (*ibid.*: 183). So it would seem that no one *could* deny realism, because it is not possible to mean (show; demonstrate) what one would want to say in *doing* so.

Now, when Searle accepts that although "certain sorts of talk ... presuppose external realism" (Searle 1995: 184) this does not constitute a knockdown argument, one might suppose that he has in mind Stroud's well-known objection to transcendental arguments; namely, that they can only reveal subjective necessities. These are, however, necessities of belief, and as noted Searle denies that the "pretheoretical commitment" (cf. *ibid.*: 195) to ER is an intentional state. It might of course be that Searle has some other understanding of the nature of transcendental demonstration in mind here – one that somehow vivifies the claim that a rejection of realism is unintelligible because the Background "embodies" "preintentional realism" (Searle 1983: 159). In this respect, recall that the reason Stroud (1968) thinks such arguments have limited efficacy is because *he* presupposes that their context is one in which the relationship of mind to world (or of subjective to objective) is in (sceptical) question; in other words, that the possible falsity of ER cannot be eliminated by them. There is no reason why one must make such an assumption, and we have seen several attempts to resist doing so. Moreover, the desire to want to avoid making something like ER a *theoretical* belief is shared by thinkers as disparate as Carnap (1967) and Wittgenstein (1969). Notwithstanding this fraternalism, although Searle rejects the claim that he shares Stroud's epistemological preoccupations (1991: 289, 292–3), ER is founded on a subjective-objective distinction that is a requirement of his methodological solipsism. Despite assertions to the contrary, it is difficult to see what a non-theoretical commitment that is both *necessarily* shared and yet widely (and meaninglessly) rejected could be.

The closest we get to an appreciation of Searle's realism is when it comes to elucidating the intrinsic/relational distinction. Here he falls back on the rather unhelpful example of what an omniscient being would and would not see. It would, for example, see a Screwdriver-*an-sich*, if what that denotes is something stripped of *all* possible, say, readiness-at-hand. Equally, it would see us "*treating*" (Searle 1995: 12) that entity as a screwdriver. But it would not see a screwdriver *qua* screwdriver because, intrinsically speaking, there's no such thing. The problem here is that we cannot *mean* what we say. We cannot *mean* that it sees us treating something *as a screwdriver* because "seeing", "us", "treating", "something" and "screwdriver" have no use in the language of the omniscient. It might be that Searle is, as some Wittgensteinians would have it, indulging in a superior sort of nonsense here and "*shewing*" us what cannot be *said*. But the readier conclusion is that one cannot say anything about what something that has no Background does or does not "see".

We can express this latter point in more fundamental terms and still remain broadly within the scope of Searle's account. Since (to recall) the Background designates the "standpoint of beings who are … inside the world that includes us as active agents", only *interpreters* "see". But if interpretation goes all the way down for the only sort of entities that matter (cf. Davidson 1984) then there's not much mileage to be got from the intrinsic-relational distinction: all facts are "linguistic". Contra Searle's suspicions, this does not make reality a social construct. That would only be the moral if one assumed, as primary, a distinction between norms indicated by brute facts and those indicated by social facts. To reject that assumption is simply to go along with the idea that ultimately there's little sense to be made of the idea of separating out in some determinate fashion the contribution made by language users and the contribution made by the world.

On this preliminary revision of the Searlean position, one can still retain the idea of the Background, and of the role it might play in explicating the related concepts of tacit knowledge and know-how (as outlined at the end of §"Ontological relativity"). Equally, the notion that ultimately the non-separation thesis derives from the fact that language users are part of the world they know is respected, although we cannot maintain that that is because the "Brute" facts are ontologically privileged. This should come as a relief. The idea that at the appropriate "level" of description the Background is neurophysiological is clearly problematic, as is the precise status of "social reality" when construed as the determinate source of the norms that agents will be inculcated with and yet contrasted invidiously with its brute superior. However, this proposed revision does present a problem. When deprived in this way of a connotative link with the *physical* attention necessarily turns to the relationship between the Background and *intentionality*. As we have seen, Searle struggles to characterize the Background, taking descriptors like "preintentional" and "nonintentional" as interchangeable terms. Such infelicities reveal the difficulties involved in construing tertium quids, issuing in such otherwise unenlightening avowals as "*Intentionality rises to the level of Background abilities*" (Searle 1991: 293).[6] The non-intentional status of the Background seems even odder when one is reminded that the "whole edifice" of adult intentionality, despite being in most of its modes essentially linguistic, "rests on biologically primitive forms of prelinguistic Intentionality" (*ibid.*: 94). Why does intentionality, as it were, *circumvent* the Background in order to express itself at a level that is made possible only by the Background? Why not amend the Dreyfus/ Heideggerian view and claim that fully fledged intentional content presupposes a "more fundamental" form of intentionality (call it *bio*intentionality) and adopt a lofty disdain when it comes to arguments about whether this should be denoted *mental* or not? One might then at least make good on the claim that since "Intentionality is … a ground floor property of the mind ... [a]ny explanation of Intentionality ... takes place within the circle of Intentional concepts" (Searle 1983: 26).

A way of summarizing these concerns is to inquire into what it is that obliges the detachment of normativity from intentionality. For Searle, it is the price (willingly) paid for responding to the threatened regress of rules *given particular theoretical assumptions*, key among which is the intrinsic/relational distinction (on which ER turns). But flushing normativity out of the intentional and into a *non*-intentional Background hardly helps matters. Discussing a suggestion strikingly similar to Searle's, Sellars notes that:

> [if one substitutes] the phrase "learning to conform to the rules ..." for "learning to obey the rules ..." where "conforming to a rule enjoining the doing of A in circumstances C" is to be equated simply with "doing A when the circumstances are C" – regardless of how one comes to do it ... (then a) person who has the habit of doing A in C would then be conforming to the above rule even though the idea that he was to do A in C had never occurred to him, and even though he had no language for referring to either A or C. (1954: 204)

No regress threatens here because there's no requirement that John has to grasp an explicit rule: the norms are implicit in John's abilities, capacities, dispositions and so on. This solution amounts to what Robert Brandom calls "regularism", the suggestion that such norms ("known tacitly") "should be understood just as regularities of behavior" (1994: 27). The worry is that on such an account the only way to license normative evaluations is on the basis of a deviation in performance from an identified regularity. Since the regularity in question cannot here be one dictated by the agent's past performances (there being good Kripkensteinian reasons to be sceptical about which pattern if any is relevant, as we noted in §"The tacit dimension in Kripke's response to Wittgenstein"), it must be one which assessors of performances determine to be correct on the basis of *their* understanding of the constitutive rule.

As we have seen, Searle does indeed maintain that all constitutive rules are in-principle codifiable; although he simultaneously acknowledges that explicit codification has its price: "it deprives us of the flexibility, spontaneity, and informality that the practice has in its uncodified form" (Searle 1995: 88). One might take the view that these characteristics are precisely what define normative command: *grasping* a rule as opposed to *conforming* to it. Indeed, the fact that the open-endedness and contextual sensitivity of skilful responses to practical exigencies seems to contradict the in-principle codifiability claim is one of the factors motivating our analysis of practical know-how in terms of PA. If A's practices lack the "flexibility" and "spontaneity" of B's then their ability to express in codified form ("tell") the rule seems beside the point: lacking (as Kant would say) the "mother-wit" to apply the rules they can recite they lack the appropriate understanding. For Searle, of course, the role of "mother-wit" is mandated to the Background, since that is required for the application of rules. But now the burden of normativity is returned to the "realm" where, it appears, only regularities can prevail.

The moral here is that if the norms are "out there" then it is not clear how we *answer* to them; but if they are "in here" then what they answer *to* remains equally obscure. In trying to make sense of what a (rival) Searlean view of the relationship between tacit knowledge and know-how would look like, we are led to the conclusion that it founders on problems deriving from the inner/outer, subjective/objective distinctions. Consequently, one can see the appeal of accounts that take the overturning of such dualisms as the diagnostic key to understanding the nature of human-being-in-the-world. On this alternative conception, *practice* – as the locus of implicit norms – takes over as the primary datum; and we have already encountered the view that it involves dealing with things that are ready-at-hand as opposed to present-to-hand, and noted how that relates to an alternative conception of the Background (§"Regress redux" in Chapter 1, and the introduction to the present chapter).

Now, we have endeavoured to demonstrate how Searle's account of the Background and of the status of norms results from his commitment to realism and its attendant dichotomies. But we have neglected hitherto an evaluation of the way that commitment *shapes his response to the rule-regress*. We can make this clearer if we examine the views of someone who takes himself to be responding to Wittgenstein's rule-following considerations and of answering the question how norms can be implicit in practice. As such, they present us with an alternative, both to the account of tacit knowledge we have been developing in Searle's name *and* to the one we have been retailing under the name practical knowledge-how. Let's look briefly, then, at "how to understand ... [the] practical normative know-how" (Brandom 1994: 25) that serves as Brandom's version of the Background.

According to Brandom, Wittgenstein is alert to two problems relating to the normativity of concept-involving activity. Against the notion that such doings are to be understood in terms of explicitly discursive rules ("regulism") he proffers the by now familiar regress of "correctness of application" (Brandom 1994: 20); against the suggestion that norm-governed activity is to be understood as regularity ("regularism") he raises considerations similar to those raised above against Searle. *Regularism*, then, is an anti-intellectualistically motivated but ultimately ill-fated attempt to respond to the problems raised by *regulism*. Given this failure,

> [the] conclusion of the regress argument is that there is a need
> for a *pragmatist* conception of norms – a notion of primitive

> correctness of performance *implicit* in *practice* that precede and
> are presupposed by their *explicit* formulation in *rules* and *princi-*
> *ples.*   (*Ibid.*: 21)

There are three things to note here:

1. Brandom thinks that there's a *positive* conception of normativity to be derived from the regress.
2. The positive conception involves a level of "primitive correctness" operating in what for the sake of argument we will call the Background.
3. The solution to the regress argument takes the form of a transcendental demonstration of sorts.

Brandom's position is thus akin to Searle's, both in thinking that the regress argument sanctions one theoretical project "rather than" (*ibid.*: 23) another and in lending support to the explanatory requirement for a Background by introducing a different "level" of normativity. The principal difference is that in so far as Brandom takes practice as primary and is unmoved by Searle's dualisms he can articulate more clearly the relationship between the Background and the Foreground.

In this regard, to be clearer means *not* to attempt Searle's shotgun wedding between causation and presupposition. Rather, Brandom takes it that although norms are not just necessary for but are indeed *constitutive of* conceptually contentful performances, the norms in question are those that are implicit (let's say *tacit*) in practices. There is no rule regress, then, *not* because – *à la* Searle – the order of derived normativity (the Background) happenstantially mirrors the hard normativity of social reality, but because *what it is* to understand a codified rule is to have mastery of the "background of practices permitting the distinguishing of correct from incorrect applications of those rules" (Brandom 1994: 22). Norms stating explicitly that this or that must be done according to the rule and which take the form of knowledge-that (cf. *ibid.*: 23) are "intelligible" in that form only because of the know-how that comprises "norms … *implicit* in what is *done*" (*ibid.*: 30). Accordingly, the theoretician who wishes to describe performances in terms of regularities answering to codified rules is simply making explicit what is always-already implicit in the performances of those who simply go on in the right way.

This is not the place to embark on a full critical evaluation of Brandom's project, and in particular on its social-practice-based deontology. Two things, however, have an important bearing on our task in this chapter. The first is that it presents us with an alternative understanding of tacit knowledge (albeit one closer in spirit to ours than to the Searlean version). To recall that earlier formulation, people can "know more than they can tell" in so far as the "implicit understanding or 'know-how'" (Brandom 1994: 658, n.40) that constitutes their mastery of practices need not be "expressible by those in whose regular conduct they are implicit" (*ibid.*: 27). If we wish to be guided by a more traditional formulation, what they know when they *know* tacitly are the rules (as expressed by someone who can make them explicit); but such knowledge is *tacit* because as understood by them it takes the form of practical mastery. Moreover, since "the properties of practice" (*ibid.*: 23) are prior (as constitutive), intentionality goes all the way down and we need no longer be vexed by having to account for some *tertium quid* betwixt "nature" and "culture".

Turning to the second point, we have noted that the implicitness of norms gives philosophy a specific project: their explication. The motivation for such an undertaking is that "implicit structures are often best understood by looking at how they can be made explicit" (*ibid.*: xiv). At first blush this methodological principle seems unproblematic; but it does raise the issue of what sort of *difference* explicit understanding, where norms are brought to concepts, makes to the *implicit* understanding that is (always) already operative. Now the nature of Brandom's explicatory project naturally brings to mind Searle's own views concerning the possibility and "cost" of cashing-in deontic commitments, and it may well be that this way of thinking about the complexity of human social and other interactions is fundamentally misconceived. We will say more about this below, but for now the concern is with the extent to which such an explicatory project is motivated by the distinction between a conceptually articulated Foreground and a more primitively normative Background.

The issue here, which picks up points 1 and 2 above, is how Brandom deploys an interpretation of Wittgenstein's regress argument to promote a *positive* conception of the Background, in which "primitive" correctness is at work in practice. To this end, he disambiguates three uses of the concept of a rule. The first two concern what agents themselves "consult" or are "guided" by: either (i) rules as "discursively articulated and propositionally contentful" (Brandom 1994: 64) statements of procedure, or (ii) rules as norms in general. The third is an observer's category: (iii) rules as forms of normative assessment. Brandom takes it that Wittgenstein, as part of his attack on regulism, is concerned with showing how (i) generates a regress; but as McDowell points out, the examples that Wittgenstein gives – like signposts – are in fact examples of (ii), which he glosses as ideas of "acting in the light of a standard of correctness" (McDowell 2009: 99). We will, thus, now take up the task outlined at the end of Chapter 3 and to offer in detail the account of rule-following we favour.

RULE-FOLLOWING REDUX

We began the previous chapter with an outline both of Wittgenstein's regress argument and the way it can be taken to support a role for tacit knowledge. The examples of correctly determining the direction that a signpost points, or of the possibility of deviant reactions to explanations of how to continue, correctly, a mathematical series, suggests that everything that can be said still allows for misunderstandings. Since everything that can be made explicit apparently underdetermines the correct understanding, such understanding must instead be based on something unsaid and implicit. It must depend on tacit knowledge of the rule. Hence, on this account, the regress argument is stopped by an appeal to tacit knowledge.

This connection appears to be in accord with Wittgenstein's own conclusion: "What this shews is that there is a way of grasping a rule which is *not* an *interpretation*, but which is exhibited in what we call 'obeying the rule' and 'going against it' in actual cases" (Wittgenstein 1953: §201). It also fits the emphasis, discussed so far in this chapter, that both Searle and Brandom place on the importance of a background against which explanations of rules and meaning or the possession of intentional mental states can be set. However, although this way of connecting the regress argument with tacit knowledge is intuitive, it is also misleading. That it is misleading can be clarified by identifying three problems it faces.

The first problem with it, as an interpretation of Wittgenstein, is that it accepts part of what he criticizes: a platonic picture of rules as rails "invisibly laid to infinity" fundamentally distinct from our capacity to articulate them. That picture is easily prompted by the case of the deviant pupil (*ibid.*: §185). What that case, and others like it, seems to show is both that any finite set of examples underdetermines a correct understanding of the rule and that such correct understanding must involve grasp of a supernatural pattern. Since no actual human enumeration of the pattern seems enough to determine it, it must be supernatural. Hence the metaphor of rails laid to infinity. With this picture of the way rules determine correct moves in place, there is a substantial role for tacit knowledge to bridge the gap between what can be made explicit in the sublunary realm and the ideal platonic rule. But if so, it seems that Wittgenstein offers support for the platonic picture he also seems to criticize. To put this point in the terms used by McDowell (1994), such a picture of tacit knowledge presupposes a *rampantly* platonic picture of rules, one in which the normative demand they place on rule-followers is conceived as independent of human thought.

A second problem concerns the communication of knowledge of rules. On this interpretation explanations are insufficient explicitly to fix a unique rule, which depends instead on a tacit understanding both by speaker and hearer. But if so, the tacit grasp of a particular rule cannot be a matter of *knowledge* even if it were, as a matter of fact, of the rule intended. Nothing could *justify* the selection from the infinite range of alternative options. The best case would be that hearers were disposed to select a particular rule because of a shared background of dispositions but this would not be a matter of justification. But even this way of putting things is put under strain because of a third problem.

The final problem, then, is one of accounting for the idea that tacit knowledge of a rule or the meaning of a word has some particular content to be *known*. Regarding what can be made explicit, this approach is in the same position as Kripke's sceptical account; but it differs from that in attempting to invoke something tacit. The problem, though, is that this means that nothing can be said by way of positive account of what the tacit knowledge amounts to since any attempt will fall prey to the objections, made particularly vivid by Kripke, to explicitness. If that is the case, what reason is there to think that what remains tacit is a "something" at all? It may justify the label "tacit" but only at the cost of undermining the idea of knowledge.

These three problems all stem from the idea that tacit knowledge is needed to plug a "gap" between what can be explained, or otherwise made explicit, and the full grasp of a rule that can be understood as a result. This, however, rests on a misunderstanding of Wittgenstein's dialectic, which aims to undermine the very idea of such a gap. He suggests, instead, that there is a close connection between what a teacher can express and what a student can grasp in the examples that manifest the teacher's meaning.

> But do you really explain to the other person what you yourself understand? Don't you get him to *guess* the essential thing? You give him examples, – but he has to guess their drift, to guess your intention. – Every explanation which I can give myself I give to him too. – "He guesses what I intend" would mean: various interpretations of my explanation come to his mind, and he lights on one of them. So in this case he could ask; and I could and should answer him. (Wittgenstein 1953: §210)

> "But this initial segment of a series obviously admitted of various interpretations (e.g. by means of algebraic expressions) and so you must first have chosen *one* such interpretation."–Not at all. A doubt was possible in certain circumstances. But that is not to say that I did doubt, or even could doubt. (*Ibid.*: §213)

In §210 the interlocutor expresses the worry that, since an explanation fails to determine the rule to be explained, a listener has to guess – from an infinite range of options – what rule was intended. The guess is needed to bridge the gap between what is actually expressed and what was really intended. But Wittgenstein's response is to equate what can be explained to another person and what might have been assumed to be epistemically optimal: what a speaker can explain to him or herself. This equation might be thought – optimistically – to offer in the third-person case the happy circumstances of the first-person case: what one knows one intends in one's explanation. But it might also be thought – pessimistically, in the context of an inquiry that undermines the efficacy of mental templates to underpin one's own grasp of a rule – to limit what is available to others to what is available to oneself. Either way, the connection undermines the idea that a guess is necessary to bridge a gap between first- and third-person cases.

§213 applies the moral of §210 to the explanation of a rule. While some explanations can fail, that is not the general case (just as, in general, signposts succeed in pointing). Although Wittgenstein rejects substantive explanations of our grasp of rules, via mental mechanisms, he does not claim that there is a gap between what can be manifested and what must be understood: a gap that has thus to be filled by a tacit element. Recognizing that our understanding can be expressed in examples undermines the gap between the sublunary and the platonic and thus that potential role for tacit knowledge. It also blocks the worry raised above that such a model of the tacit understanding of rules or meanings would put under pressure the idea that there is something to be known, a content grasped. There is a content that can be expressed in examples or ongoing practice.

That might suggest that, on a proper understanding, Wittgenstein's regress argument offers no support for tacit knowledge. And indeed, an interpretation, perhaps inspired by Kripke, which concentrates on the potential failures of explanations or the lack of efficacy of signposts seems to have things almost exactly the wrong way round. A pointing sign can be a paradigm case of what it is to make a direction explicit not implicit. Some ostensive examples can explicate the meaning of a word. Such phenomena, in which understanding is made perfectly explicit, might seem to suggest no connection between the regress argument and tacit knowledge. But that is not the case either: there is a tacit dimension to rule-following.

Consider a rule which can be partly codified in an informal statement such as that the digits always follow the pattern: "0, 2, 4, 6, 8, 0, etc.", or more fully codified in an explicit mathematical formula or principle. Someone who understands such a rule may understand such a general principle or perhaps a set of related principles using some of them to explain others. They may thus be able to articulate what they understand the rule to be in general and context-independent terms. Nevertheless, understanding even with such a codifiable rule cannot be independent of understanding its instances. One needs to know, in Wittgenstein's phrase, how to go on; and this is a form of personal and practical knowledge in the sense articulated in Chapters 1 and 2 of this book.

Wittgenstein gives an example of someone who grasps a series either with, or without, having a formula in mind:

> It is clear that we should not say B had the right to say the words "Now I know how to go on", just because he thought of the formula – unless experience shewed that there was a connexion between thinking of the formula – saying it, writing it down – and actually continuing the series ...
>
> We can also imagine the case where nothing at all occurred in B's mind except that he suddenly said "Now I know how to go on" – perhaps with a feeling of relief; and that he did in fact go on working out the series without using the formula. And in this case too we should say – in certain circumstances – that he did know how to go on. (Wittgenstein 1953: §179)

The passage makes a connection between understanding and an ability to take part in a practice explicit. But there is also something implicit in this example: it involves particular cases. Whatever the general criteria there may be for understanding a rule, such as restating or summarizing it in general terms, such understanding also requires grasp that *this particular* number, for example, is the next number in the sequence. One needs to know how to recognize or proffer a particular number which – whatever its size, colour and font – counts as an instance of the rule because it is an instance of the next number, for example 8.

Consider the case of being able to recognize, without perhaps coming up with, an appropriate next number in a more complicated series than "plus 2". In such an example, knowing how to go on involves recognizing correct numbers and thus knowing of that! number that it is correct. So, on the one hand, it involves context-dependent judgement. But, on the other, it is an example of knowledge-that, and thus does not seem to be a candidate for the practical personal knowledge we have identified as tacit.

The moral of Wittgenstein's regress argument, however, is not that anything is hidden in explanations of rules which has instead to be tacitly added in. On that account, which we have rejected, knowledge of a rule, or the meaning of a word, would violate what we have called the *Principle of Articulacy*:

PA   All knowledge can be articulated, either in context-independent terms or in context-dependent terms.

Because knowledge of the meaning of the word involves an inarticulate guess – inarticulate because nothing that can be put into words is sufficient for understanding, on this view – it involves a form of knowledge that resists expression. But on the view that we have put forward the connection to tacit knowledge is through the idea of context-dependent practical knowledge. It involves, for example, knowing in a context that this! number is the right continuation of a series, or calling that! object red accords with grasp of the meaning of "red". Such knowledge *can* be articulated in context through practical demonstrations.

We have argued that the conception of tacit knowledge as conceptually structured but context-dependent practical knowledge still merits the label "tacit" because it cannot be put fully into words. It requires the assistance of context, whether in the form of a chick to be sexed or a sea to be navigated. In the case of a mathematical series, the context is in recognizing particular intances, particular numbers, as correct. But it may be thought that such cases do not fit our analysis because, although they accord with PA, they also accord with the *principle of codifiability*:

> PC   All knowledge can be fully articulated, or codified, in context-independent terms.

They thus count as explicit, rather than tacit, knowledge.

But that objection fails to grasp the priority of practice that is the conclusion to Wittgenstein's discussion. *Once* one can recognize what it is for a new case to be an instance of a general rule (whether of a mathematical or empirical concept) *then* codifications can subsequently be built. But the codification of rules that can be expressed independently of context-dependent abilities is by itself insufficient to guide the novice rule follower. The negative force of the rule-following considerations targets the idea that such codifications in themselves can underpin practice. The positive descriptions of practice remind us that the knowledge we exchange in explanations by example can, nevertheless, be articulated in context.

CONCLUSION

If the foregoing is right, the regress argument proper relates to any sort of understanding that introduces a gap between the expression of what's understood and the behaviour on the basis of which evaluations of normative correctness are made. Wittgenstein's regress argument thus complements both Ryle's and also the idea, outlined in Chapter 2, for equipping a subject not only with context-dependent or demonstrative *thoughts* but also context-dependent or demonstrative *concepts*. It is not an attack on the range of knowledge-that. Nor does it aim to suggest that there is something mysterious about our understanding and communication of rules. In other words, "acting in the light of a standard of correctness" does not require that the burden of interpretation be shifted into a normatively "primitive", pre-discursive (rule-constituting) or "ineffable" background. Rules can be said to go all the way down; or, perhaps more felicitously, all the way *out*; precisely because they are *not* the sort of things that are (ordinarily) subject to interpretation. The terminus of philosophical explanation of our grasp of rules is knowledge-how, which manifests itself *directly* in one's mastery of the appropriate rule-governed activity. Enabled by such know-how, a subject is then able to express and articulate their practical knowledge to those at least with eyes and ears to see and hear in context-dependent conceptually structured ways.

Returning now to §"Into the foreground", it should be clear that it is because Brandom distinguishes (i) (rules as discursively articulated statements of procedure) from (ii) (rules as norms in general) in advance, and restricts the regress argument to (i), that he can offer some variant of (ii) as a *solution* to the regress argument. As with Searle, a prior commitment to a particular account of normative correctness informs Brandom's characterization of the regress argument and determines that it is seen as something that promotes a *positive* conception of the background. But understood aright the rule-regress sanctions no such (putatively explanatory) domain: nothing is (in principle) hidden from view.

In the light of this, we can reconsider Dreyfus's understanding of the Background (introduced in Chapter 1, §"Regress redux", and returned to in the introduction to the present chapter) and what transcendental claims like Dreyfus's/Heidegger's (and quasi-transcendental evidential "considerations" like Searle's) might be thought to achieve. Now, what Heidegger describes as the "primordial transcendence" that makes intentionality possible and constitutes "the understanding-of-being" (Heidegger 1984: 135, 136) equates, for Dreyfus, to a Background (BB) of "'abilities', 'practices' and 'capacities'" that comprise a "general skilled grasp of our circumstances" (Dreyfus 1993: 11). As part of a "traditional" transcendental story this invocation of skills can seem rather mysterious; especially when it appears to move effortlessly from the rather specific skills a janitor has to those of *Dasein*. However, if one regards talk of absorbed coping, practical mastery and the like as on a par with other prompts concerning the ways in which we go about our business it seems less problematic;[7] as, indeed, does Searle's "consideration" relating to the "skillful body". Moreover, taking the view that transcendental arguments and their kin are not *general* demonstrations to the effect that certain concepts are impossible to do without, but rather show that *particular* alternatives are *parasitic* (see Rorty 1971) on the linguistic resources we do in fact *use*, we can regard them as "reminders" assembled by the philosopher for the "particular purpose" of dealing with the revisionist-intellectualist (Wittgenstein 1953: §127).[8] Accordingly, even Searle's realism can be domesticated, although not in any way that validates its metaphysical foundations.

On this account, the rule-regress is a vertigo-inducing response to theory-driven searches for an illusory depth (in the form of an explanatory "background" to our practices), and transcendental arguments are a return to the quotidian. It suggests that we deflate those aspects of Heidegger's transcendental inquiry that pertain to the insights into the being of *Dasein* and regard the invocation of skills and other bodily achievements in the more Wittgensteinian light suggested above, according to which it is Foreground all the way (which is to say, there's neither foreground nor background). As it stands, however, there is an option that remains unexplored, pertaining to what Dreyfus refers to as that "more fundamental" form of intentionality (FI) that is presupposed by conceptually articulated intentional states (RI). Although this is not formally designated the Background (BB) by Dreyfus, and is not what he contrasts with Searle's account of the same, it is nevertheless the real explanatory competitor and the one of obvious interest here.[9] What is of concern, then, is the "involved" or "absorbed" coping of that more "primordial" form of intentionality, which involves what Dreyfus, following Merleau-Ponty, calls motor intentionality. As a naturalistic account of our basic ways of dealing with our environment it aims to show how the transmission and acquisition of skills might be construed in a way that does not involve the mastery of practices viewed as conceptually structured activities. And that would reinstate the sort of account of tacit knowledge and of its relation to know-how that we have canvassed (and opposed) in connection with talk of the background. In Chapter 5 we will discuss in detail this non-conceptualist alternative.

5. SECOND NATURES

INTRODUCTION

Drawing on two clues from Michael Polanyi – that "we can know more than we can tell" and that knowledge is an "active comprehension of things known, an action that requires skill" – and on arguments for the priority of practical knowledge from Ryle and Heidegger, we have argued for a conception of tacit knowledge as a context-dependent, conceptually structured form of personal or practical knowledge. In Chapter 2, we attempted to draw the sting of a recent "intellectualist" backlash by accepting that, like knowledge-that, practical knowledge has a content even as we defended the (Rylean) argument supporting its priority. This gives rise to a conception of tacit knowledge that deserves the label "knowledge" because of its content and "tacit" because it runs counter to what we called the *principle of codifiability*:

> PC All knowledge can be fully articulated, or codified, in context-independent terms.

In Chapters 3 and 4 we examined and rejected a number of possible routes towards a more radical conception of tacit knowledge drawing on both Wittgenstein's rule-following considerations and responses to it which deploy the notion of a background. These run counter to both PC and the *principle of articulacy*:

> PA All knowledge can be articulated, either in context-independent terms or in context-dependent terms.

That is, in related but differing ways, they subscribe to the claim that:

> PI There can be knowledge that cannot be articulated.

We have argued, however, that they are untenable both as conceptions of knowledge and as satisfactory interpretations of Wittgenstein's regress argument.

However, this still leaves a possible source of support for PI hinted at earlier. Chapter 1 (§"Schemata") mentioned the constructivist notion of nonconceptual content. What counts *as* nonconceptual content depends in large part on how one conceives of the conceptual and proponents of nonconceptual content often take as their target McDowell's brand of conceptualism. Since that account of the content of *experience* introduces the demonstrative trick we have deployed as part of our account of *knowledge* one aim in what follows is to explain why the conceptual content of tacit knowledge is not undermined by criticism of McDowell's conceptualist account of perceptual experience.

But more importantly, the aim of this chapter is to rebut attempts to use an account of nonconceptual content to motivate a rival understanding of the kind of worldly *coping* that we have associated with tacit *knowing*. The main target here is the sort of naturalistic appropriation of the phenomenological tradition one finds in the work of Hubert Dreyfus. As observed in Chapter 1 (§"Regress redux) and in the introdution and conclusion to Chapter 4, one oddity of Dreyfus's position derives from the fact that, following Heidegger, the background proper (BB) relates not to the primary level of intentional coping (FI) but to the understanding of being that makes it (and reflective knowledge) *possible*. Like Kant, Heidegger was embarked on a particular sort of project: to demonstrate the structure of the understanding that beings like us must have of the world (or of being) and of themselves in order for both to "appear" as they do. Necessarily, the self-understanding sought (the sort of story devised) in pursuit of that project is of the sort of entity that would *seek* such understanding: *a person*.

In this respect the transcendental-phenomenological project is at odds methodologically with an explanatory project that centres on the non-rational, prelinguistic abilities we appear to *share*, on the face of it, with other animals. But the contemporary strand of phenomenology associated with Dreyfus and epigones like Sean D. Kelly, John Haugeland and others sets great store by its anti-intellectualist willingness to identify features we have in common with other sentient creatures. In so far as their emphasis is on the basic cognitive structures for coping with the world that characterize FI, their "naturalism" is in tension with the obligation to give an account of how things "appear" *to us* and risks the *abandonment* rather than the revision of the category of the *personal*. As we will see below, this becomes particularly apparent in the treatment of freedom.

Given the requirement to (i) distinguish our use of demonstratives from McDowell's and (ii) resist a defence of PI in terms of nonconceptual content, a useful starting point is the work of Sean D. Kelly. Later we will evaluate how Kelly combines an argument against the McDowellian use of demon-strative concepts to account for the conceptual content of experience with the suggestion that this lends support to a *non*conceptualist account of coping/unreflective understanding derived from Merleau-Ponty's idea of bodily intentionality, or motor intentionality. This phenomenologically moti-vated attempt to confute what is perceived as a reactionary intellectualism comes to the fore in a recent exchange between McDowell and Dreyfus, which will be the topic of the penultimate section of this chapter. We will conclude by arguing that whatever naturalistic imperative there might be for invoking in an explanatory context some background to our reflective practices can be captured therapeutically by exploiting an understanding of Aristotle's account of second nature, albeit one disburdened of McDowell's empiricist ambitions. We will begin by outlining in broader terms the notion of content.

THE CONTENT OF "CONTENT"

One hitherto neglected way to defend an account of tacit knowledge in accord with PI turns on contrasting the sort of conceptually articulated con-tent associated with knowledge with a *non*conceptual variant. The possibility of nonconceptual content is a touchstone for both reductively and phenom-enologically minded naturalists. For example, in pursuit of an explanatory programme that aims to accommodate the thought that other animals have knowledge, one could assimilate tacit knowing to the externalist's "brute" or "apt" knowledge – of the sort to be distinguished from a person's higher level "reflective" knowledge (cf. Sosa 2007) – and then proceed to deny that a creature's "brute" contentful states have to be conceptually articulated in order to be judged as knowledge *per se*. On the other (by now more famil-iar) hand, it might be contended that our fundamental way of being in the world – our *intentional* relatedness to or "intra" it – operates "below" the level at which (conceptually contentful states of) knowledge-that appear. That "fundamental" way could in turn be used to elaborate the notion of tacit knowledge.

The notion of nonconceptual content was first introduced by Evans (1982) in the context discussed in Chapter 2 (§"Knowing how and know-ing that"), and subsequent work has reflected an ambiguity at the heart of Evans's own account: whether we are to regard such content as oper-ating *in* experience at the level of conscious awareness, or *below* the level of consciousness at a modular, sub-personal level. Addressing directly the underdetermined nature of Evans's position in the face of McDowell's (1994) criticisms, Richard Heck (2000), for example, proposes we distinguish "state" from "content" nonconceptualism. On the "state" view, distinctions between the conceptual and nonconceptual depend only on whether or not the state-holder "possesses" (or "grasps") the concepts required to *specify* the content of the state (*ibid.*: 487–8). Crucially, then, there is no distinction in content-*type* between perceptual states and the fully (conceptually) articulated states governed by the generality constraint (cf. Evans 1982: 104). On the "content" view, however, the content of perceptual states is "different in kind" (Heck 2000: 485); or, with an alternative emphasis: "the thesis that perceptual content is nonconceptual … implies the claim … that one can be in perceptual states an adequate specification of whose content would *necessarily* employ concepts one does not possess" (*ibid.*: 488, emphasis added).

We are not concerned to advance an account of the content of experience,[1] but "merely" of a certain sort of putative *knowing*. But the relevance of the former can be gleaned from exploiting an unintentional ambiguity attending the modal nature of Heck's implied claim. In sympathy with the naturalistic explanatory project, the overt interpretation is that *content*-nonconceptualism is allied to the modular, sub-personal approach to understanding perception. In other words, the concepts that are required to specify the content of perception belong to a different region to those related to percipience, to whatever the sciences require. But there is also an (unintended) sense, according to which the concepts required (that are *necessary*) to understand the nature of nonconceptual content derive not from a bottom-up, constructivist, *empirical* standpoint but from a *philosophical* standpoint. In other words, when experience or perception is being invoked it is *not at all the same sort of thing* for the reductively and the (transcendental) phenomenologically inclined.

This is the origin of the tension referred to above between the "transcendental" and "naturalistic" strains in contemporary phenomenology. It surfaces in the discussion of freedom, to which we will return below There is, however, a more obvious way in which perceptual nonconceptual content is relevant to our concerns. To clarify this, we can go along with the various criticisms of Heck's state/content distinction[2] and help ourselves to a slightly less freighted contrast: Speaks's (2005) distinction between *relative* and *absolute* nonconceptual content. Where the latter is characterized by a "different kind of content" from that possessed by the propositional attitudes, the former "includes contents *not* grasped (possessed) by A at *t*" (*ibid.*: 360, emphasis added) and "corresponds roughly" (*ibid.*: 392, n.5) to "state" nonconceptualism. Since *relative* nonconceptual content turns essentially on the "relations between … contents and agents" (*ibid.*: 360) it says nothing about the nature of content *per se* and thus does not lend direct support to PI over PA (or PC).

Speaks's desiderata for an adequate account of relative nonconceptual content are rather restrictive, since they involve *mental* content that is *not grasped* by the agent (at a particular time). The idea that such content should be construed as mental is contentious, as is the idea that such content is best characterized as "grasped". Similarly, one might take issue with the attempt to construe the relation in question in *wholly negative* terms: it refers to (presumably conceptually individuated, mental) content *not* grasped by the possessor of the state. All in all, this makes the case against relative nonconceptual content rather too easy to prosecute.[3] Of course, one might choose to construe the relation in less *privative* terms. Accordingly, if the "content" of tacit knowledge is *personal* and *situation*-specific in the way we have suggested it would be entirely appropriate for some R who lacked the relevant know-how to classify the cognitive achievement of some (tacit) knower S in terms of a content the concepts for expressing which R lacks. *Ergo*, S's cognitive state (of tacit knowing) has *non*conceptual content (for R).

In so far as one finds the concept useful, then, the interpretation of know-how (in terms of PA) we have offered is consistent with an account of *relative* nonconceptual content. Or to put it another way, tacit knowledge as personal knowledge-how offers a way of making sense of (the concept of) *relative* nonconceputal content. What, then, of absolute conceptual content? Speaks takes a great deal of time lingering over the problems involved in making sense of this, but for our purposes the conclusion is twofold. First, terminological distinctions notwithstanding, for the majority of defenders of nonconceptual content it is the *absolute* version that is key. This is the version Heck strives to vindicate (2000, 2007), and it is what Robert Hanna (2011a) defends as the view that "the perceptual mental contents, had by human and non-human animal cognizers alike", are disjunctive in semantic structure and function with what is conceptual (*ibid.*: 338). Henceforward, reference to nonconceptual content and to nonconceptualism will imply the absolute version of the position, and this leads to the second point: in defending PI one must elucidate the notion of *absolute* nonconceptual content.

As Hanna reminds us, part of the appeal of nonconceptual content is that it does justice to the intuition that, given our phylogenetic history, we must share something with animals at the cognitive level; something that is, as it were, *given*. This raises the problem of how such content interacts with or in some way gives rise to conceptual content. We have already remarked one complication here. What appears to distinguish us from the beasts is that our experience of the world seems pervaded by the sense of our *freedom* not to be "captured" by it in the same way. Correlatively, it seems odd to think of such freedom as something that comes onto the scene *only* with reflection; that we are, as it were, free *only* when we take up the (nonconceptual; given) contents of perception and *conceptualize* them.

Given this concern with freedom, it is not surprising that the requirement for a bottom-up account of rationality that respects our natural history has taken the particularly Kantian turn it has in recent years; although one cannot overstate the significance in this respect of the appearance of

McDowell's syncretic *Mind and World*. Both conceptualists and nonconceptualists alike are keen to recruit Kant's support. This division is not for our purposes, however, exhaustive. It often denotes positions that share a similar sort of epistemological project; to wit, naïve or direct realism. As indicated above, we do not intend to take a *direct* stand on whether or not the content of perceptual experience is or is not conceptual. However, the way that Kant figures in this debate is important in so far as it hinges on whether or not objects can appear to us independently of the involvement of understanding; whether or not, to scramble the oft-quoted phrase, intuitions do in fact require concepts to "see".

To see the significance of this let us turn again to Hanna, who has recently argued that nonconceptual content is, as Ismael (2007) terms it, "situated content ... mental content that is inherently sensitive to the egocentrically-centred orientation, intrinsic topology (etc.) ... of actual essentially embodied minded animal subjects" (Hanna 2011a: 371, 370). According to Brady Bowman, the superiority of Hanna's "Kantian essentialist" version of *absolute* nonconceptualism means "the case for non-conceptualism stands or falls with his position" (Bowman 2011: 419). What is important for our (dialectical) purposes is that content is "situated" in this way principally because of the role pure forms of intuition (space and time) play in "conditioning" sensibility *prior* to the subsumption of intuitions under concepts.

Much of the controversy in this area revolves around how Kant should be interpreted, with attention focusing on one or two purportedly key passages where he appears to reveal his true intent. Although Kant exegesis is not our concern, Hanna acknowledges that any interpretation of Kant as a *non*conceptualist is predicated on rejecting the idea that the "I think" must accompany our representations,[4] thus detaching the objects of experience from the categories of the understanding that would otherwise be constitutive (Hanna 2011b: 407). This detachment of the "I think" and thence of the *understanding* from their formal roles in constituting experience combines with the emphasis on the *non*conceptual nature of the pure forms of intuition to advance the concept of a given, nonconceptual content that is essentially *sub*-personal. In so doing, it eliminates the central role of the schematism in the constitution of experience, since that is where conceptually structured experience – or, for our purposes, *knowledge* – comes into play.

By eliminating the role of the schematism, Hanna's account of *absolute* nonconceptual content becomes irrelevant to our concerns, since it offers no justification for PI and hence for a rival account of tacit knowledge/practical knowledge-how. However, one might go a little further here. Evidently, the circumvention of the "I think" that is required to make sense of the nonconceptual is promoted by way of a (*sub*-personal) corrective to Kant's account of the *subject* of knowledge. But the considerations raised in Chapter 1 in relation to Heidegger's criticism of Kant and to Ryle's anti-intellectualism were intended to help elucidate a "thickly" personal account of knowledge-how that does all that is required to capture the "situational" character of content. Moreover, it does so without *any* requirement to dig deeper in search of some nonconceptual substratum.

DEMONSTRATIVES, GIVENNESS, AND MOTOR INTENTIONALITY

In the previous section the relation between relative and absolute nonconceptual content was clarified. We then proceeded to reject the suggestion that PI might be justified by using the situational character of experience to motivate a *relevant* account of nonconceptual content. The error here (call it conjunctivitis!) is to think that in challenging an excessive intellectualism to find a ready place for the knower in nature one must see the *animal* part of the human animal – that pertaining to the nonconceptual – as shared with other creatures, and the *human* part – that pertaining to the conceptual – as disjunctive. But depriving a human of the sensory/social conditions necessary for initiation into the "space of reasons" would not sediment out some "animal" underpinning or ground, something shared with (say) a gorilla and a mouse. There is nothing *privative* about the concept of an animal. Consequently, classifying persons as animals is no more illuminating of the *human* way of being than classifying gorillas (or mice) as animals is of *their* distinctiveness.

Given its origins in Heidegger's work on the ontological distinctiveness of personhood (*Dasein*), the foregoing does however leave open the possibility of a phenomenologically motivated conception of nonconceptual content that can offer a rival account of what comprises skilful coping (as know-how), which we have associated with tacit *knowing*. To constitute a genuine alternative it will have to clarify how nonconceptual content gives us an account of know-how that links up with our self-understanding, even if that self-understanding is subject to revision. More specifically, it will have to show us how, on an account that assimilates *our* skilful doings to those of other sentient animals, the freedom that we (phenomenologically) take to distinguish us from them is nevertheless *possible*.

With that in mind, let's turn to Kelly's attempt to associate a *non*conceptualist account of coping/unreflective understanding with Merleau-Ponty's idea of bodily or motor intentionality. Now, the dialectic here is potentially confusing for two reasons. Firstly, Kelly aims to forge the link between nonconceptual content and motor intentionality by providing an argument against the McDowellian use of demonstrative concepts to account for the conceptual content of *experience*. Since we have no horse in that particular race, our objective is merely to show that the attack on conceptualism does nothing to make plausible an account of *non*conceptual content that has any sort of bearing on our understanding of tacit knowledge as practical knowledge-how. By defending not conceptualism (about experience) but *anti*-nonconceptualism, we aim also to liberate our exploitation of the demonstrative trick from its McDowellian origins. The second complication is that Kelly's attempt to vindicate nonconceptual content proceeds by way of a criticism of Christopher Peacock's similarly motivated project. Since the perceived shortcoming of Peacock's account is key to understanding what Kelly hopes to wrest from the notion we will start with the former.

In "Nonconceptual content defended", Peacock suggests that when it comes to the perception of, say, a shape there are "three levels of description" (1998: 381) relevant to the disagreement between the conceptualist and the nonconceptualist:

1. The shape itself (the objective shape).
2. The shape perceived.
3. The demonstratively conceptualized shape.

For Peacock, demonstrating that levels 2 and 3 can come apart is sufficient for establishing the existence of nonconceptual content. As it stands, this would be consistent with the content in question being *relatively* nonconceptual, which, in the wake of the previous section, is of limited interest. Nevertheless, it is clear from subsequent work (Peacock 2001a, b) that what interests Peacock is *absolute* nonconceptual content, captured in the familiar thought that if non-linguistic animals have perceptual states with contents in common with ours then "some perceptual representational content is nonconceptual" (2001b: 614). In brief, then, Peacock's argument is that since a (*particular*) shape or other perceived property (level 2) can be picked out in various ways using different demonstrative expressions (level 3; "that diamond"; "that shape"; "that pointed figure"), demonstrative concepts "slice *too* finely to capture the ways of level" (level 2; Peacock 1998: 382).

To clarify the significance of this argument for our purposes it is best approached by foregrounding an assumption that Peacock makes respecting level 2; namely, that the content of experience (the particular this or that) is in some sense passively *given* to perceivers (including animals in some cases), wholly independently of their conceptual repertoires. Let us call this assumption the *assumption of givenness*. The argument then takes the following form: If the *assumption of givenness* is made, then in order to prevent levels 2 and 3 coming apart, introducing thereby the gap required to make sense of the notion of *non*conceptual content, the *conceptualist* must hold that level 2 bears the burden of all the articulations that are possible at level 3 ("that diamond"; "that shape"; "that pointed figure", etc.). And that, contends Peacock, is "quite implausible" (Peacock 1998: 382).

Presented this way, it is of course open to the anti-nonconceptualist to reject the *assumption of givenness*. One will then view the different contents of demonstrative expressions as precisely that. In other words, if one commences from the level of description 3 one will accept the distinctions made using the phrases "that diamond", "that shape", and so on, and let one's account of the purported content of experience 2 flow thence (or not at all). This becomes clearer once one considers the broader context of usage that level 3 enshrines, since it is evident that one would be intending to express different things with the phrases "that shape" and "that pointed figure". Indeed, if one insists on starting at the level of linguistic use, it becomes apparent just how metaphysically exacting Peacock's characterization of 1–3 as *levels of description* is.

All this is by the by, however, for it is evident that Peacock's rather attenuated view of the nonconceptual *given* is – like Hanna's – irrelevant to our epistemic concerns. It does however suggest that to motivate an account of the nonconceptual given that will sustain an alternative to our analysis of practical knowledge-how the gap between levels 2 and 3 needs to be opened up in the *opposite* direction and the *assumption of givenness* supported by considerations that justify the "thicker" account required. It is for this reason that Kelly, despite declaring himself "sympathetic to the project" on which Peacock is engaged (Kelly 2001a: 601), nevertheless offers various criticisms of his attempt to impugn McDowell's conceptualism before embarking on what he takes to be the real weakness of the use of demonstratives: that they are "too coarse-grained, not too fine-grained, to capture perceptual content" (*ibid.*: 608). Given the requirement for that "thicker" account, the considerations he raises are, of course, phenomenological.

Kelly's piece is rather convoluted. He *assumes*, for the purposes of argument, that one *might* be able to provide a more convincing case than Peacock that demonstrative concepts are too fine-grained, and then aims to show that the two possible responses that Peacock offers on behalf of the conceptualist are vulnerable, not to Peacock's rebuttals, but to his own. However, since there *is not* a more compelling opening argument on offer there's no obligation to respond to it in the manner outlined (on the conceptualist's behalf) by Peacock and as a consequence no reason to think that Kelly's rebuttals have any bearing on the matter at hand. As we will see, however, this is relevant to the case Kelly attempts to construct in favour of nonconceptual content.

With that in mind we can present Kelly's argument in the form of a challenge. The anti-nonconceptualist either:

A rejects the *assumption of givenness* by impugning "Peacock's intuition that the possession of fine-grained concepts doesn't change experience" (Kelly 2001a: 605); or

B accepts the *assumption of givenness* and aims to "explain perceptual content in terms of demonstrative concepts of the medium-grained"

141

("that shape"; "that colour") sort that everyone can be assumed to possess (*ibid.*).

With respect to A, Kelly assumes that the rejection of the *assumption of givenness* requires an argument (rather than a shrug) against Peacock's "passivist" intuition; with respect to B, we have the thought, paralleling Peacock's, that closing the gap between levels 2 and 3 puts pressure on the use of demonstratives to nominate the content of experience.

Kelly offers a view on how one might defend A, and then introduces a detail that Peacock has purportedly neglected in his own attempt to drive a wedge between levels 2 and 3; namely, that the perception of properties is sensitive to two distinct factors.

I The property perceived is context-dependent.
II The property perceived is object-dependent.

Factor I is said to count against B and factor II against the proffered defence of A (and thus, for Kelly, against A itself).

Turning first to factor II, Kelly argues that the anti-nonconceptualist can reject Peacock's *assumption of givenness* and defend the view that the possession of a concept conditions the contents of one's experience *only if* she has a specific account of colour perception. According to that account, when experiencing a particular shade of red, *what* S sees and what P *fails* to see results from S's noticing that the shade "looks like" (Kelly 2001a: 604) the objective colour sample red_{112} and not (say) red_{113}. But, continues Kelly, the property one attributes to an object – the fact that it is a certain shade of blue, say, or that it has a certain length – cannot be abstracted from the object that bears that property. Merleau-Ponty (1962: 313), for example, remarks that the blue of a carpet is essentially a *woolly* blue and not (say) a *metallic* blue; and Peacock (1989: 307) notes that a line and a bar on wallpaper may both appear and indeed be the same length but a percipient nevertheless judge that they might not be.[5] "The basic idea," then, is that the "dependency of the perceived property on the object is so complete" that it simply makes no sense to talk of "independently determinable propert(ies)" (Kelly 2001a: 607). That being the case, the anti-nonconceptualist defence of A does not work because there are no purportedly "objective" properties like red_{112} to serve in the explanation of *how* S's experience can be conceptually contentful.

Kelly does not indicate why, in the absence of a stronger preliminary argument, the anti-nonconceptualist is *required* to motivate an objection to the *assumption of givenness* or to give an account of colour perception. Equally, although he does not claim that this is the *only* account of colour perception available to the conceptualist, he offers no other. This omission seems particularly sinful when one considers the following line of argument:

(i) If one grants the legitimate use of demonstrative concepts and of conditions for their possession then one must hold that those conditions involve bringing instances of properties under concepts.
(ii) If there are no "independently determinable properties" then from (i) it follows that the properties, instances of which are to be brought under concepts, must be understood differently.

The relevance of this is that, in what is in effect a companion piece to the one under discussion, Kelly endorses the following: "in order to possess a demonstrative concept for x, a subject must be able consistently to re-identify a given object as falling under the concept if it does" (2001b: 403).

Notwithstanding the merits of this account,[6] it suggests that there is a less troublesome understanding of properties to be had. That being so, it seems unwarranted to encumber the anti-nonconceptualist with the invidious option presented above; not least because that model seems wrong, whatever one's account of the status of properties, for the very reasons discussed in connection with rule-following.

The sense that factor II carries little weight by itself is implied by Kelly when he notes that the attack on the idea of "independently determinable properties" is similar to that relating to factor I, which turns on the idea of colour constancy. Consider the inside wall of a library, judged to possess colour uniformity but "experienced" nevertheless as being lit differently at various points due, say, to the local preponderance of natural or of artificial light. We might call what this phenomenon draws our attention to the "sensory" (Peacock 1983) or "informational" (Merleau-Ponty 1962) content of experience, but the point is clear enough. If the (conceptual) content of our *judgement* is that the wall is uniformly white and yet our *experience* is of diversity then the content of the latter cannot exhaust that of the former: level 3 is not coextensive with level 2. Specifically, the thought is that medium-grained demonstrative concepts like "that colour" cannot determine the content of experience and close the gap because they cannot distinguish the way *that* colour "appears" differentially in the sun and the shade: there is a "sensory" or "informational" surplus, which outruns the content of the majority's demonstrative repertoire.

Two claims are being combined here. The assertion that medium-grained demonstrative concepts are insufficient to capture the phenomenological richness of experience piggy-backs on the following contention: "the complete and accurate account of my perceptual experience of the color of an object *must contain some reference* to the lighting context in which that color is perceived" (Kelly 2001a: 607, emphasis added).

Recall, however, that the only reason the anti-nonconceptualist is being restricted to a repertoire of medium-grained demonstrative concepts is in response to the contention that *finer*-grained varieties are disallowed because they involve an inadmissible rejection of the *assumption of givenness*. But since neither Kelly nor Peacock have any argument to that effect at their service nothing prevents the anti-nonconceptualist from availing herself of all the linguistic discriminations required to express the different things she wants to say. From *this* perspective talk of "containing some reference to the context" is irrelevant; but Kelly seems to be suggesting that the context is somehow *constitutive* of the experience in such a way that it must of necessity fall outside the experiencer's conceptual repertoire. Speaks concludes on this basis that Kelly must be arguing for the existence of *relative* non-conceptual content (Speaks 2005: 22; cf. n.37), but this is clearly wrong. As Kelly concludes, "perceptual content is non-conceptual—because it is situation dependent, and situations are not specifiable in conceptual terms" (Kelly 2001a: 608); which is to say that Kelly is drawing on the sort of ontological considerations familiar from our discussion of Heidegger in Chapter 1.

Kelly makes clear that this contextual factor is key to defending the account of nonconceptual content, and it is similarly evident that, notwithstanding the discussion of demonstratives, it has to do *all* the work here. We have already attempted to demonstrate how one can do justice to this sort of phenomenological consideration without invoking the need for transcendental phenomenology of the Heideggerian variety. However, Kelly's assumption is that one can manifest discriminatory *abilities* in perception that cannot be accounted for in demonstrative terms.

The immediate problem this confronts is that it appears to deny a condition of possibility of its formulation, maintaining that R can say of two colour samples *a* and *b* that they are experienced *as* being different without it being the case that in saying *that*$_a$ is different from *that*$_b$ R is manifesting possession of the demonstrative concepts at issue. The tactic, then, is to aim to show that there is a prima facie tension between the demand that a demonstrative concept be sufficiently *contextual* to characterize in its multiformity the content perceptual experience, and the requirement that it satisfy some possession condition requiring that one can "entertain" (Kelly 2001b: 417) it when not in the appropriate perceptual context. But there seems to be an obvious response here; namely, that Kelly has overlooked[7] the one feature of a situation that can square this apparent circle:

III The property perceived is *observer*-dependent.

It is the addition of the *person* to the situation that shows how the "radical" contextuality required to make good on the diversity in perception can be linked to the "context-independent" (*ibid.*: 416) possession of such demonstrative concepts. It is R's *ability* to discriminate between *a* and *b* that constitutes their possession of the requisite demonstrative concepts. Absent that ability, there *is* no concept possessed: R cannot mean *that*$_a$ shade by using the expression, although they can of course, like S, mean $that_{a\&b}$ shade (assuming a and b "look alike" to S[8]). Moreover, it is this ability that R possesses when they leave the context: an ability that *is*, and can only be explained in terms of, the possession of the relevant (demonstrative) concepts, where this is to be understood in terms of their knowledge-how.

One might counter that the ability in question makes *possible* the concepts possessed, but is somehow distinct. At this point we would leave behind any attempt to demonstrate *directly* that the limitations of demonstrative concepts to do justice to the content of experience necessitates the introduction of nonconceptual content. But it would see us back on more familiar territory, since the foregrounding of abilities in this way is correlative with the promotion of the significance of knowledge-*how* over knowledge-*that*. That this is where Kelly ought to have been focusing his attention is clear from his conclusion that a successfully prosecuted case against the explanatory completeness of demonstrative concepts requires an account of how nonconceptually contentful experience that can stand in non-"justificatory or reason-giving relations to" thought (Kelly 2001b: 419). And as he goes on to lament, "I have no idea what such a nonjustificatory relation could be" (*ibid.*). Taken at face value, such humility might engender a degree of scepticism concerning the arguments leading to the need for such "content", but it is not entirely ingenuous. Kelly *does* have something to say in this general area, which comes more clearly into focus when the flirtation with post-Evansian thought is set aside and his phenomenological orientation is emphasized. His primary concern is then revealed as the understanding that we manifest in our skilful dealings with objects, which he maintains is of "a kind that we cannot reflectively access as such" (Kelly 2002: 389). This is the sort of understanding that Merleau-Ponty (1962) calls "motor intentional".

Motor-intentional understanding relates to the way in which one deals with objects in a skilful, everyday way. Although many skills are common they are not made manifest in the same way; and although all are grounded in shared human capacities, the more complex the skill the more apparent this difference is. Since this essentially *bodily* understanding reflects and instantiates divergent experiences and training regimes it captures the *personal* aspect registered in factor III. But there is another reason why this "personal" aspect needs to figure in the account. In his contribution to a Dreyfus festschrift, Kelly remarks of phenomenology: "Its goal is completely and accurately to describe the phenomena of human experience without the interference of metaphysical presuppositions inherited from psychological, scientific, historical, sociological, or other theoretical frameworks" (Kelly 2000: 162). Needless to say, there is a useful metaphilosophical get-out here: since Heidegger, following Kant, contends that the inquirer is constitutively complicit in those metaphysical wrongdoings, the correct description might often *appear* radically revisionary (as opposed to "descriptive"[9]). But even

145

the existentially neutered version of phenomenology retailed by Dreyfus, Kelly and others requires a certain methodological commitment to the effect that it is an "essentially descriptive" (*ibid.*) endeavour that cannot afford to lose touch with "human experience" altogether lest it risk degenerating into a dogmatic search for "independently identifiable properties".

The risk alluded to here is readily discerned in the work of those neuroscientists who have been impressed by the possibility of using concepts deriving from Merleau-Ponty and Heidegger to avoid the extremes of mentalism and behaviourism, the one assimilating the intentional content of an action to the propositionally structured states that cause it and the other to the bodily movements that would satisfy it. In a widely cited paper, Rizzolatti and Sinigaglia (2007) for example claim that our understanding of the intentions of others – our "motor knowledge" (*ibid.*: 205 and *passim*) of their motor intentionality – is based on the existence of visuomotor neurons that fire during both action and the observation of action.[10] S "understands" – which is to say, possesses non-propositional "motor knowledge" *of* – R's "grasping-for-drinking" as opposed to "grasping-for-clearing away" because the "frontal node of the human mirror neural system … codes" for these differences in R's guiding "motor intention" (*ibid.*: 208).

Rizzolatti and Sinigaglia are not interested in satisfying the formal requirements of a phenomenological *description*. But their account is intended to explain how a particular phenomenon – unreflective understanding of another's intentions – is *possible*. However, any sense that this is an account of a *person's* understanding turns on the slippery assimilation of a neuronal structure to a form of *knowledge* through the notion that it encodes the contextually sensitive possibilities. The fact that different regions of the cortical motor system "light up" in response to different sorts of actions does not mean that pattern μ is "coding" for "grasping-for-drinking" as opposed to "grasping-for-clearing away". The idea that the "properties of the motor system and the mirror neuron mechanism" (*ibid.*: 209) are sufficiently fine-grained to make all the distinctions one would wish to is not only deeply implausible, it presupposes the discredited idea that our *understanding* of such motor-intentional contents is explicable in terms of "independently identifiable properties".

Although it is evidently all too easy to lose sight of the *personal* when one trades in talk of neurons, one would not expect such a degree of unsophistication from Kelly. He does, however, maintain that "certain neural network models of action … are much better … than standard cognitive science … at accounting for … the phenomenological features of certain skillful bodily actions" (Kelly 2000: 161–2). We have no interest in defending "standard cognitive science" of course; but Kelly is disposed to associate the "intellectualism" or "cognitivism" of those early researchers with the conceptualism of McDowell,[11] so his account of why the phenomenology eludes the intellectualist is relevant. It also offers us the opportunity to say a little more about the all-too-important concept of motor intentionality.

According to Merleau-Ponty (1962), to avoid the allure of either an intellectualist or an empiricist *account* of skilful coping the concepts required to undertake a phenomenological description of have to be *created*. Key to this is the recognition

> of something between movement as a third person process and thought as a representation of movement – something which is an anticipation of, or arrival at, the objective and is ensured by the body itself as a motor power, a "motor project" (*Bewegungsent-wurf*), a "motor intentionality". (*Ibid.*: 126–7)

As Kelly observes, there is a clear distinction to be made between reflex responses and intentional acts like grasping. While the first sort of motion is *undergone*, the latter has *satisfaction* conditions (whether or not one is conscious of them at the time). From the phenomenological perspective, then, the empiricist *reduction* of action to mere behaviour makes no sense. The case against the intellectualist, however, is a little more difficult to make, and Kelly enlists the support of the oft-invoked case of Schneider.

As reported by Merleau-Ponty, the severe brain damage he suffered in the First World War left Schneider "unable to perform 'abstract' movements ... not relevant to any actual situation ... with his eyes shut", although able to perform the situation-specific tasks that his job as a wallet maker comprised and "in living his life ... with extraordinary speed and precision" (Merleau-Ponty 1962: 118). Merleau-Ponty goes on to focus this pathology on Schneider's (apparent) inability to point to a particular part of his body when asked to, despite being able to grasp the things needed when absorbed in activity. The conclusion is that "'grasping' ... is different from 'pointing'" (*ibid.*: 119).

Kelly is clear about the intuitive appeal of cases like Schneider's: "One good way to determine the phenomenological characteristics of a behaviour is to consider the behavioural pathologies that can occur" (Kelly 2000: 168). There are good reasons for being suspicious of this. One might have thought that if phenomenological inquiry is to turn on the possibility of descriptions purged of metaphysical prejudice then these sorts of pathologies should be avoided like the plague, not least because one must rely for the most part on accounts of behaviour that are (1) other people's and (2) cannot be checked against whatever constitutes the norm. So, for example, we have no account of whether or not Schneider's *absorbed* behaviour included acts one might readily characterize as *pointings*. This is significant because it is central to Kelly's anti-intellectualist case that grasping be seen not just as a "distinct and independently experiencable" (*ibid.*: 171) but as a more *fundamental* mode of understanding or "knowledge of where something is" (Merleau-Ponty

1962: 103–4) than that characterized by pointing.[12] It is on this basis that he associates the motor-intentional understanding that Merleau-Ponty identifies with grasping with what Goodale and Milner (1992, 1995) interpret as the function of the dorsal pathway or stream for visual "information"; namely, to process "how" as opposed to "what" information. For Kelly, this differential "encoding" of visual information explains "at the neural level" (Kelly 2000: 172) Merleau-Ponty's phenomenological distinction.

A recent literature survey concludes that the "perception-action dissociation" that is supposed to "explain" the phenomenology in the above case "is difficult if not impossible to test" and posits the explanatory superiority of "one single processing stream" (Cardoso-Leite & Gorea 2010: 89). But this merely draws attention to the problematic nature of the relationship between phenomenological data and theory. The key point is that "appearances" *must* come first if "descriptive phenemenology" is to have *any* function at all, let alone one fulfilling the grandiose claim that it provide the "data" that the brain sciences subsequently "model" (Kelly 2000: 165). As we have seen, the case made for the phenomenological distinction rests on Kelly's interpretation of Merleau-Ponty's account of Goldstein's report of what *he* took to be descriptively relevant about the behaviour of a severely brain-damaged patient! And while there are clear differences between *normal* cases of pointing and grasping, that phenomenological distinction does little to sustain the claim that these involve fundamentally different sorts of understanding.

The problem naturalistically orientated phenomenologists confront is revealed by that term "fundamental". Merleau-Ponty follows the Heideggerian line in maintaining that the motor intentionality/knowledge associated with grasping (FI) is fundamental in the sense of being the *condition of possibility* of the reflective intentionality associated with pointing (RI). But as Kelly notes, the evidence suggested by patients who appear to be able to point but not grasp implies that optic ataxics "are not actually pointing at objects when they appear to be" (Kelly 2000: 367, n.33), hence the rival assumption that "fundamental" must connote some essential neurological feature. But characterizing complex cases of motor dysmetria in such crude terms as non-grasping-but-pointing seems to belie the phenomenology of both normal and pathological cases. Indeed, the sense that they are different seems to be driven by the prior conviction that since pointing often takes place in response to a request and is thus associated with deliberation, it must in some way be analogous to the mental "pointing" to some to inner representation of the disembodied Cartesian cogito. Such an interpretation seems constrained by the phenomenologist's own "presuppositions" concerning the "metaphysics" of intellectualism rather than anything "given" (*ibid.*: 165) in experience. From the standpoint of phenomenology, then, invoking the differential "informational encoding" of the dorsal and ventral pathways – even *if* it were neurologically sound – would at best gesture towards sub-personal and thus phenomenologically irrelevant processes. These would no more be cases of "knowing" or "understanding" than those outlined by the Parmigiani.

We noted above that Merleau-Ponty introduces the term "motor intentionality" as an alternative to the then prevalent empiricist and intellectualist paradigms, the implication being that the collective *blindness* of these to the relevant phenomena derives from a privileging of the behavioural and the intellectual respectively. In other words, motor intentionality becomes a third, mediating and yet fundamental term precisely because phenomenology is the mediating methodology. What is evident from this is that the purposes served by the concept of motor intentionality are determined in large part by what phenomenology opposes; and in this respect Kelly and Dreyfus[13] share Merleau-Ponty's orientation. Or, rather, their concern to make phenomenology relevant to "brain science" means they are apt to view intellectualism as the greater opponent, and construe motor intentionality in a way that pushes it closer to the (sub-personal) fundamental-as-biological than the (transcendental) fundamental-as-ontological. We will return to this theme in the final section of this chapter, but it is clear at this point that, notwithstanding the foregoing criticisms, there is one, very clear price to be paid for it. To see this, recall that, following Merleau-Ponty, the principle phenomenological consideration Kelly raises against the empiricist account of skilful coping is its failure to account for the difference between reflex movement and action; specifically, the fact that while the "success or failure of the reflex act" turns on "the relevant muscular contractions" (Kelly 2000: 167), the latter has a normative directedness. However, this way of drawing the distinction fails to bring out fully the fact that in reflex movements we experience our movements as falling outside the domain of our *freedom* – that is why we characterize them as nonnormative.

By emphasizing the unreflective, coping skills that we putatively share with other animals, Kelly *et al.* make it difficult to explain where human freedom comes onto the scene. The simplistic model we get from the facile distinction between grasping and pointing is that while the former corresponds to absorbed, unreflective coping the latter sees the introduction of the sort of deliberative distance one associates with *freedom*. It would be odd to think that freedom emerges at some "higher" level, leaving the nonconceptual or pre-predicative or motor-intentional understanding untouched. And yet if the former is something we *share* with animals there must be a way of characterizing it that makes evident its essential *un*freedom, otherwise we would be left with the mere assertion that some animals can do some of the things we can do if the relevant behaviour is decontextualized sufficiently. It would be foolhardy to deny that a chimpanzee can be taught to ride a bicycle, for example, or to drink a glass of beer. But it would be equally rash as things stand to characterize such behaviour in terms appropriate for describing the complex ways in which they figure in the freely undertaken action of *persons*. In this regard, the possibility of accounting for the emergence of freedom or agency from unreflective coping is correlative with showing how conceptual content can issue from nonconceptual content; and, indeed, with how knowledge how can be characterized as *knowledge*, other than by the sort of analogy we employ when one says that one's dog knows where its bone is buried.

The *desire* to account for freedom within the constraints of the kind of naturalism pressed upon us by an awareness of our facticity is one of the motivating factors behind a conceptualism like McDowell's. Since we are concerned not with the content of experience but with the status of tacit knowing, our interest has been merely to demonstrate that the positing of nonconceptual content is either irrelevant to cognition or raises more problems than it purports to solve. Correspondingly, we showed that the variant on McDowell's "demonstrative trick" we deploy as part of our account of know-how helps to block the move made against the use of demonstratives in the attempt to argue for nonconceptual content *as long as that use is understood as articulating the know-how* of the percipient. Being rather more anti-nonconceptualist than conceptualist, then, we feel no need to defend McDowell's empiricist sympathies. However, that dialectical positioning does involve a particular role for second nature and for the way in which McDowell relates it to the similarly Aristotelian concept of *phronesis* or practical wisdom. We can help clarify it by examining a recent exchange between McDowell and Dreyfus. In this, the latter aims to repeat Kelly's strategy of arguing against McDowell's intellectualism in order to motivate the requirement for a notion of nonconceptual content. Dreyfus is interested in such content only in so far as it characterizes the sort of coping skills that for him we share with other animals and which he associates with *phronesis*. Since coping skills are for us to be explicated in terms of tacit knowing (as practical knowledge-how) the attack on McDowell is directly relevant both to our overall position and to the use we wish to make of practical wisdom.

DREYFUS AND MCDOWELL

Dreyfus first came to prominence for applying phenomenology to a debate in artificial intelligence concerning the nature of the so-called "frame problem". Basically, the conceit of traditional AI was that a machine, programmed with a representation of the world in the form of fact-stating sentences, would be able to match human intelligence. As such, the frame problem can be seen under two aspects. Daniel Dennett (1984) gives a good example of the first. Imagine programming a robot so that it has to fetch its replacement battery from a room before a bomb goes off, and it pulls out the wagon with both the bomb and the battery on it! The simple point is that the robot had not deduced one of the consequences of its action. It is easy to imagine how to correct this particular shortcoming. But now imagine, for example, that the bomb is connected by string or balloon to the battery, or triggered by movement of the wagon or by the increase in the ambient temperature of the room or by detected motion of the air. Under its other aspect, the frame problem relates to how many of a machine's states it needs to update once it has carried out an action in order that its "representation of the world" continues to be sufficiently accurate to ensure future success. Is the shape of the world affected by the fetching of a battery? Are the laws of physics? Is the ambient temperature? This is sometimes referred to as "Hamlet's problem": when to stop trying to deduce the consequences of an action and actually act.

In the case of a simple machine, the represented "world" will perhaps consist of only a few thousand facts and that may not cause operational problems. But for a machine to be as intelligent in principle as we are the world as "represented" would comprise an enormous number of propositions, and problem of calculating consequences insurmountable. What the frame problem highlights, then, is the importance of *relevance*. Any rule we programmed into the machine to determine the relevant consequences of its actions would itself only have significance within a *context*, and it would require another rule to specify that context. We have, in other words, a familiar regress.

Historically, what Dreyfus takes from this is twofold. Firstly, that the "intellectualist" or "conceptualist" model of AI is based on a pervasively Cartesian (or Cartesian–Platonic) view of the mind, which regards it as essentially context*less*/disembodied. Trivially, the "world" that the robot consults is a purely intellectual representation of the world, an analogue of Descartes' representational mind whereby the contents of thoughts are fixed independently of how things go with the external world. The second point is that existential phenomenology of Heidegger and Merleau-Ponty serves as a corrective to this view of the mind and (by implication) phenomenological data should thus provide the lead in formulating a non-"intellectualist" AI. The argument here is simple: if the disembodied conception of intelligence gives rise to the frame problem by failing to show how systems select for relevance and, phenomenologically, we humans do *not* experience the relevance problem, then the world is *not* presented to us in the form of an "internal" set of sentence-like representations of contextless facts that we are free to reflect on (a Hamlet sort of freedom). Rather, we experience the world as something that we are always-already at home in, coping skilfully with Frisbees, doors and one another without (much) reflection.

On Dreyfus's account, humans have a dual structure: on the one hand "a ground-floor level of preconceptual, preobjective/presubjective, prelinguistic

151

coping" (2007a: 364) that is shared by "animals, prelinguistic infants, and everyday experts" (2005: 57); on the other hand, an ability to engage in abstract rational thought. Since the "background" proper (BB) relates *Dasein's* self-understanding (Chapters 1 and 4), we have a shift in metaphors towards the architectural. Nevertheless, detached rational reflection (RI) is only possible because it is held in place (as it were) by the preconceptual grounding in coping (FI). What we have here is the familiar structure of regress (applied to the intellectualist conception) followed by a positive recommendation founded on getting "clear concerning the phenomena that need to be explained" (Dreyfus 2005: 50). Or, to be more precise, "returning to" the phenomena is meant to show us *why* the regress (the relevance problem) does not arise for us.

As we saw with Searle (who takes his account of intentionality to be the only alternative to that impugned by the rule-regress), to work together in this way the phenomenological and intellectualist possibilities have to be exhaustive. To find out whether or not the "phenomena" do support the phenomenology, let's look at the considerations Dreyfus raises in opposition to McDowell, which take two basic forms:

I The relation between rule-following and expertise;
II Reflective thinking as the enemy of skilful doing.

Form I recalls the line taken against AI above; form II is familiar from our discussion of Polanyi in Chapter 1 (§§"The tacit dimension" and "Tacit knowing so far"). Both aim to use the "phenomena" themselves to motivate the need for some account of nonconceptual content.

Turning to form I, Dreyfus begins by imagining the transition from journeyman to expert, from mere competence to skilful accomplishment. The details are not particularly important; what matters is the claim that the cognitivist is wrong in assuming that any rules that might be formulated either for the purposes of instruction or by the neophyte herself are in some sense "internalized" in order to be subsequently applied in practice. We have encountered many formal arguments to that effect, but the line Dreyfus takes here is different: an "emotional involvement," he says, is necessary to effect the move from "detached, analytic rule-following" to an "engaged, holistic mode of experience" (2005: 52). Although many accomplishments require a stage at which "one needs reasons to guide action," the "phenomenology suggests" that the expert arrives at a "entirely different" state wherein "a way of coping" with exigencies has been arrived at "in which reasons play no role" (*ibid.*).

By way of further (presumably *non*phenomenological) evidence for this distinction, Dreyfus cites brain-imaging research that purports to show that the brains of grandmasters and amateurs exhibit different distributions of focal activity. As presented, this purports to show that since "rules needn't play any role in *producing* skilled behaviour" (*ibid.*: 54), reason, in the guise of the mastery of concepts, is entirely absent. What the chess master "sees" when she looks at the pieces on a board; what the skilful bowler of googlies does when (among other things) he twists his wrist anticlockwise to get the break from off to leg (and the accomplished batter "sees" when he does); all these have "a kind of *intentional* content; it just isn't *conceptual* content" (*ibid.*: 55).

We are not so much interested in defending the integrity of conceptual content but in impugning the notion that nonconceptual content bears on our understanding of the mastery of skills. From *that* perspective it is reasonable to inquire what exactly is the *content* of (nonconceptual) content. In light of the discussion of the previous section, the answer is perhaps unsurprising: it rests, suggests Dreyfus, on the extent to which we can revive the notion of *givenness* while avoiding both traditional attacks on empiricism *and* the scoundrel's last refuge, psychological nominalism: "a Given that is *nonconceptual* but not *bare*" (Dreyfus 2005: 55). To this end, Dreyfus deploys a term of art derived ultimately from Merleau-Ponty and introduced by Gibson (1977, 1979): *affordances*. Affordances are highly situational features of objects and environments that present, at the level of everyday doing, opportunities for action. A hole in the wall affords the possibility of escape for the incarcerated; the acorn on the floor the promise of a stored meal for a scavenging squirrel. *Qua* the contents of experiences, affordances are unthinkables; but it is the expanded range of affordances in a situation that, for Dreyfus, constitutes the skilful coping of the expert, or *phronimos*. It is not a case of the Inuit, as it were, having many different names for snow; rather, it is the way some creatures "see" more in an environment than others because it *affords* them more opportunities for absorbed activity. "In their direct dealing with affordances," then, "adults, infants, and animals respond alike" (Dreyfus 2005: 55).

This talk of affordances is one way that (what we called) Peacock's *assumption of givenness* might be made more plausible. Likewise, one can detect some similarity with the understanding Polanyi associates with tacit knowing (nor is it surprising given their shared origins in gestalt psychology); especially if one thinks that the patterns of affordances to which creatures respond involve features that, "although available to the perceptual system, needn't be available to the mind" (*ibid.*: 54). Indeed, when Dreyfus invokes talk of the skilful mastery in terms of "the brain" detecting "high order invariants in the optic array" (*ibid.*: 58) Polanyi's suggestion that the tacit knower grasps the pattern of firing neurons does not sound quite so fanciful.

According to the first "phenomenological" objection (I), then, the fact that expert responses to situations do not involve the awareness of rule-following motivates (a) the conclusion that reasoning plays no role, and (b) the consequent need to invoke nonconceptual content *qua* affordances. As Dreyfus acknowledges, however, McDowell does not think that skilled behaviour is caused by unconscious rules. It is granted that his position is "much more subtle and plausible, namely that, thanks to socialization, experts conform to reasons that can be retroactively reconstructed" (Dreyfus 2005: 54).

A great deal here turns on what precisely Dreyfus understands by "conforming to reasons". If it means something other than "applying rules" (something Searlean, perhaps) then one might have expected that a different type of phenomenon would be invoked to embarrass McDowell. However, although the excursus on affordances is intended to show that we can make sense of the responsive actions of the skilled coper without seeing them as reasonable, Dreyfus offers no grounds for thinking that responsiveness to reasons can mean *anything other than following a rule*. Indeed, the provisional conclusion confirms that view "if we understand concepts as context-free principles or rules that could be used to guide actions ... a phenomenology of expert coping shows concepts to be absent" (*ibid*.: 58).

The all-too familiar pattern here is of nonconceptual content being invoked to block the rule-regress, where the latter is driven by a specific understanding of what the intellectualist (purportedly) takes conceptual mastery (or for us, knowledge) to consist in (something akin to PC). Of course, as McDowell might say, that characterization of conceptual mastery "misses his thinking" entirely.

Before turning to Dreyfus's second phenomenological consideration (II), it is worth dwelling a little longer on the first (I). The claim is that when one moves from mere competence to skilful mastery one shifts from a domain in which concepts are applied to an "entirely different" state in which they are not. First off, it seems unwarranted to motivate this distinction on the basis of phenomenological considerations (a similar point was made against Stanley and Williamson's use of Ginet in Chapter 2). Granted, one might not be *aware* that one is applying a rule when one is bowling a googly, but it requires a very specific understanding of what it would be *like* to apply a rule for this to prove decisive.[14] One is unaware of all sorts of things that are, cognitively speaking, closed to us, and given that affordance-detection can purportedly take place at the neuronal level it would be churlish to contend that it is the "phenomena" that reveal the truth here. Likewise it seems unmotivated to assert that whatever achievement-related abilities the journeyman manifests suddenly sublimate without trace when, at some point, the transcendent state of expertise is achieved! Even Searle allows for a *trace*. And yet how else are we to account for the claim of radical "difference"? Notwithstanding the empirical (that is to say, non-phenomenological) evidence relating to brain-activity, presumably the organism is not so contrived that there are two routes to performance that are only coincidentally related, that of the competent exhibiting reason and that of the skilled no reason at all. Is it flattering to liken the move of the grandmaster to a cat's pounce while his less able opponent is merely being *reasonable*?

Restricting reasoning to the application of general reasons/rules may well be required if one is predisposed to leave the nonrational account of skilful coping as the only option. But whether one characterizes it in terms of the phenomenology, logic or "mere sanity" the results of such a restriction makes the defence of conceptualism (if one were so inclined) *easier* not harder. The situation is similar with respect to affordances. The intention is to introduce a basis for the weakened, nonconceptual normativity of the "ground-floor level"/background by giving it some worldly friction without nominating things that are nameable. To preserve the non-rational and therefore potentially pan-species status of the ground-floor level of coping, however, the patterns that affordances make have to be *real* (cf. Dennett 1991). We must possess criteria of individuation independent of the reidentifying powers of language. However, we can make the fine discriminations we do concerning the doings of animals – fill out the details of the affordances their environment presents them with – only through the use of language. Note that one does not need to go the whole conceptualist hog here, and claim the following:

> our relation to the world, including our perceptual relation to it, is pervasively shaped by our conceptual mindedness ... affordances are no longer merely input to a human animal's natural motivational tendencies; now they are data for her (practical and theoretical rationality).   (McDowell 2007a: 346, 344)

Rather, one can simply insist that the phenomenological appeal deriving from affordance talk is parasitic on the linguistic resources (context-sensitive demonstratives) brought to bear in showing how rich in detail and complexity actual situations are compared with those some philosophers deal in. Indeed, it is the foundation of phenomenology in the knowledge-how that constitutes our linguistic practices that compels Dreyfus – as, indeed, it did Kelly – to shift the way an affordance "shows itself from itself" from the domain of authentic *Dasein* (person talk) and into the arms of the brain imager.

Returning to Dreyfus's critique of McDowell, the inapplicability of "concepts as context-free principles or rules" (PC) is entirely irrelevant. The exercise of reason is essentially situational. The difference between the merely competent and the highly skilful *phronimos* marks the same sort of difference as that between the ethically tolerable and the truly virtuous. In both cases an expert's understanding of what to do in specific situations – their know-how – are manifest in the responses that for them are second nature. Indeed, it is the very situatedness of reason that forms the response to the problem we raised in connection with Brandom and Searle. While for them making something explicit means codifying the deontic commitments, for McDowell the norms are there *in* the practices. There is nothing to unpack. To say that the norms are there *in* the practices is to say that there's nothing *hidden* from view. In the epistemological terms we favour, the possession of (tacit) knowing does not turn on "inner" process, nor does it require adverting to some "background" or "ground-level" explanatory resource. Or to put it another way, the peculiar *mindedness* of (tacit) knowers is part of the phenomenology of embodied cognition.

On our account, the mindedness of persons is inseparable from the account given of tacit understanding or knowledge-how and hence with skilful coping. For Dreyfus, however, the latter equates with an unreflective responsiveness to affordances. This brings us to the second phenomenological consideration (II) raised against McDowell. Dreyfus's contention is that in characterizing skilful coping as *minded* in a way that *ipso facto* eliminates the "minds" of non-linguistic animals, McDowell is being "untrue to the phenomenon". Being – phenomenologically speaking – "the enemy of embodied coping" (McDowell 2007a: 353), mindedness is consequently the theoretical obstacle to the recognition of the need to posit nonconceptual content in order to account for the "ground-floor level" coping skills we share with animals. The principal example Dreyfus gives in support of the "phenomenology" is, needless to say, of a behavioural pathology; namely, that of Chuck Knoblauch, a baseman for the New York Yankees who developed what's sometimes called "Steve Blass disease" or "Steve Sax syndrome", or, to illustrate more fully its diagnostic bona fides, "the yips". This is how Dreyfus describes the situation:

> Knoblauch was so successful he was voted best infielder of the year, but one day, rather than simply fielding a hit and throwing the ball to first base, it seems he stepped back and took up a "free, distanced orientation" towards the ball and how he was throwing it – to the mechanics of it, as he put it. After that, he couldn't recover his former absorption.   (Dreyfus 2007a: 354)

Now, the aforementioned talk of being "untrue to the phenomenon" is one of those irritating methodological tics inherited from the phenomenological tradition. Dreyfus (*ibid.*: 359) quotes Merleau-Ponty to the effect that "nothing is more difficult than to know precisely *what we see*. There is ... a dialectic whereby perception hides itself from itself". He also notes, in a Heideggerian tone, that the nature of the transformation from nonconceptual coping to reflective thought "covers up the nonconceptual perception and coping that made our openness to the world possible in the first place" (Dreyfus 2005: 61).

The imputation is clear. McDowell has fallen victim to this self-concealing/ revealing nature of the transformation of preconceptual to conceptual that is the hallmark of the human way of being. Like his conceptualist forebears, he regards reason as the measure of all things, whereas in fact reason comes late onto the scene, and messes things up when it does so. To put the accusation at its crudest, McDowell is a sort of philosophical Knoblauch, unable to immerse himself in the phenomena, and thereby unable to throw straight and true: he is unable to see the impotence of rule-seeking rationality.

Dreyfus gives no source for his description of the all-important "phenomenology" other than the above allusion to Knoblauch's report and the fact that he has been *told* that "in some replays of … easy throws one could actually see Knoblauch looking with puzzlement at his hand trying to figure out the mechanics of throwing the ball" (Dreyfus 2007a: 354). Nevertheless, the conclusion drawn is that "in this case we can see precisely that the enemy of expertise is thought" (*ibid.*). According to Dreyfus's reading of the phenomenology, then, when reflection comes on to the scene a performance stops being a matter of absorbed, skilful coping (shared with animals and infants) and becomes at the very best competent. Since whatever skilful coping *is* is changed when it becomes an object of reflective thought, Dreyfus concludes it cannot be conceptual: "expert coping … [is] direct and unreflective, which I take to be the same as being nonconceptual and nonminded" (Dreyfus 2007a: 355).

The paucity of Dreyfus's description might not matter if it were not for the accusation that McDowell is being "untrue to the phenomenon".[15] First, it is odd to think that in such cases one must as it were "inspect" the phenomenon while undergoing it if one is to maintain veracity. This is not a problem in the case of mere competence of course, since that *is* accompanied by reason. But if reflection destroys the skilful coping of the expert then reflection destroys the very phenomenon that one is aiming to describe in aiming at a phenomenology of expertise! Presumably memory does not help here, since memory, as a process of re-presentation, seems to necessitate reflection. Can we invoke the phenomenology of observation? Well, the expertise of the observer is not the same as the doer, but that does not rule out that seeing an action *as* expert requires expertise of its own. Indeed, it is central to the case that we have been making that this sort of "seeing" is, like that of the chick-sexer, an example of tacit knowing. But reflecting on *that* expertise does not cause one's experience of the active sort of expertise to sublimate. Of course, one might counter that this line of objection is disingenuous, that we draw on other resources when being "true" to the phenomenon. And of course, this must be correct; although since it is not clear what it would mean to be "true" to some nonconceptual "given", it is not evident how one would know that one's description satisfied a criterion of truth.

Although Dreyfus does not make the point directly, what he must describe is the experience of *disruption*, the moment of transition from absorbed coping to reflective evaluation. Such moments must be, to mis-quote Leibniz, pregnant with both the past and the present. Returning to the quotation above, *that* point seems to be where one "steps back and takes up a 'free, distanced orientation'" towards the object one has hitherto being coping expertly with. Dreyfus's inclusion of this phrase is rather telling, since it is one McDowell takes from Gadamer (1992: 445) to illustrate the thought that "man's relation to the world is absolutely and fundamentally verbal in nature" (*ibid.*: 475–6): how our possession of a *language* transforms what would otherwise be the *environment* of an animal into a *world* (cf. McDowell 2007a: 346).[16] However, Dreyfus insists on interpreting this, not as some hermeneutic mantra but as a specification of the *moment* at which we step back and bring to bear on the (nonconceptual) "content" of absorbed coping the linguistic resources of conceptual thought.

This interpretative obtuseness would be of less consequence did it not reveal Dreyfus's views relating to human freedom. Dreyfus grants that even when absorbed in our activities we must have the ever-present *capacity* to step back and evaluate them (2007a: 354). Now, *if* it were the case that these absorbed activities *were not* fundamentally changed by the disruption brought about by reflection, then it would be hard to make the case that the ability (*not* shared with animals) to disengage from absorbed doing was not always-already bound up with such doing. In other words, since the freedom to reflect is associated with the bringing to bear of concepts, the *lack* of a caesura between expert coping and mere competence/reflective appraisal would imply that the ever-present possibility of freedom to disengage from one's activities indicated that such activities were *themselves* exercises of conceptual capacities (and therefore *not* part of a "ground-floor level" shared with animals). The desideratum for the nonconceptualist, then, is to elucidate the claim that a *human* capacity to act freely does not vitiate the status of the coping skills putatively shared with nonhumans. And that in turn relates to the requirement to demonstrate *how* nonconceptual content becomes conceptualized.

Dreyfus's contention is that the freedom to "step back" that characterizes the moment of disruption "presupposes a truly pervasive human freedom". He continues: "Unlike mere animals, we have a freedom not to exercise our freedom to step back but rather to let ourselves be involved" (2007a: 355). This clearly has no basis in the phenomenology of coping. It would be odd indeed to think that in such circumstances one is "aware" that one is freely *not* exercising one's freedom to step back: that skilful coping is pervaded with (or haunted by) the awareness that one is (as it were) *choosing* not to choose. On the one hand, that sounds like the sort of reflective awareness that destroys the phenomenon one is describing; on the other, it invites a variation on the existentialist maxim to the effect that in choosing not to choose one is still making a choice. More importantly, since Dreyfus invokes with approval Heidegger's notion that "our free experience of the world is different from an animal's unfree experience of an environment" (*ibid.*) it not only fails to show how such a capacity can be conceptually *separated* from the unminded doings of animals, it seems to assert their essential co-dependence. Unlike us, then, animals "can never step back" (*ibid.*). But that seems to imply that the *possibility* of freely stepping back is always present because the activities in which we are engaged in skilful coping are exercises of conceptual capacities and linked thereby to *reflection* on such capacities.

Although, paradoxically, this makes Dreyfus appear committed to a form of conceptualism, that is not the *real* point here. Before addressing that, note first that since one does not "experience" the disruption of absorbed coping as one wherein one chooses to trade in a more fundamental form of freedom for a lesser (because reflective, linguistically constituted) one Dreyfus's account fails to be "true to the phenomenology". But it should be recalled that it is *Dreyfus* who interprets the Gadamerian point about linguistic creatures in this phenomenological/occasionalist manner when in point of fact the claim is that the "free, distanced orientation" that language brings characterizes the standpoint of the agent presented with the world in which they *act*. For McDowell, this means that phenomenology has no methodological priority; rather, it operates within a framework constrained transcendentally by the need to account for the objectivity of thinking and doing – for the possession of a world. Since we do not share McDowell's concern to establish the objectivity of our thinking, the Gadamerian point restates in another idiom the point made above: that the solicitations and affordances that might be thought to give content to the "ground-floor level" of pre-conceptual coping can escape the reach of language and thus of tacit knowing only on the assumption that they somehow nominate the sort of "independently determinable properties" that phenomenologists should disdain.

We come, then, to the real moral of that imputation of "conceptualism", which has two aspects. First, the point is not that Dreyfus is unwittingly committed to some Cartesian (ego) or Kantian ("I think must accompany ...") account. Rather, it is that he is obliged to make sense of what skilful doing must be like *on the assumption* that such an account of explicit, propositional, theoretical knowing is correct. In other words, the requirement *for* and character *of* the "ground-floor level"/background is determined jointly by a specific conception of the "upper level" and the assumption that the intellectualist is required to explain *all* phenomena in its terms. This is why we get such a contrived account of freedom. *Authentic, persistent* freedom has to be defined in terms of the *absence* of reflective freedom; *real* freedom ends at the point of disruption, when the ever-threatening possibility of reflective freedom is actualized. The "ground-floor level"/background is defined as the (free) willed absence of reflective freedom: it is as if the phenomenologist, its spiritual denizen, were herself haunted by it.

159

Although he does not put the point in quite this way, one finds a similar conclusion in Joseph Rouse's (2000) criticisms of Dreyfus's project. In the areas of social norms, theoretical understanding, and (explicit) linguistic representation it is Dreyfus's anachronistic account of the "intellectualist" alternative that determines both the requirement for a Background and the character of what is to be found in it. But there is of course no obligation to conceive of the ("intellectualist") upper level in this way, and consequently to need to characterize a "ground-floor level" in the guise of an alter ego. Indeed, there is no obligation to characterize the upper level so that one *needs* a background (or vice versa) in order to respond to the rule-regress that such a characterization seems to invite. In this sense our criticism parallels that levelled against Searle in Chapter 4.

Returning to McDowell, the self-awareness that underpins the moment of disruptive reflection is not due to a free non-"I think", itself defined in some complex relation (of "determinate negation"?) to a reflectively free "I think" whose "I" "it" (*Dasein*, possibly) rejects. Rather, it is the practical self-awareness of an "I do", which captures the "essentially first-person character of the realization of practical rational capacities". If we acknowledge this much, we can see that a descriptively rich account of the phenomenology of everyday/skilful coping simply makes no requirements on us to eliminate the role of concepts if among them are practical concepts realized in acting. Consequently, nothing stops the anti-nonconceputalist from agreeing with McDowell that what Knoblauch was trying to do when he interrupted his flow was not strive for a clearer view of what he was already doing – the "pathological" equivalent of striving under the sway of some transcendental illusion to bring under concepts that which, being part of the Background coping skills, can never be fully explicated. Rather, what Knoblauch was trying to do was to bring an action under a different intentional description, akin to trying to play tennis blindfolded. He simply lost the ability to exercise the practical concepts ("of things to do"; McDowell 2007b: 367) involved in acting. In our terms, he no longer had the know-how.

This brings us to the second of the two aspects mentioned above. Recall that what is supposed to distinguish Dreyfus's position from Searle's is that for the former the background is "the understanding-of-being" (BB) that makes possible the "ground-floor level" of skilled coping (FI). Although Dreyfus downplays this in relation to his account of expertise, it is a *sine qua non* of the accusation that, as we somewhat facetiously put it, McDowell is a philosophical Knoblauch. What that "understanding-of-being" is supposed to reveal is that we are at one with the animals in respect of skilled coping, and that it is a perverse intellectualism that "conceals" that from us. But for Heidegger that "understanding-of-being" reveals to us that we *are* different from the beasts. Persons inhabit a (linguistic) *world*, not a (dumb) *environment*, and it is the phenomenology of freedom that makes that evident.

Accordingly, it is not intellectualism – at least as *we* have defended it – that conceals/reveals the "truth" in phenomena. That lot falls to the (reductively) naturalized phenomenology that is compelled to deny the role of freedom in order to resist an unnecessarily restrictive account of knowledge-that. In doing so, its adherents fail to see that the best way to do justice to the way of being in the world of *persons* is to see their know-how not as something that stands in opposition to their reflective knowing but as having the same fundamental basis. If there's a philosophical Knoblauch, then, it is Dreyfus: left looking confused when he stops acting and starts to reflect.

WHAT LIES BENEATH

At the end of §"Demonstratives, givenness, and motor intentionality" we noted that Kelly and Dreyfus share Merleau-Ponty's sense that motor intentionality has to be understood in such a way that in resisting reduction to both behaviour and propositionally structured thought it establishes phenomenology as the methodological corrective to empiricism and intellectualism. Getting the phenomenology of motor-intentional action right establishes that phenemenology is right and in so doing establishes the explanatory need for and character of the Background. We then went on to indicate two concerns, which (in the light of the previous section) can be seen as related. The first is that Kelly's and Dreyfus's understanding of the phenomena is constrained by a restrictive understanding of what the threat from intellectualism encompasses. The second is that the function of freedom in the "description" of the phenomena is underdeveloped. Combined with the desire to enhance the status of phenomenological descriptions by viewing them as the "data" for the brain sciences, these push this particular naturalistic variant of phenomenology into the sub-personal. Despite protestations of phenomenological orthodoxy, then, the phenomena are being shaped to fit the (brain) science and not the other way round. Nothing remains of the transcendental; it is Kelly and Dreyfus that are "untrue to the phenomena".

The first thing to note in this respect is that Merleau-Ponty need not be interpreted this way. There are, for example, those who, critical of Kelly and Dreyfus, want to reconsider his account of embodied intelligence or cognition by accommodating the sorts of phenomena they appear to leave out of the picture. Rietveld (2008b), for example, claims that the freedom immanent in skilful coping needs to be characterized in its own terms (see also van Grunsven 2008, who draws on Rietveld 2008b). Unfortunately, he proceeds to simply *assume* that what he calls "situated normativity"[17] (Rietveld 2008a *passim*) is the defining characteristic of "'non-propositional'; 'tacit' ... 'know-how', etc." (*ibid.*: 975) and blithely presupposes that a reading of

Wittgenstein on rule-following sanctions the conclusion that "a bedrock of immediate unreflective (viz., nonconceptual) action underpins" our discursive practices (*ibid.*: 983). More revealingly, for our purposes, when confronting the conceptualist challenge Rietveld (2010) assumes that the former must give us *reasons* for thinking that "conceptual capacities are operative in unreflective action" (*ibid.*: 197) because the phenomenology points us in a different direction (*ibid.*: 195). Or more to the point, since it *is* part of the "phenomenology" that we can give accounts of why we did what we did, Rietveld assumes that the only way to get from this to the claim that conceptual capacities are operative is by way of an adventitious bit of conceptualist *theory*. But when one says why one acted as one did, one does not understand oneself to be describing the action from a perspective of theoretical retrospection. Rather, one takes oneself to be describing why one did what one did when one did it. From that standpoint it looks like the Phenomenologist is the one struggling beneath a theoretical burden, which turns on a decidedly unphenomenological and by now familiar division between the "intellect" and "bodily coping".

With that division in mind note that for Rietveld (2010: 183) there's an "Aristotelian–Wittgensteinian common ground" in the positions of Dreyfus and McDowell, a courtesy we can assume he would extend to Kelly. Wittgenstein comes in many flavours, so it is not worth contesting the claim that any random fraternity can be said to share Wittgensteinian *sympathies*. The more interesting claim turns on the precise concatenation, for that is precisely wrong. Part of the reason Kelly and Dreyfus have problems addressing the related problems of freedom and of how nonconceptual content becomes conceptual is because they share an essentially *Platonic* outlook. As we saw in this chapter, Kelly, for example, quite happily distinguishes the following:

I   Reflex movements.
II Unreflective motor actions (like grasping).
III Deliberate cognitive actions (like pointing).

The distinction between II and III in particular is drawn as starkly as it is precisely because of the way in which II is determined by the (over-intellectualistically) accredited nature of III. But in this respect the division reflects Plato's distinction between the appetitive, spirited and rational parts of the soul. And it is of course this tripartite model criticized in *De Anima* (Aristotle 2004) to the effect that the soul is unified and actualized in different ways.

The appeal of Aristotle is in giving us a way of thinking about the naturalness of the person that does not set bodily coping over and against the intellect. In this respect, the related concepts of second nature and *phronesis* or practical wisdom have returned somewhat to the fore. In his *Ethics* (2009) what has come to be called second nature registers the way in which character is formed through the acquisition of the habits that conduce to virtuous behaviour. Although there is a tradition in contemporary interpretations of Aristotle[18] that see the dispositions, habituations and what have you as "non-intellectual motivational propensities" (McDowell 1998a: 38) put at the service of the practical intellect McDowell proposes instead a more Wigginsian view (Wiggins 1975). There is no fortuitous match between the disciplined body and its deliberating pilot, no set of desire-harnessing sub-routines matching the needs of the *phronimos*. Rather, the "practical intellect's coming to be as it ought to be *is* the acquisition of a second nature, involving the moulding of motivational and evaluative propensities" (McDowell 1998a: 185, emphasis added).

This interpretation of second nature plays a central role in the larger project outlined in *Mind and World*. The ambition here is to get back "behind" the distorting influence of the modern epistemological tradition to an understanding of nature that helps to elucidate a *philosophical* thought to the effect that there *ought* to be no mystery in the idea that our thinking has objective purport (that in an oft-repeated phrase, "our thinking is answerable to the world"). For McDowell, this thought has been "deformed" (1998b: 366) by association with the notion that what the world delivers up to us in the way of experience ("the receptivity of sensibility") is independent of the concepts we use to arrive at a world-view ("the spontaneity of the understanding"). But since, on this dualistic account, nothing *rationally* constrains our thinking, we arrive at "an intolerable oscillation" (McDowell 1994: 23) between two positions: either one appeals to something "Given" in experience that offers ultimate justificatory grounds for empirical judgements, or one rejects the need for rational constraint on thought "from the outside" and embraces a fully fledged coherentism. While the first is unacceptable for standard Sellarsian reasons, the second "cannot make sense of the bearing of thought on objective reality" (*ibid.*).

McDowell's aim, then, is to give us an account of experience wherein it is not held absolutely distinct from conceptual thinking, "a notion of experience as an actualization of conceptual capacities in sensory consciousness itself" (1998b: 366). And it is in this Kantian-cum-Hegelian context that a generalized account of the concepts of second nature and *phronesis* come into the picture. To acknowledge constraints on our thinking from experience is to acknowledge the role of our physical nature – the "potentialities that belong to a normal human organism" (McDowell 1994: 84) – in our understanding of the world. Although other animals share some of the potentialities or propensities that constitute part of second nature, McDowell follows Sellars in holding that "conceptual capacities are not merely natural, but acquired along with acquiring mastery of a language" (McDowell 2003: 76).

What it is to be inculcated into a stretch of reality, be it perceptual, ethical or "institutional", is to become initiated into the associated normative space of linguistic practice. It becomes "second nature" to respond as one ought, not because the associated habits "blindly" track the institutional facts but because *what it is* to have those habits is to have had one's "eyes opened" to the correct view of things (*ibid.*). Since we are "animals whose natural being is permeated with rationality" (*ibid.*: 85), what it is to be skilled, to cope in a masterful way, to know *how* to go on – to be, in short, a *phronimos* – is a matter of having had one's animal potentialities "shaped" in the way the constitutes understanding of the relevant concepts.

This suggests that there are two accounts of second nature available. The first is conditioned by the idea that we must do justice to a basic empiricist intuition[19] and leads to an Aristotelian-inflected Kantian conceptualism. The second account takes it that when we remark the skilled coper's "understanding of the relevant concepts" we are evoking Aristotle's observation that they "perceive" that things are the way they are and do what they do because they have "*knowledge* of the ultimate particular thing" unattainable by "systematic knowledge" (Aristotle 2009: 1142a:25–7, emphasis added). It is this second account that is the more authentically Aristotelian–Wittgensteinian, and, according to this, second nature plays a therapeutic role. It is invoked descriptively to avoid the felt need to have recourse to something like a background or "ground-floor level" to account for the "naturalness" of our normative practices. It is, as it were, all we need to talk about if want to talk (naturalistically) about schematism.

According to this, the *phronimos* acts as they do because that is what is demanded by the full concrete situation, and in acting as they do they exhibit the practical rationality demanded by it. It is second nature to respond in that way, not because one's second nature can be hypostatized as the background against which such choices and actions take place but because calling it second nature characterizes (phenomenologically, if you will) the unreflective way in which one does what one does. If we take it that Aristotle's "systematic knowledge" denotes that which is subject to PC, the knowledge in question is *tacit* knowledge, subject to PA. Tacit knowledge is personal, practical knowledge-how because of the second nature possessed by the knower.

In the previous section we noted that, for McDowell, phenomenology is constrained by the need to account transcendentally for the objectivity of our thinking. It is for that reason that, he maintains,

> Phenomenological attention to embodied coping should not be conceived as Dreyfus conceives it—as a way to answer the question "how the nonconceptual given is converted into a given with conceptual content". That question should be rejected, not answered. (McDowell 2007b: 349)

This is quite right. However, it is difficult to reject that question if one insists on holding a view on the *content* of experience and takes it that both the following conditional *and* its antecedent are true:

CC   If experience has representational content then (experience has conceptual content or experience has nonconceptual content).

For McDowell the self-awareness exhibited by the skilful coper in the exercise of their practical rational capacities is that of the I-that-does. If one rejects the antecedent of CC then one makes available the Aristotelian–Wittgensteinian account of second nature outlined above and avails oneself of the resources to "exorcise" rather than merely reject the desire to explain the emergence of concepts from the primordial soup of the nonconceptual. In doing so one can embrace the epistemological standpoint we have been recommending and hold that the first-person nature of the "I do" indicates the *personal* aspect of the (tacit) knowing one exhibits when, as a result of the second nature one has acquired, one knows how to do something.

6. TACIT KNOWLEDGE AND LANGUAGE

INTRODUCTION

Drawing on two key slogans from Michael Polanyi and "regress arguments" for the priority of practical knowledge over theoretical knowledge (or practical knowledge-how over knowledge-that) put forward by Polanyi, Gilbert Ryle, Martin Heidegger and Ludwig Wittgenstein, we have argued that the idea of tacit knowledge should be thought of as context-dependent but conceptually structured practical or personal knowledge.

The stress on balancing conceptual structure with both context-dependence and practical knowledge addresses a potential worry that knowledge has to have a content. *Tacit* knowledge is *knowledge*. Thus, unlike accounts of context-dependent skilled coping, our account of tacit knowledge presupposes a rational subject. At the same time, unpacking the conceptual structure requires both context-dependent demonstratives and practical demonstration. It cannot be put into words alone. Tacit *knowledge* is *tacit*.

The equation of "personal" and "practical" flags the fact that such knowledge can only be articulated practically and from within. It requires not just a context, which would be sufficient for context-dependent spectator knowledge, but also a skilled agent both to perform the practical demonstration (in the role of the teacher) and also to have "eyes to see" the import of the demonstration (as the "learning-ready" pupil).

This chapter considers what might appear a surprising connection: a positive relation between tacit knowledge and language. It might seem surprising because we have approached what is tacit by a suitable contrast with what is "tellable" or what is explicit, and what can be codified in general (i.e. context-independent language) has been paradigmatic of the explicit. But one connection between tacit knowledge and language has already been set out at the end of Chapter 4. To grasp the meaning of a word (which is presupposed by general codifications of explicit knowledge) is to be able to recognize and deploy the right word in the right context: an ability which, according to

Wittgenstein's regress argument, goes beyond the limits of what can be codified. This is an important point, worth repeating, and we will develop it in the next section, which addresses what, to many philosophers, is the obvious claim about the connection between language mastery and tacit knowledge; namely, that to understand a language is to have tacit knowledge of a theory of meaning. We will summarize that project in order both to emphasize the differences between the connection of tacit knowledge in play there and our own account and the very substantial challenges it faces.

This familiar project addresses the question:

1. To what extent is language mastery a matter of tacit knowledge?

There is, however, a second connection between tacit knowledge and language, which goes to the heart of what can be taught and prompts the question:

2. To what extent does tacit knowledge depend on linguistic mastery?

Addressing question 2 will help us draw some conclusions for the teaching, transfer and maintenance of tacit knowledge.

One focus of this chapter will be the work of the sociologist Harry Collins. Collins and Robert Evans argue, partly on the basis of experiment, that mastery of the language of a practice can carry a form of "practical understanding" (in their phrase) that stops short of practical ability. Despite being linguistically mediated, it is not explicit knowledge; but neither does it imply practical ability or know-how, which they call "contributory expertise". Their own account of how this might be is, however, underdeveloped. After giving a brief account of the testimonial transmission of explicit knowledge, we argue that providing that tacit knowledge fits the *principle of articulacy*, as Chapters 2–4 have stressed, it can also be communicated in practical demonstrations. But something less than full-blown practical knowledge can also be communicated in the experimental designs outlined by Collins and Evans.

TO WHAT EXTENT IS LANGUAGE MASTERY A MATTER OF TACIT KNOWLEDGE?

The conception of tacit knowledge set out in this book is a form of personal knowledge or "active comprehension of things known" in Polanyi's phrase. We have argued that tacit knowledge is best thought of as context-dependent, conceptually structured, practical know-how. It stands opposed to knowledge that can be made explicit in situation-independent general terms. Tacit knowledge stands opposed to the *principle of codifiability* (PC) but not the *principle of articulacy* (PA). Thus, in general, tacit knowledge cannot be conveyed by situation-independent linguistic instruction. But there has, historically, been an appeal to tacit knowledge precisely in connection with language. This is the idea that a speaker's understanding of a language consists in "tacit knowledge" of a theory of meaning, or a grammar, for that language. There are two main threads for this idea in the philosophy of language. One derives from Chomsky's project to articulate an innate, universal grammar for human natural language.

> If a person who cognized the grammar and its rules could miraculously become conscious of them we would not hesitate to say that he knows the grammar and its rules, and that this conscious knowledge is what constitutes his knowledge of language.
>
> (Chomsky 1980: 70)

The other is Donald Davidson's aim to set out a theory of meaning for natural language based on an inversion of Tarski's semantic conception of truth. Such a theory of meaning would contain a finite set of axioms, giving, for example, the reference of primitive terms and a recursive procedure to derive an instance of the T-schema (such as "Snow is white" is true iff snow is white) to serve as a meaning theorem for any declarative sentence of the language.

> In Tarski's work, T-sentences are taken to be true because the right branch of the biconditional is assumed to be a translation of the sentence for which truth conditions are being given. But we cannot assume in advance that correct translation can be recognised without pre-empting the point of radical interpretations; in empirical applications, we must abandon the assumption. What I propose is to reverse the direction of explanation: assuming translation, Tarski was able to define truth; the present idea is to take truth as basic and to extract an account of translation or interpretation. The advantages, from the point of view of radical interpretation, are obvious. Truth is a single property which attaches, or fails to attach, to utterances, while each utterance has its own interpretation; and truth is more apt to connect with fairly simple attitudes of speakers.   (Davidson 1984: 134)

Under the general constraint that such a theory delivers true instances of the T-schema – true meaning theorems – across the board, individual instances will, Davidson argues, unpack the meaning of sentences of the object language.

In fact, the cognitive status of meaning theorems in Davidson's project is not clear. He makes two relevant comments. One is that knowledge of such a theory would *suffice* for understanding (Davidson 1984: 125). The other is that it is a *necessary* condition for languages to be learnable that a constructive or compositional account of the language could be given (*ibid.*: 3). But he does not say overtly, for example, that speakers have implicit knowledge of a theory of meaning which *explains* their ability. Others, however, have made this claim.

Michael Dummett, for example, argues that the best interpretation of Davidson's approach is as "full-blooded" rather than "modest". The requirement for full-bloodedness for a theory of meaning is the requirement that it does not presuppose key facts about content by merely giving the meaning of the basic terms of one language in another language. Instead, it gives an account of the meaning of the primitive terms of a language, its basic predicates and referring terms, by describing the practical abilities that an understanding of those terms gives to a speaker. This, in turn, presupposes a form of tacit or implicit knowledge.

> A theory of meaning will, then, represent the practical ability possessed by a speaker as consisting in his grasp of a set of propositions; since the speaker derives his understanding of a sentence from the meanings of its component words, these propositions will most naturally form a deductively connected system. The knowledge of these propositions that is attributed to a speaker can only be an implicit knowledge. In general, it cannot be demanded of someone who has any given practical ability that he have more than an implicit knowledge of those propositions by means of which we give a theoretical representation of that ability. (Dummett 1993: 36)

The recursive structure of a theory of meaning of such a form reflects "our intuitive conviction that a speaker derives his understanding of a sentence from his understanding of the words composing it and the way they are put together" (*ibid.*: 11).

In a recent overview, Alexander Miller (2007: 274) suggests that this project aims at answering three questions:

(a) How is it possible, given the finitude of their capacities, for speakers of a natural language to understand a potential infinity of sentences?
(b) How is it possible to understand utterances of previously unencountered sentences?
(c) How is it possible for a natural language to be learnable? (i.e. how is it possible for explicit training with only a relatively small number of sentences to secure competence with a possibly very large set of sentences outwith that initial set?)

Dummett's outline answer to these questions depends on the cogency of thinking that speakers have some kind of knowledge of the axioms that encode understanding of the language and which fix the derivation of suitable, interpretative, instances of the T-schema.

There is, however, a problem with thinking of "knowledge" of the axioms as *knowledge* in any ordinary sense. The problem was first highlighted by Gareth Evans who argues that "It is of the essence of a belief state that it be at the service of many distinct projects, and that its influence on any project be mediated by other beliefs" (Evans 1981: 132). He then considers the ascription of a belief, that a particular substance is poisonous, to a rat:

> It is true that many philosophers would be prepared to regard the dispositional state of the rat as a belief. But such a view requires blindness to the fundamental differences which exist between the state of the rat and the belief of the man – differences which suggest that fundamentally different mechanism are at work. We might begin with this disanalogy: the rat manifests the "belief" in only one way – by not eating – whereas there is no limit to the ways in which the ordinary belief that something is poisonous might be manifested. The (rational) subject might manifest it ~by, for example, preventing someone else from eating the food, or by giving it to a hated enemy, or by committing suicide with it. These variations stem from the different projects with which the belief may interact, but similar variations arise from combining the belief with other beliefs. It might, for example, lead to the subject's consuming a small amount of the food every day, when combined with the belief that the consumption of small doses of a poison renders one immune to its effects.
>
> (Evans 1981: 131–2)

So although the rat and the rational subject may share some dispositions to behave (in general: avoiding eating the poisonous substance), for the rat, the dispositions are tied to a narrow range of behaviours whereas, for the rational subject, there is no limit to the actions to which a belief that something is poisonous may contribute. Ascribing a belief to the rat adds nothing to a more minimal stimulus response account of its behaviour. This then presents a problem which Crispin Wright summarizes as follows:

> someone who is credited with implicit knowledge of a meaning-delivering theorem may express his knowledge in an indefinite variety of ways, including, in appropriate contexts, lying, assent and silence. But the (implicit) knowledge of a meaning theoretic *axiom* would seem to be harnessed to the single project of

171

> forming beliefs about the context of sentences which contain the
> expression. (Wright 1986: 227–8)

Thus while the *output* of a theory of meaning, codified as a potentially infinite set of instances of the T-schema or meaning theorems, can play a role in the broader life of a rational subject and thus can be the objects of intentional states or propositional attitudes, the axioms on which such a theory is based cannot.

Evans himself continues to speak of the speaker's relation to axioms as a form of "tacit knowledge" even though it is not, according to him, a propositional attitude. It is *sub-doxastic*. Further, because the form of generalizability that is missing is, according to him, a condition on *conceptual* understanding such tacit knowledge is also non-conceptual. So on Evans's picture, a speaker's grasp of the axioms of a theory of meaning is a form of non-conceptual, sub-doxastic tacit knowledge.

Evans's argument leaves a potential problem concerning the distinction between different possible theories of meaning for a language. Consider a language with a simple subject–predicate structure, and ten names and ten predicates yielding 100 different possible sentences of the form Fa. Two distinct theories of meaning would be possible. One comprises a list of one meaning theorem for each of the 100 sentences. The other has one axiom for each of the names, one for each of the predicates, and one setting out the meaning of a subject–predicate combination.[1] Given that the speaker does not stand in any intentional attitude to the axioms and need not possess the concepts in which they are expressed, what is the rationale for preferring one theory over the other? What makes it true that a speaker has "tacit knowledge" (under Evans's interpretation) of one theory rather than another?

Evans's suggestion is that the second theory should be preferred if it turns out that a speaker has a disposition for each of the expressions given by the theory. For the list-like theory, that is 100 distinct dispositions linking each sentence to its truth condition. For the theory that articulates an underlying structure, Evans argues that there are 20 dispositions: one for each of the names and the predicates. For each name, then for each predicate, the speaker will be disposed to judge the corresponding sentence composed of name and predicate is true if the object named satisfies the predicate. Likewise, for each predicate. Using Π as a universal substitutional quantifier, a speaker U has tacit knowledge that a names or denotes John if and only if U has a disposition such that:

> $(\Pi\phi)(\Pi\psi)$ (if U tacitly knows that an object satisfies ϕ iff it is ψ; and if U hears an utterance having the form ϕa; then U will judge that: the utterance is true iff John is ψ).

Tacit knowledge that F means bald corresponds to this disposition:

> $(\Pi x)(\Pi\alpha)$ (if U tacitly knows that the denotation of α is x, and U hears an utterance having the form $F\alpha$, then U will judge that: the utterance is true iff x is bald).

As Wright puts it:

> "Tacit knowledge" ought to be a disposition which constitutes understanding; and what is it to understand a sub-sentential expression ... except to be disposed to make the right judgements about the truth conditions of sentences containing it provided one understands the accompanying name or predicate?
>
> (1986: 230)

Hence the 21 axioms yield 20 inter-defined dispositions. If there is evidence that a speaker possess just these dispositions, then it is evidence that the second, structural theory, mirrors their competence.[2] But, as Wright points out, even the 20 dispositions are dispositions to make judgements about whole sentences. So, still, why prefer the structured theory over the unstructured list? Both will yield the same dispositions. Evans's response is to stress the underlying causal structure that grounds the dispositions.

> The semanticist aims to uncover a structure in the language that mirrors the competence speakers of the language have actually acquired. This does not mean that he aims to uncover a theory that he supposes his subjects *know*, in any acceptable sense of that word. It means merely this: if (but only if) speakers of the language can understand certain sentences they have not previously encountered, as a result of acquaintance with their parts, the semanticist must state how the meaning of these sentences is a function of the meanings of those parts. He must assign semantical properties to the parts and state the general significance of the construction in such a way that a statement of what those sentences mean is deductively entailed. There may be more than one way of doing this. (Evans 1975: 343–4)

Martin Davies develops this thought further in what he calls the "mirror constraint":

> The salient structural facts about the competence of speakers are here presented as being of the following form: speakers who understand sentences s_1, s_2 ... s_n are able, without further

> training, to understand sentence s. And the salient structural facts about a semantic theory are of this form: the resources used in derivations of meaning specifications for s_1, s_2 ... s_n are jointly sufficient for the derivation of the meaning specification for s. The constraint on semantic theories ... is just that these two structures should match. (1987: 446)

"Tacit knowledge" of one theory of meaning rather than another consists in the fact that the structure described by one, rather than the other, is the causal explanation of the speaker's ability.

> To conceive of semantic structure as psychological, rather than abstract, is to conceive of it as the causal-explanatory structure of the semantic ability of actual speakers. It is the kind of cognitive structure that permits speakers to recognize the meanings of previously unencountered sentences. (Davies 1986: 132)

Evidence for this should include, not just patterns of sentence use but also patterns of acquisition and loss of linguistic understanding as well as revision of meaning. Such a strategy, however, presupposes rather than explains why the structural facts about the competence of speakers picked out by the mirror constraint deserve to be called psychological rather than abstract *explanations* of abilities. Davies stresses the role of the structure in explanations but provides no insight into why these count as psychological as opposed to abstract neurological (or other sub-doxastic) explanations.

There are two other relevant concerns about this general approach to ascribing "tacit knowledge" of the axioms of a theory of meaning on the basis of sub-doxastic dispositions. One worry that Wright develops, for example, is whether any account can be given of the dispositions governing either names or predicates in the example above (Wright 1986: 232–3). The account of the disposition that corresponds to understanding a name has to presuppose the disposition corresponding to understanding a predicate and vice versa. Hence the objection is: no non-question-begging account has been offered of what these dispositions are.

Miller, however, argues that this worry can be assuaged by a comparison with the role of beliefs and desires in rationalizing action. In that case, an account of the role of either belief or desire has to presuppose the other. But we, rightly, do not take that to threaten the elucidation of either (or both) but rather demonstrate the holism of the mental. "Tacit knowledge" of the axioms governing a language has to be ascribed as a whole relative to the mirror constraint (Miller 1997: 158–9).

But this response to the objection that the dispositions corresponding to states of "tacit knowledge" of a theory of meaning cannot be given non-vacuous clarification does not undermine the earlier point. "Tacit knowledge" of the axioms of the theory is no form of intentional state *for the subject*. Given that, as we said at the start of this book, talk of tacit knowledge is not very well established in natural language and thus its use is a matter, in part at least, for stipulation, there is no very firm objection to calling the relation between a subject and his or her dispositional grasp of the axioms of a theory of meaning a matter of "tacit knowledge". But it is worth stressing the difference between this use of that phrase and the use we have articulated.

First, "tacit knowledge" of the axioms of a theory of meaning is not a matter of belief or any other intentional attitude. It is not conceptually articulated *for* the subject and thus not personal knowledge. It is, obviously, conceptually articulated in theories of meaning and thus conceptually articulated for the theorist. But, aside from their outputs, the contents of such theories are not objects of awareness for subjects.

Second, since they are constituted by dispositions that are not at the service of a variety of distinct projects, what is tacitly known does not play a rationalizing role in the life of the subject merely a causal role (Byrne 2005: 79).

Third, it is open to question whether such states carry content or meaning at all. All that the mirror constraint clearly does is establish that a theory of meaning tracks causal and enabling states of a subject's physiology. Evans even suggests that neurophysiological data would be decisive in matching a theory of meaning to a subject. But that surely supports only a causal-structural approach rather than a content-laden one.

This reflects a more general problem of reducing meaning or content to sub-personal states or processes, which has been the central aim of reductionist theories. But that project, examples of which (like Searle's) we have encountered in earlier chapters, faces a general explanatory challenge outlined by William Ramsey in his book *Representation Reconsidered* (Ramsey 2007). Ramsey points out that a lesson from the history of the philosophy of mind is that, as Daniel Dennett noted, it is nearly always *possible* to describe physical processes in representational terms but it is never *necessary*. Just as one can avoid biological descriptions by describing biological systems in lower level physical and chemical terms, so representational terms need not be used. What then justifies the use of representational terms for complex systems? What is the explanatory benefit? Ramsey calls this the "job description challenge". He argues that all the dominant approaches to explaining intentionality fail this test.

Take the case of a Venus flytrap, which according to Fred Dretske's teleosemantic analysis is supposed to have an internal trigger that responds to movement and thus *signals* the presence of insects (Dretske 1988). Dretske says "there is every reason to think that this internal trigger was selected for its job because of what it indicated, because it told the plant what it needed to know" (*ibid.*: 20). But Ramsey asks why we need think of this in representational terms in addition to thinking that because of the law-like connection between movement and plant closure plants with the trigger would be selected: "there is no reason to think that structures recruited because their states have the property of being nomically dependent on some condition are also recruited because they carry information about that condition" (Ramsey 2007: 135). This mirrors the case of the firing pin in a gun, which bridges the gap between pulling the trigger and firing the round. That law-like connection is why the pin is part of the design. But there is no reason to think that the firing pin is a representation of anything.

Thus despite the fact that sub-personal elements of a speaker realize a particular nomic dependence is not in itself enough to show that the sub-personal "grasp" of an axiom of a theory of meaning is content-laden. In the terms of a by now familiar dilemma, such a conception may merit the description "tacit" but only at the cost of failing to count as knowledge. By contrast, the account we have given is pitched at the level of the person, is conceptually structured and has a content albeit one which can only be expressed in context-specific ways. That third point is consistent with the fact that there may be lower level explanations of the motor skills presupposed by such practical knowledge.

There is a further and interesting difference. The project of articulating a theory of meaning for a natural language is one of formalizing the knowledge that a competent speaker has. It aims to codify the know-how that is exercised in particular situations in situation-independent and universal terms. Thus what we have taken to be at the heart of tacit knowledge – its situation-specificity – is what this alternative conception aims to trump. Situation-specific expertise is explained through the provision of a general theory. But for the fact that the theory itself is merely "tacitly" known, the project aims to turn what is tacit knowledge at the level of the person for most speakers into explicit knowledge, of speakers' sub-personal dispositions, for theorists.[3] Thus, if the arguments set out in Chapters 3 and 4 are correct, this project is threatened by the fact that nothing that can be codified in the form that Evans's theory requires is sufficient to explain mastery of the right response to a new case.

If one does not follow Evans in calling sub-personal causal dispositional states "tacit knowledge", is there any sense in which linguistic understanding involves tacit knowledge? Yes. As we argued in Chapter 4, the right response to Wittgenstein's regress argument balances what is explicit in explanations of meaning with what is tacit in the sense of situation-specific practical ability. To grasp the meaning of a word is to have a potentially unlimited competence in its use even if it is explicable, to those with eyes to see, in finite and particular explanations. But such grasp of the meaning involves the recognition of any particular use that *that!* use is correct, accords with its meaning. Such recognition is a context-dependent demonstrative thought which accords with what we take to be the most promising understanding of what is tacit.

There is a further line of argument that we will mention, although a proper assessment lies outside the scope of this book. According to Charles Travis, it is a feature of concepts (or of "the conceptual" as he puts it) that they apply to, or can be realized by, a range of different actual and counter-factual cases. This is an implicit feature of Wittgenstein's regress argument and, as we saw in Chapter 3, rules out explanation of our open-ended abilities to recognize how concepts apply in new instances in terms of mental templates or talismans. But while divergent ways of responding to explanations can seem to be merely philosophical possibilities, Travis argues that, although it often goes unnoticed by philosophers, our words generally admit of quite different, and conflicting, understanding. Thus, for example, the claim that something is a piece of meat or judging that there is meat on the rug can both be understood in quite different ways.

> Handing you a packet from the butcher's I say, "Here's the meat I bought for dinner". You open it and find the kidneys. "I don't call that meat", you say. "Meat, for me, is muscle". "Well, I do", I say helpfully. Again one of us may be demonstrably wrong. Lamb's kidneys are no more meat than wool is, to one who knows what meat is. But perhaps not. In fact, there are various understandings one might have of being meat, consistent with what being meat is as such. In that sense, being meat admits of understandings. We sometimes distinguish (e.g., in good markets) between meat and offal. Then if the kidneys wound up in the meat section they are in the wrong place. On the other hand, one would not (usually) serve kidneys to a vegetarian with the remark, "I made sure there would be no meat at dinner" … There are various ways being meat *admits* of being thought of. (Travis 2007: 187)

The way that the meat is being thought of, or the circumstances that obtain for meat to be on the rug (wrapped or unwrapped and bleeding), or shoes to be under the bed (exactly or partly; on the same floor or a lower floor), or someone to be at home (when, for example, his house has been in a landslip) are the sorts of cases that Travis stresses can be taken in different ways in different contexts. The right understanding is not fixed by the meaning of the words alone, nor the concepts so expressed, but by the occasion of utterance and by facts as to what it would be reasonable, in such a case, to be taken to be saying. What is said is, according to Travis, "occasion-sensitive".

A philosopher working in the tradition of formal theories of meaning will complain that Travis's claims may be important contributions to the study of pragmatics but not the semantics of languages. Thus the project of articulating a theory of meaning is not undermined as it concerns the semantic properties of words. Travis, however, argues that even once one fixes, for example, that the word "green" speaks of green, there are still different understandings of what it is for things to be green, and thus what it is for them to be called "green" to be true. A painted leaf may not count as a green leaf in a garden centre but might in a theatrical props department. So the stable division between semantics and pragmatics cannot be drawn.

To repeat, this is not the place to assess Travis's occasionalism. If it is correct, however, it suggests that the basic moral of Wittgenstein's regress argument may often be understated. It is not just that codifications (by contrast with articulations) of rules fail to determine what is properly grasped. Rather, there is always a real gap to be filled in by a context-dependent judgement about what is reasonable to understand in the circumstances. But if correct, Travis's view does not offer support for a view of tacit knowledge as hidden or ineffable (a view we have rejected) since, in the context, it may be perfectly clear what is the right understanding. It does, however, reinforce the answer we have offered to the question of whether language mastery is a matter of tacit knowledge. Although we have cautioned against the mainstream philosophical view that speakers have tacit knowledge of a theory of meaning for a language in virtue of their sub-personal dispositions, their knowledge of how to deploy words is tacit because it resists codification in context-independent general terms.

TO WHAT EXTENT DOES TACIT KNOWLEDGE DEPEND ON LINGUISTIC MASTERY?

At the start of this chapter we introduced two questions:

1. To what extent is language mastery a matter of tacit knowledge?
2. To what extent does tacit knowledge depend on linguistic mastery?

Having focused so far on question 1, we now turn to question 2.

We have already mentioned the work of Harry Collins in both the introduction and Chapter 3. His early work focused on the tacit knowledge involved in such practical cases as knowing how to build a working laser (Collins 1985). More recently Collins, with co-author Robert Evans, has suggested that his earlier study had an important omission (Collins 2010a; Collins & Evans 2007). Even though his discussion of Wittgenstein's regress argument, discussed in Chapter 3, invokes linguistic enculturation (Collins 1985: 15–23), he neglected the role of such enculturation as an important *source* of a distinct form of tacit knowledge. Thus he neglected the role that acquiring a language has for also acquiring a further form of tacit knowledge, which he calls "interactional expertise". In this section, we will examine this idea and address the question of whether linguistic mastery underpins such a distinct kind of tacit knowledge.

Interactional expertise is introduced both as marking a distinction between humans and other animals, and as playing a role in the communication and constitution of aspects of tacit knowledge:

> humans are unique in the way they share tacit knowledge. Humans have an ability to develop and maintain complex bodies of tacit knowledge in social groups that is not possessed by non-human entities. Humans can share this knowledge with new members of the group in ways they cannot explicate.
>
> (Collins & Evans 2007: 7)

As will become clear, the last sentence provides their reason for taking this to be tacit. Although it is supposed to be a form of tacit knowledge, interactional expertise contrasts with practical skills. Those who have the ability to perform a skilled practice or to do something have "contributory expertise" because they can "contribute to the domain to which the expertise pertains" (*ibid.*: 24). Taking the example of tennis, a *contributory* expert is someone with practical knowledge how to play the game. This includes a practical knowledge of how to execute a variety of shots, to navigate the court, to anticipate an opponent and so on. An *interactional* expert need not have any of those abilities. Nevertheless, he or she does have an understanding not just of the "theory" of the game, its rules and so on, but also the practice. A non-playing commentator might thus have a kind of practical understanding, according to Collins, without being able to wield a racket.

Collins and Evans's bold hypothesis is that it is possible to acquire this form of "tacit knowledge" of a field (whether tennis playing or gravitational wave physics) without having direct practical know-how. According to Collins:

> The idea of interactional expertise implies that it would, for example, be possible to come to understand, say, tennis – to have a practical understanding of tennis – without ever having played tennis, held a tennis racket or bounced a tennis ball. Imagine a person who has been blind and confined to a wheelchair from birth. The claim is that such a person could acquire a practical understanding of tennis solely from extended and intensive discussion of tennis in the company of tennis players, without watching tennis or stirring from their wheelchair; such a person could, in principle, *understand tennis as well as someone who had played it all their lives.* (2010a: 272, emphasis added)

Thus on their account, although it is still a form of tacit knowledge, interactional expertise is distinct from contributory expertise. It is tacit but, unlike our account of tacit knowledge, it carries no practical implications. This is a bold hypothesis because it attempts to introduce a new kind of tacit knowledge. But it may prompt the following *a priori* objection. There is simply no conceptual space for such a form of tacit knowledge. If the interactional expert lacks practical know-how and acquires their expertise linguistically then it must be explicit knowledge. If it is not explicit but involves no practical mastery then it is no form of knowledge at all.

There are two aspects to Collins and Evans's reply: one empirical and one more philosophical. The philosophical picture is that interactional expertise is tied to linguistic ability and although it carries no implications for contributory expertise (our form of tacit knowledge) it is nevertheless a form of *practical understanding*. We will return to this idea and what further clarification they can offer shortly. But against the background idea that one acquires interactional expertise through the encultured acquisition of a language, they suggest that if this is true it should be testable through a kind of Turing test or imitation game. Under the test conditions of Turing's imitation game, can those with practical mastery of a field or discipline tell the difference between others of their number and those who do not? Anyone who passes the test without possessing the practical mastery has interactional expertise. If there is a substantial group who lack practical mastery and also fail the test this implies that the interactional expertise of those who do pass it is both substantial and tacit. Everyone should be able to pick up the *explicit* knowledge.

Having outlined this hypothesis, Collins and Evans have gone on to carry out a variety of imitation game tests. By testing colour-blind and non-colour-blind subjects, for example, and contrasting this case with those with and those without perfect pitch, they aim to show that because the colour-blind have been surrounded by the non-colour-blind community, colour-blind subjects will have fully mastered its language (although they do not have contributory expertise) while those without perfect pitch will not have mastered the language of the perfect pitch minority. Initial evidence, at least, suggests that this is, indeed, the case. If so, it raises the question of the nature of the kind of expertise possessed by the colour-blind of colour vision but not of those with ordinary hearing of perfect pitch.

In light of the connection to language and enculturation, Collins and Evans connect this question to what can be conveyed by non-practitioner coaches to athletes or students. They say:

> one of the standard motifs in critiques of artificial intelligence is
> the mistakes made my coaches of any practical activity, the point
> being that the coach, whether mechanical or human, cannot

express in words what the athlete or other kind of learner can only master by action. The idea of interactional expertise gives us a better idea of what some human coaches might be doing and how they succeed despite the gap between language and practice. As we now see, the human coach *can* teach some things through the medium of spoken language because the coach shares some of the non-explicit skills of the student: the shared linguistic skills can transfer mutually understood tacit meanings that would not be available to those with levels of expertise below interactional.

(Collins & Evans 2007: 30)

This connection does not in itself shed light on what it is that is conveyed in such instruction. However, in work written since *Rethinking Expertise*, Collins addresses this question explicitly. How is it possible that practical understanding could be contained in language? His answer begins by denying that such understanding can be codified in symbolic representations "because the fluent lived language discussed here is itself laden with tacit knowledge" (Collins 2010a: 280). Thus the answer to how practical understanding can be contained in, and conveyed by, spoken language starts with the idea that language possession is itself a tacit skill.

Traditionally, language, at least in its relationship to practical and technical matters rather than artistic or expressive matters, has been thought of as the domain of the explicit as opposed to the tacit. The tacit is often exemplified by a practical ability, such as balancing on a bicycle. But acquiring native fluency in a language – as opposed to learning the shell of a language from its explicit grammar and the dictionary – always involves the acquisition of tacit knowledge. That is, it involves the acquisition of far more in the way of understanding than what is said or even could be said. (Collins 2010a: 280)

This view that language mastery is itself a piece of tacit knowledge is illustrated through the example of mastering verb placement. Children learn to do this as they learn to ride a bicycle: by doing it. "To that extent and more, language speaking is a practice. Having acquired verb placement, the child then 'knows' how to do something, even though they usually cannot say what they know" (*ibid.*: 280).

That final comment links back both to Polanyi's slogan, but also to Collins's approach to tacit knowledge: that it is what cannot be made explicit. Children do not have a codified grammatical theory of verb placement so they cannot account in general terms for their knowledge. In the terms introduced in this book, this violates the *principle of codifiability*. But they do have context-dependent demonstrative knowledge of where or when the verb comes in what they want to write or say. Thus, contra Polanyi and Collins, they can say what they know in each specific case, albeit it only in context-dependent terms, even if they cannot summarize that knowledge in general terms. The know-how fits the *principle of articulacy*. Still, since that knowledge is context-specific and tied to practical mastery, it is tacit in our sense as well as Collins's contributory expertise.

This point, however, merely addresses question 1. It does not address question 2. While language mastery is itself tacit, that fact does not explain how it can be used to convey tacit "practical understanding", albeit an understanding that does not amount to practical knowledge of how to do something. In fact, this remains mysterious even on Collins's further account. The most explicit answer he gives is contained in these passages:

> We do not know how practical understanding is contained in language. It might be contained in the arrangements of words, phrases and sentences. It might also be contained in wider patterns and frequencies of usage in the community as a whole. For example, the frequency with which a word or phrase is uttered by the entire body of speakers may indicate something of practical importance. (Collins 2010a: 281)

In learning to use words as the community around one uses words, one is learning things of practical importance. One is learning what and who is to be taken seriously, and such things are some of the crucial components of practical judgements – they teach what does and does not exist and what can and cannot be done. Speakers are mostly unaware of the frequency and nuance of words and names in their speech, and in this case most would be unable to provide a scientific explanation of why this could be said, and that could not be said, nor how they were creating scientific understanding in the course of their speech. Yet the pattern of usages they acquire and promulgate contains things that affect practical judgements and physical practices:

> as the tacit knowledge of the understanding of a practice is acquired through the development of fluency in the domain language, there are subtle changes to the metaphorical muscles, and metaphorical nerve pathways of the spoken language and in the, metaphorical, "synapses of society". (Collins 2010a: 282)

Thus, on the one hand, language is of key importance. It is, Collins thinks, "more important to practical understanding than practice" (*ibid.*: 283). Given that language can be shared, that provides a route to the sharing and teaching of tacit knowledge. But, on the other hand, the role it plays is mysterious. Speakers are unaware of how they convey (or even "create") practical understanding in speech.

Further light can be shed on this, however. First, on the account developed in this book, while tacit knowledge is context-dependent and practical, it is also conceptually structured. Collins comments that "nearly the whole of even a *contributory* expert's expertise in a practice is interactional expertise" (*ibid.*: 284). As he also concedes, there is no way to quantify relative contributions or components but the thrust of his claim accords with the idea that all tacit knowledge is conceptually structured. It is, of course, also possible to possess a great deal of the relevant conceptual knowledge without having practical knowledge of how to do something. It is possible to have a great deal of explicit knowledge about a practice without having the practical ability involved in enacting the practice. In answer to question 2, then, there is thus no mystery about the general connection between language possession and possession of practical knowledge.

But what of the idea that an understanding – which still merits the label "practical understanding" under some interpretation – of the practice of tennis or gravity wave physics can be conveyed through linguistic enculturation? We will explore that by forging a connection between discussion of tacit knowledge and knowledge by testimony. The first issue is how enculturation can provide the basis for knowledge, of some sort or other, of another person's tacit knowledge. It can seem that there is an impediment in the communication of aspects of tacit knowledge from a practitioner to a non-practitioner. Surely, goes the worry, the recipient can never acquire any practical *knowledge* because, *ex hypothesi*, they lack the right kind of practical experience. The second element of an answer to this is to adopt a suitably externalist account of testimony in general. A good account of tacit knowledge goes in hand with an externalist account of testimony.

TESTIMONY AND EXTERNALISM

Following established use in philosophy, by "testimony" we mean any form of transmission of knowledge through the reports of others. It thus contrasts with perception, reasoning, whether inductive or deductive, and memory.

That we can acquire knowledge by testimony is hard to reconcile with an internalist model of knowledge and justification. Roughly it is the view that justification for knowledge claims must be available or accessible to those who frame them. The problem with combining testimony and internalism is that an individual cannot in general do enough to vouch for the status of knowledge transferred. Suppose, for example, that internalist accounts could be given of perception and induction. An internalist account of testimony would then be possible provided that testimony could be reduced to a combination of perception (of others, of their utterances, etc.) together with inductions from their previous reliability, for example. David Hume attempted to outline just such a defence of testimony in his *Enquiries Concerning Human Understanding* (Hume 1975: 109–16). But as Anthony Coady convincingly argues, no such attempt can work (Coady 1992: 79–100). We will mention just two of Coady's criticisms of Hume, which suggest the principled difficulty of any such attempt.

The first objection is that Hume's defence depends on establishing inductive correlations between past instances of testimony and the truth of beliefs successfully communicated. But there is, in fact, much less evidence available to individuals than Hume supposes. Summarizing Coady, Peter Lipton puts the point thus:

> Hume's discussion systematically hides the fact that our evidential base is far too slender to underwrite in this way even a small fraction of the testimony we rightly accept. Perhaps the main device Hume uses here is to appeal to the correlations we have observed to obtain between various types of testimony and the facts. This appeal to communal observation closes a vicious circle, since you can only in general know what others have observed on the basis of *their* testimony. The only evidence that you can legitimately appeal to consists of correlations between what you yourself have heard and what you yourself have seen, and this provides far less evidence than would be required to support inductively the wide range and variety of generalisations that would cover all the unchecked testimony you actually accept. (Lipton 1998: 15)

A second line of objection is that the observations that an individual might make are not themselves free from past testimony and thus cannot be used to justify it independently. The quickest argument for this is that observations are framed in language and language is taught through testimony, given the definition above. One might argue that observation *statements* are linguistic and thus depend on the teaching of language by testimony. Equally, one might argue that observation itself is conceptually structured by a learned language and hence depends on past testimony. For either reason, there seems to be no way that one could frame relevant observations of successful knowledge transfer by testimony without having acquired, also by testimony, a language.

Thus it seems that there is little hope of offering a non-question-begging justification of testimony, or an account of testimony in internalist terms. Instead, whatever local checks might be carried out, we have to take the general reliability of testimony as a whole on trust. Successfully learning something by testimony is simply hearing in another's utterance that something is the case and taking that at face value. While the ignorance or insincerity of a witness undermines such transmission of knowledge, one does not, and in general cannot, first ensure their knowledge and sincerity in non-question-begging non-testimony-based terms.

Defending an externalist account of testimony is beyond the scope of this book but we will outline a summary of one such account in order to show how it could be used to shed light on the communication of aspects, at least, of tacit knowledge. Because it is tailor made to fit our preferred response to Wittgenstein's regress argument and the idea that action is conceptually structured, the account we will outline is John McDowell's.

Like traditional internalists McDowell does think that reasons have an important role in knowledge. Internalists, however, construe justification as something under the complete control of a subject, although Gettier cases suggest that luck is needed to promote a justified belief to a truth. McDowell rejects the view that: "reason must be credited with a province within which it has absolute control over the acceptability of positions achievable by its exercise, without laying itself open to risk from an unkind world" (McDowell 1998a: 442). On his account, even to have a justification – a "standing in the space of reasons" – requires some luck. One is lucky not to be looking at an unrepresentative physiology or in distorting lighting conditions or not to be in the presence of a capricious lecturer. But given that initial luck, no further luck is required to transform one's situation-based justification into true belief and hence one has knowledge. This idea is clarified by three further points:

- A comparison with practical reason.
- An anti-intellectual view of knowledge.
- An anti-reductionist view of the kind of philosophical insight needed in epistemology.

First, McDowell's proposal about our authority over our justification can be compared with a view of practical reasoning that already seems natural:

> The concept of what one does, understood as applying to one's interventions in the objective world, cannot mark out a sphere within which one has total control, immune to luck. It is only if we recoil from this into a fantasy of a sphere within which one's control is total that it can seem to follow that what one genuinely achieves is less than one's interventions in the objective world. (McDowell 1998a: 406, n.16)

Although our actions are the result of an interplay between, on the one hand, our beliefs and desires and, on the other, contingent or lucky features of the world which shape the possibilities for action, this is not taken in general to undermine our responsibility for our actions. Likewise our epistemic status.

Second, McDowell combines his view that having an epistemological standing depends at least in part on a relation to the world with an anti-intellectualist view of knowledge. It can be brought out by considering his attitude to a contrast between what he terms "mediated" and "unmediated epistemic standings". If it existed, an unmediated standing would be one which was foundational, or an "absolute starting point" of the sort hoped for by the Logical Positivists. That, sadly, is mere myth and leaves only mediated standings, by contrast, which stand in rational relations to each other. Even perception is a "mediated standing" because observation is theory dependent.

On one view of them, a mediated standing in the space of reasons is one for which an *argument* can be given, by the knower, from premises which do not beg any questions to a claim to knowledge. The argument might thus move from premises about how things look – their mere appearances about which one supposedly cannot be mistaken – to a conclusion to the effect that the subject can see that things really are thus and so. On this view, the space of reasons in general consists in the explicit arguments subjects can offer for their beliefs.

McDowell does not deny that there are *some* arguments relevant to one's epistemological status. If a subject sees (or has seen; or hears; or has heard) that something is the case, then it must be the case. Furthermore, to be a subject capable of knowledge at all, he or she must be sensitive to the power of reasons. But he does reject the idea that the epistemic position of seeing or hearing that something is the case can be *reduced to* or *constructed out of* something more basic via an argument that the subject of the position could provide.

In the case of testimony, it is particularly clear that a hearer is not in general in a position to rule out possible sources of error in what a speaker says or other factors that would imply that a speaker does not *know* what he or she affirms. Thus, in general, a hearer cannot provide an *argument* from what he or she hears said to its truth. Nevertheless when unbiased by mistaken assumptions about the nature of knowledge, it seems clear that testimony can indeed provide knowledge.[4]

McDowell's response to this tension is to suggest that the attempt to give a reductionist account of having justification is mistaken:

> The idea is, then, that one's epistemic standing with respect to what one comes to know by testimony consists in one's, say, having heard from one's informant that that is how things are; not in the compellingness of an argument to the conclusion that that is how things are from the content of a lesser informational state. (1998a: 436)

So – and this is the *third* point flagged above – the tenor of the analysis runs in the opposite direction to what is normal. Rather than attempting to build up an analysis of knowledge by asking what more primitive concepts need to be combined to yield it, he takes knowledge to be a basic concept and then explores its relation to other concepts such as reason, justification and truth.

TESTIMONY AND TACIT KNOWLEDGE

With that brief outline of an externalist account of testimony in place, we can now return to the question of how it would apply to the sharing of tacit knowledge: of context-dependent practical knowledge-how. Can it shed light on the empirical claims made by Collins and Evans that mastering the language associated with a practice can, somehow, carry with it a form of practical understanding of the practice, as measured by their imitation games?

First, combined with the view set out in this book of tacit knowledge as context-dependent practical knowledge-how, the above sketch of testimony avoids the potential worry that tacit knowledge cannot be transferred because the basis or justification for tacit knowledge cannot be transferred in mere demonstrations, that it needs, additionally, the direct transfer of relevant experiences. That worry can be turned aside, however. Given that even tacit knowledge can be *expressed* – in practical demonstrations – then it can also be shared. When all goes well, context-dependent practical knowledge can be expressed in something like the way that context-independent general knowledge can be expressed and shared. In the face of Wittgenstein's regress argument in Chapters 3 and 4, this was a key reason for preserving the *principle of articulacy*:

PA   All knowledge can be articulated, either in context-independent terms or in context-dependent terms

rather than its opposing *principle of inarticulacy*:

PI   There can be knowledge that cannot be articulated.

If grasp of a rule is a matter of having to "guess the essential drift" of explanations (as Wittgenstein puts it), if understanding cannot be articulated, this puts the transfer of knowledge under threat.

There are some differences, however, between the transfer of context-dependent practical knowledge and context-independent theoretical knowledge. Consider the communication of a particular type of tennis shot likely to outfox a particular player. If the type of shot has a name (such as "American twist"), a non-playing coach can communicate knowledge by saying "you can beat him if you use the American twist". In an appropriate context, a player with the relevant understanding can acquire theoretical knowledge of how to defeat an opponent, even if there will never be any such match, by attending to these words.

If the necessary shot is a specific variant of the American twist serve, it may be necessary for the coach to demonstrate its execution either by showing examples of other players using it or by performing it herself. That, however, can still be sufficient, in the right context, for the transfer of *theoretical* knowledge of how to defeat the particular opponent. A non-playing spectator may be able to learn from the coach's demonstrations what the winning shot looks like and thus be able to recognize it in other games while unable to play it herself.[5]

Both such cases can also transfer *practical* knowledge of how to defeat the opponent, providing that the player has the right context of other know-how. For a skilled player, with an armoury of practical knowledge of shots, simply knowing *which* shot to play in combination with a prior knowledge of *how* to play that shot (among others) is sufficient for the player to have practical knowledge of how to defeat his opponent. For an intermediate player, without such an extensive prior armoury, the coaching will need to combine demonstrative knowledge of which shot to play with a practical demonstration of how to play the shot. But, if it is a minor variant on a familiar basic shot, the player's "glad start" and confident claim that he knows how to do it may be enough. For a student player, by contrast, instruction may require lengthy practice and feedback by the coach and the student's claims of self-knowledge may not be reliable.

Given the different relations between practical and theoretical knowledge and luck, outlined in Chapter 2, the transfer of knowledge through its expression will behave differently in both cases. Nevertheless, there is no principled block to its testimonial transmission.

Second, while tacit knowledge can be transmitted through testimony when all goes well, things can go less well. Such cases are what Collins and Evans's account of interactional expertise highlights. Non-playing tennis commentators, for example, will not be able to gather as much from a demonstration of tennis skills as players. Even lengthy practice and feedback may not be enough to transfer practical skills. In such cases, however, sedentary commentators can still acquire *something* from practical demonstrations. They may learn that a serve that looks like *that!* can outfox a particular player without being able to begin to do it themselves. If so, their ability subsequently to pass this knowledge on will be hampered. Even if they have accurate visual memories for what the correct movements look like, they will need to make use of pictures or film clips to express what they know.

The imitation game, deployed by Collins and Evans to test interactional expertise, restricts things still further. The resources available to an interactional expert to express her expertise are, in effect, context-independent; although any particular situation will suggest context-dependent possibilities of expression. So both commentators and players have somehow to translate what they know – and what, under other circumstances, they could articulate through pictures or through practical demonstrations, respectively – into the reduced "vocabulary" of the imitation game. Still, there is reason to think that those whose knowledge of tennis (whether that of the commentator or the player) could be articulated in a variety of context-dependent terms will have more to say than those who have always been restricted to context-independent knowledge. Knowledge whose expression requires access to tennis rackets and balls, or films of others playing (or for chick-sexing, access to chicks) does not cease to exist in the absence of those forms of expression. And so those with knowledge that is context-dependent have greater resources than those without, even in the context of the imitation game.

In combination with the idea that even context-dependent knowledge can be articulated, testimony suggests a simpler account of the results of the imitation game than Collins himself proposes with his talk of "subtle changes to the metaphorical muscles, and metaphorical nerve pathways of the spoken language and in the, metaphorical, 'synapses of society'". It is not so much that practical understanding is carried by knowledge of the language of a practice as by judgements made about that practice which can be passed on or transferred through testimony. Language offers opportunities to share context-dependent judgements with a varying degree of transparency. While echoes of it can also be overheard in less than optimal circumstances, practical knowledge can be fully demonstrated by skilled teachers to pupils with the right capacities to grasp what is articulated. Although we know more than we can tell, we can articulate, and hence (in principle) transmit to others, all that we know.

CONCLUSION

In this book, we have outlined a conception of tacit knowledge as context-dependent, conceptually structured, practical knowledge. We have taken as two key clues Polanyi's early emphasis on the importance of personal knowledge as "active comprehension of things known, an action that requires skill" and his slogan that we can know more than we can tell. Tacit knowledge is practical knowledge or know-how. Further, in some sense at least, it resists being put into words. Respecting this second element is more difficult than the first, however, because of a dilemma that an account of tacit knowledge faces.

Any plausible account of tacit knowledge must respect its status both as tacit and as knowledge. But if one addresses the former by adopting what we called the *principle of inarticulacy* and assuming that there are states of subjects that are cognitive but which are not articulable, then one makes a mystery of *how* such states should count as knowledge. What is the content of such knowledge? For that reason, we have defended a view of tacit knowledge according to which it does have a content, but not one that can be captured in context-independent or purely linguistic terms. The articulation of the content requires practical demonstration. But, following late-twentieth-century developments in the philosophy of language and thought, this does not imply that the content lies outside the space of concepts.

Thus the truth of Polanyi's slogan is that one knows more than one can put into words without the aid both of one's environment and one's skills, whether bodily or not. With that aid, however, what one knows *can* be articulated. Articulation, however, is not codification. Tacit knowledge is a species of the genus of knowledge without being either an instance of context-independent knowledge-that nor even context-dependent knowledge-that. Its articulation – what a subject with it knows – is also practical. There is no prospect of a reduction of it in favour of either form of theoretical knowledge.

This emphasis on the personal or the practical is what underpins the connection between Polanyi and the other major figures in this book, all of whom can be seen as proposing a regress argument that prioritizes knowing how over knowing that. But again, it would be a mistake to interpret their regress arguments as subsuming theoretical under practical knowledge, a reduction in the opposite direction to that mentioned above. An intellectualist attempt to ground practical know-how in the entertaining of inner signposts or the purely contemplative grasp of a proposition fails; but this does not show that what is grasped is ineffable and merely a matter of tacit doing instead. What one knows, when one knows how to go on, can be articulated, demonstrated, and thus seen and heard in the moves one makes and the words one utters. Nothing need be silent or hidden in the sense of inexpressible.

We have thus attempted to balance one further set of opposing constraints. Tacit knowledge is both ordinary and surprising. It is ordinary because it is merely a practical species of knowledge, sharing with the rest of that genus a reliability, although not infallibility, which goes beyond luck, although in this case that is based on a standing capacity or skill rather than any other form of justification (and thus threatened by distinct variants of Gettier cases, for examples). Its tacit status depends on the fundamental nature of its context-dependence rather than a deeper mystery. Thus, for example, the famous cases of chick-sexing and Polynesian navigation do indeed seem to be forms of tacit knowledge in our sense because an explanation of the knowledge involved has been given in context (with chicks or on the water) and involves the exercise of skills not easily shared with an unskilled audience. The subjects or knowers of such knowledge need not be baffled by their inability to offer explanations in general terms to count as having tacit knowledge. It need not be as mysterious as these examples are generally taken to suggest it is.

But it remains surprising and even subversive in a culture in which explicit codification is taken increasingly to be the norm. As empirical examples discussed have indicated, even if there are no principled barriers to the transmission of tacit knowledge, its personal nature can sometimes make its transfer difficult. Particular demands may be made on an audience who may need to have particular educated sensitivities and skills. While, as we hold, tacit knowledge can be articulated without remainder, it cannot be codified without loss. That fact can seem threatening in a culture that assumes that knowledge and expertise can be fully accounted for in a manual or a guideline. In that context, a defence of tacit knowledge is both a contribution to the rebalancing of views of knowledge and a defence of the exercise of good judgement.

NOTES

1. THREE SOURCES FOR TACIT KNOWLEDGE

1. The most frequently cited works in the following sections are abbreviated as follows: *PK = Personal Knowledge* (Polanyi 1958); *SM = The Study of Man* (Polanyi 1959); *KB = Knowing and Being* (Polanyi 1969); *TD = The Tacit Dimension* (Polanyi 2009).
2. For biographical details see Jha (2002: pt I).
3. Works of varying value include Allen (1990), Gill (2000, 2010), Jha (2002), Mitchell (2006), Prosch (1986), Scott (1985) and Scott and Moleski (2005).
4. Another is Meno's paradox of inquiry (of learning), to which Polanyi (in *TD*) presents his view of tacit knowledge as a solution.
5. See, for example, Brueckner (1994), discussed at length by Pritchard (2007).
6. For more on this see, for example, Reber (1976), Dulany *et al* (1984) and Reber *et al* (1985). For a useful overview of the phenomenon and its relation to "implicit" expressions of memory and knowledge see Schacter (1987).
7. Since the *ordo essendi* and the *ordo cognoscendi* are not really distinct, it turns out that Polanyi's solution to Meno's paradox (see note 4 above) is not that different from Plato's: we do not need to recollect *a priori* truths because the world is there to whisper them to us; although rather more work is required to make out what it is trying to say.
8. Grene is reporting criticisms made of Polanyi by Dreyfus in a three-way conversation.
9. However, it might give succour to the identity theorist struggling to make sense of topic neutralism.
10. See Burge (2010: 430) for related thoughts on the legitimacy of assuming an "armchair" understanding of the concept of perception (specifically, perceptual warrant).
11. See Prosch (1986: ch. 15) for a detailed (if unprepossessing) rebuttal of Harré's points.
12. For more detail see, for example, Pippin (1976).
13. See Schaper (1964).
14. Pendlebury acknowledges that this is a rather free interpretation, but does adduce some textual evidence.
15. For an explicit statement of this see, for example, Hanna (2005). See also Allais (2009).
16. For related criticisms of a different sort of "constructionalist" approach to subcognition see Ginsborg (2009).
17. To more fully elaborate a Kantian account of this requires attention to reflective judgement, in which "only the particular is given and judgement has to find the universal for it" (Kant 1987: 18–19).
18. We might want to contrast someone's possession of a recognitional concept (their ability to identify a kudu) with the concept possessed by someone who knows an

inordinate amount about kudu but would be unable to identify one in the field. But this contrast seems artificial: could one identify kudu without knowing something about their behaviour, seasonal colouring and so on. If much of this sort of thing goes into "recognizing" kudu then the sorts of the considerations Polanyi brings to bear on the synthesis involved in concept application seems more relevant: "Our conception of a tree … arises by the tacit integration of countless experiences of different trees and pictures and reports of still others … they are all used subsidiarily with a bearing on the conception of a tree" (*KB*: 191).

19. If it is not already clear from the line taken here, we should emphasize that, since we are interested in knowing, we are *not* taking a view on whether the content of experience is conceptual or nonconceptual. We will, however, return to the relation some might see between nonconceptual content and tacit knowing in Chapter 5.

20. For a similar view see Rorty (1979), and the responses of Dreyfus (1980) and Taylor (1980).

21. There is an interesting link between the "whole" that is grasped in tacit knowing for Polanyi and the metaphysical relation of "resultance" deployed by Dancy and (before him) Ross. Here's Ross: "An act that is right is right in virtue of its whole intrinsic nature and not of any part of it. In respect of certain elements in its nature it may be prima facie right and in respect of others prima facie wrong; whether it is actually right or wrong, and if it is wrong the degree of its wrongness, are determined only by its whole nature" (quoted in Dancy 1981: 368). From this perspective, the association of tacit knowledge with know-how amounts to what one might call cognitive particularism.

22. With the intention of denying that know-how is reducible to know-that one might challenge the view that there are any propositions at all. Although not his stated intention, Ryle (1929–30) offers both (i) an account (in a diagnostic spirit) of why, in retreat from subjectivism, one might reify the intentional objects of consciousness and – under the sway of Frege – invent the proposition as independent object, and (ii) a *reductio* against the plausibility of such objects.

23. Indeed, one might conclude that the account of know-how – like tacit knowledge for Polanyi – solves the Meno paradox: the knowledge Plato thought must be recollected because it could not be taught is knowledge how, not knowledge that (something which, under his tuition, the slave-boy comes to acquire). Although Ryle does not refer to it as such, the reference to what puzzled Socrates (Ryle 1945–6: 14) fits the bill.

24. See Ryle (1929–30) for early thoughts on how *not* to respond to this "trend".

25. For those inclined to object to an imputed attempt at "translation", note that in assimilating *Dasein* to *personhood* the target is the meaning of the latter.

26. *Being and Time* (Heidegger 1962) is referred to as *BT* hereafter, with the two sets of page references denoting the translated and original pagination, respectively.

27. Cf. contemporary "diagnosticians" like Clarke (1972) and Williams (1991). For a story influenced by Heidegger's views see Rorty (1979).

28. With Polanyi in mind, this is what Heidegger's solution to Meno's problem would look like.

29. Cf. Strawson (1966), and for criticisms Allison (2004) and Bird (1962).

30. For relevant interpretations of Heidegger see Han-Pile (2005).

31. For a critical discussion of Kant's use of time as the mediating element see Krausser (1976).

32. Reformulating Heidegger, the interesting question of the relationship between knowing how and knowing that is not the "logical" issue which "understands science with regard to its results" (true/valid propositions; *BT*: 357/408) but the "existential" issue concerning what it is about us that makes such inquiry possible.

33. The general criticism is rooted in Heidegger's own response to Husserl. See Dreyfus (1992: 34–6) for more detail.
34. Cf. Stroud's (1968) response to Strawson (1959). Rorty (1971) is a useful corrective.
35. Compare Davidson's transcendental response to cognate concerns: the very idea of a conceptual scheme makes no sense because (to simplify) constraints on interpretation determine that most of anyone's beliefs must be true. Now even in Davidson's terms, the fact that beliefs are not held to be usefully enumerable ([1983] 1990: 121) raises concerns. Viewed from a Heideggerian perspective, however, we can see the problem: belief, as a theoretical term, is categorically inappropriate for describing the necessary fundamental nature of worldly being. In this respect, Davidson's later account in terms of triangulation (1991) is more appropriate; where, as Rorty puts it, the norms "so to speak, hover(ing) over the whole process" relating self, others, and world (2000: 376).

2. KNOWING HOW AND KNOWING THAT

1. We shall use "that!" to signify a demonstrative utterance or thought.
2. Bengson and Moffett (2007: 33) suggest that in the latter case there is some sort of entailment from the knowledge to the ability even if there are exceptions with large numbers and so on.
3. Some theoretical knowledge-how can be given fully linguistic, context-independent specification. By contrast, all practical knowledge-how, or know-how, relies on a demonstrative element.

3. WITTGENSTEIN'S REGRESS ARGUMENT AND PERSONAL KNOWLEDGE

1. Moore himself reserves the idea of "tacit" knowledge for something distinct, about which he remains agnostic.
2. Ryle (1949: 112–47) shows a similar sensitivity to this distinction, which will also reappear in the discussion of Searle in the next chapter.
3. A focus on the nature of knowledge itself rather than just limits on what we can know is also present in the discussions of Ryle and Polanyi in Chapter 1.
4. That justifiable conclusion is not even as strong as the claim that when we speak of causation we do not *mean* such a relation. To reach this further claim we would require additional argument, since the implication from what we cannot know to what we cannot mean is by no means straightforward. Hume deploys an empiricist semantics to ground this move.
5. This is again akin to Hume's account where individual causal relations depend on general relations of constant conjunction.
6. According to a resolute reading, Wittgenstein cannot and does not attempt to offer metaphysical insights through strictly nonsensical assertions. Nonsense is simply nonsense (Conant 2000).
7. Whether a notion of correctness can actually be recovered is disputed.

4. BEING IN THE BACKGROUND

1. It is not clear what "it" denotes here. Consider a coin placed between two others: one might say that *it* has the position *it* does (being in the middle) only relative to the other coins. But the "it" here is independently specifiable – there are criteria for picking out coins independently of their position in a pattern. But how does this apply to

the state in question? There are no criteria for picking out a state independently of its position, so no way of giving content to the thought that there's something to possess something here (an "it").

2. Searle does invoke phenomenological considerations when it comes to the "logical" account of intentional causation: the experience of acting (intentionally) is the experience of one's bodily movements being caused by {the representation of the satisfaction conditions for fulfilling one's intention, where these conditions include that the intention brings about the action}, and the content in curly brackets is the intention in action.

3. In this respect, note other responses to the "we–I" reduction such as that of Gold & Sugden (2007), claiming "I" and "group" are the primitives. See Gold & Harbour (2012) for discussion of "ambiguity" around what "primitive" connotes.

4. Searle quotes an example from Werner Kummer's *Primate Societies*: Imo the macaque (Kummer 1971: 118).

5. Searle mentions what we might call the no-account account of Wittgenstein, but rejects it as unsatisfying because it does not tell us what the role of the structure of constitutive rules is (by which he means causal role). We indirectly address this below.

6. This is offered as part of Searle's "logical analysis" of how the component movements of, say, an intention to bowl a googly, can have intentionality in spite of the fact that it is only the overall act that has conditions of satisfaction and that can consequently be said to result from an intention in action. For a "phenomenological" response to this point see Dreyfus (1993).

7. As a phenomenologist, Dreyfus ought not to be antagonistic to this suggestion (cf. Dreyfus 1991: 4; 1992: 56–7), since the Background has a transcendental structure that can be arrived at by analysing its manifestations.

8. On this view, the question of whether such "considerations" are empirical or transcendental clearly does not arise: they are reminders of what practices of certain sorts involve. From this perspective, the debate between Searle and Dreyfus over the respective merits of phenomenology and logical analysis (and in particular over whom is doing what) becomes otiose. See Searle (2000, 2001); Dreyfus (1993, 2000, 2001).

9. As noted above, Dreyfus sometimes makes it difficult to see the difference and/or relation between the phenomenological characterizations of the Background (as being-in- and understanding-being-in-the-world) and of the level of primitive intentionality. Our assumption in what follows is that invocation of skills is intended *either* to "remind" us of the diversity of normative practices *or* to explain how conceptual content is possible. Only the latter is important here.

5. SECOND NATURES

1. Bermúdez & Cahen (2011) offer a useful overview.

2. See for example Bermúdez (2007) and Toribio (2008). For responses to his critics see Heck (2007).

3. This is not to say we disagree with the apparent moral of Speaks's paper, which is that since no convincing case can be made either for nonconceptual content or against it, and since, moreover, the idea of nonconceptual is essentially contrastive, we ought not to set too much store by content-talk per se.

4. For a discussion of this point in relation to Hanna's article see Bowman (2011).

5. Kelly takes these cases to express the same point, but it should be noted that Peacock's has a particularly Fregean setting. See Crane (1988) for another example. Speaks has a useful discussion (2005: 10–13).

6. Kelly attempts to show that this possession condition is insufficient to explain the content of experience but it turns on the rather counter-intuitive claim that one cannot possess the demonstrative concept of a shade even when one is confronted directly with that shade in experience and can refer to it as *that* shade. (Kelly 2001b: 412, n.27).

7. See Shieber (2010) for a (conceptualist) response to Kelly that focuses on defending McDowell's account of concept possession. Since that is not our primary concern we omit a more detailed discussion.

8. Needless to say, there is no suggestion that *a* and *b* are "independently determinable properties".

9. On the revisionary/descriptive distinction see Strawson (1959).

10. See Cappuccio (2010) for an overview of the literature in this area.

11. In this respect he deviates little from Dreyfus, as we will see in the next section.

12. Kelly (2002) gives a more detailed account of the relation between grasping and motor intentionality.

13. See Dreyfus (2004) on Merleau-Ponty. In addition, various online papers on Merleau-Ponty can be accessed through http://philpapers.org/s/Hubert%20L.%20Dreyfus.

14. One could claim that rules can only be followed in the first place because of background skills, but that either reinforces some connection between the two levels or gestures towards the rule-regress. In neither case need the "phenomenology" be invoked.

15. Whether or not one *should* be true to the phenomenon is a point of dispute between Searle and Dreyfus. For reasons why one might disdain fidelity to the phenomenon of expertise, see Luntley (2009).

16. For a similarly Gadamerian view, although from a more pragmatist perspective, see Rorty (1979).

17. Presumably this stands over and against "unsituated" normativity; but this involves characterizing the reflective in just the way that leads to a restrictive understanding of the "unreflective".

18. For more on this see Burnyeat (1980), Cooper (1988), McDowell (1998a: essays 2 and 9) and Forman (2008). For McDowell on second nature see Bübner (2002) and McDowell (2002).

19. Rouse offers a way of avoiding the empiricist constraints on McDowell's approach by supplementing a "top-down" conceptualism with a recognition that "discursive expression extends practical/perceptual intra-action with the world all the way up" (Rouse 2005: 58).

6. TACIT KNOWLEDGE AND LANGUAGE

1. For example, "a sentence coupling a name with a predicate is true iff the object denoted by the name satisfies the predicate" (Evans 1981: 123).

2. The fact that there are 20 rather than 21, including the axiom of compositionality, is the subject of a criticism by Wright and response by Davies that need not detain us (Davies 1987).

3. Of course, knowledge of an axiomatized structural theory of meaning for a natural language cannot be a matter of explicit knowledge for most speakers. If it were, the project would not be as difficult as it has proved.

4. Likewise, one may not be able to frame an *argument* from the nature of the lighting conditions to the reliability of appearances, but, in good lighting, seeing how things look can furnish one with knowledge.

5. Such a recognitional ability is a case of practical knowledge of how to recognize it, but, in this case, merely theoretical knowledge of the serve.

BIBLIOGRAPHY

Allais, L. 2009. "Kant, Non-conceptual Content and the Representation of Space". *Journal of the History of Philosophy* **47**(3): 383–413.

Allen, R. 1990. *Polanyi*. London: Claridge Press.

Allison, H. E. 2004. *Kant's Transcendental Idealism: An Interpretation and Defense*, rev. and enlarged edn. New Haven, CT: Yale University Press.

Aristotle 2004. *De Anima*, H. Lawson-Tancred (trans.). London: Penguin.

Aristotle 2009. *The Nichomachean Ethics*, L. Brown (ed.), D. Ross (trans.). London: Penguin.

BBC Radio 4 2008. "Thinking Allowed". Broadcast 6 February. London: BBC Radio 4.

Bengson, J. & M. Moffett 2007. "Know-how and Concept Possession". *Philosophical Studies* **136**: 31–57.

Bermúdez, J. 2007. "What is at Stake in the Debate about Nonconceptual Content?". *Philosophical Perspectives* **21**(1): 55–72.

Bermúdez, J. & A. Cahen 2011. "Nonconceptual Mental Content". *Stanford Encyclopedia of Philosophy*, summer edition, http://plato.stanford.edu/archives/sum2011/entries/content-nonconceptual (accessed 15 November 2012).

Bird, G. 1962. *Kant's Theory of Knowledge*. London: Routledge.

Blackburn, S. 1984. "The Individual Strikes Back". *Synthese* **58**: 281–301.

Blackburn, S. 1993. *Essays in Quasi-Realism*. Oxford: Clarendon Press.

Bowman, B. 2011. "A Conceptualist Reply to Hanna's Kantian Non-Conceptualism". *International Journal of Philosophical Studies* **19**(3): 417–46.

Brandom, R. 1994. *Making it Explicit*. Cambridge, MA: Harvard University Press.

Brueckner, A. 1994. "The Structure of the Skeptical Argument". *Philosophy and Phenomenological Research* **54**: 827–35.

Bübner, R. 2002. "*Bildung* and Second Nature". In *Reading McDowell on Mind and World*, N. Smith (ed.), 209–16. London: Routledge.

Burge, T. 2010. *Origins of Objectivity*. Oxford: Oxford University Press.

Burnyeat, M. F. 1980. "Aristotle on Learning to Be Good". In *Essays on Aristotle's Ethics*, A. O. Rorty (ed.), 69–92. Berkeley, CA: University of California Press.

Byrne, B. 2005. "Three Notions of Tacit Knowledge". *Agora: Papeles de Filosofía* **23**: 61–85.

Cappuccio, M. 2010. "Mirror Neurons and Skilful Coping: Motor Intentionality between Sensorimotor and Ideo-motor Schemata in Goal-Directed Actions". In *Research on Scientific Research*, R. Pietrobon & M. Maldonato (eds), 59–100. Eastbourne: Sussex University Press.

Carnap, R. 1967. *The Logical Structure of the World and Pseudoproblems in Philosophy*, R. A. George (trans.). London: Routledge.

Cardoso-Leite, P. & A. Gorea 2010. "On the Perceptual/Motor Dissociation: A Review of Concepts, Theory, Experimental Paradigms and Data Interpretations". *Seeing Perceiving* **23**(2): 89–151.

Carroll, L. 1905. "What the Tortoise Said to Achilles". *Mind* **4**: 289–90.

Cavell, S. 1976. "The Availability of Wittgenstein's Later Philosophy". In his *Must We Mean What We Say?* Cambridge: Cambridge University Press, 44–72.

Chomsky, N. 1980. *Rules and Representations.* New York: Columbia University Press.

Clarke, T. 1972. "The Legacy of Skepticism". *Journal of Philosophy* **68**: 754–69.

Coady, A. 1992. *Testimony: A Philosophical Study.* Oxford: Clarendon Press.

Collins, H. 1985. *Changing Order: Replication and Induction in Scientific Practice.* London: Sage.

Collins, H. 2010a. *Tacit and Explicit Knowledge.* Chicago, IL: University of Chicago Press.

Collins, H. 2010b. "Tacit Knowledge: You Don't Know How Much You Know". *New Scientist* (31 May): 30–31.

Collins, H. & R. Evans 2007. *Rethinking Experience.* Chicago, IL: University of Chicago Press

Conant, J. 2000. "Elucidation and Nonsense in Frege and Early Wittgenstein". In *The New Wittgenstein*, A. Crary & R. Read (eds), 174–217. London: Routledge.

Crane, T. 1988. "The Waterfall Illusion". *Analysis* **48**: 142–7.

Dancy, J. 1981. "On Moral Properties". *Mind* **90**: 367–85.

Davidson, D. [1983] 1990. "A Coherence Theory of Truth and Knowledge". In *Reading Rorty*, A. Malachowski (ed.), 120–34. Oxford: Blackwell.

Davidson, D. 1984. *Inquiries into Truth and Interpretation.* Oxford: Oxford University Press.

Davidson, D. 1991. "Three Varieties of Knowledge". In *A. J. Ayer: Memorial Essays* (Royal Institute of Philosophy Supplement 30), A. Phillips Griffiths (ed.), 153–66. Cambridge: Cambridge University Press.

Davies, M. 1986. "Tacit Knowledge and the Structure of Thought and Language". In *Meaning and Interpretation*, C. Travis (ed.), 127–58. Oxford: Blackwell.

Davies, M. 1987. "Tacit Knowledge and Semantic Theory: Can a Five Percent Difference Matter?". *Mind* **96**: 441–62.

Dennett, D. 1984. "Cognitive Wheels: The Frame Problem in Artificial Intelligence". In *Minds, Machines and Evolution*, C. Hookway (ed.), 129–51. Cambridge: Cambridge University Press.

Dennett, D. 1991. "Real Patterns". *Journal of Philosophy* **88**(1): 27–51.

Descartes, R. 1986. *Meditations on First Philosophy.* Cambridge: Cambridge University Press.

Dobzhansky, T. 1955. "The Fate of Biological Sciences in Russia". In *Proceedings of the Hamburg Congress on Science and Freedom*, Congress for Cultural Freedom (ed.), 212–23. Boston, MA: Beacon Press.

Dretske, F. 1988. *Explaining Behavior.* Cambridge, MA: MIT Press.

Dreyfus, H. L. 1980. "Holism and Hermeneutics". *Review of Metaphysics* **34**(1): 3–23.

Dreyfus, H. L. 1991. *Being-in-the-World.* Cambridge, MA: MIT Press.

Dreyfus, H. L. 1992. *What Computers Still Can't Do.* Cambridge, MA: MIT Press.

Dreyfus, H. L. 1993. "Heidegger's Critique of Husserl's (and Searle's) Account of Intentionality". *Social Research* **60**(1): 17–38.

Dreyfus, H. L. 2000. "Responses". See Wrathall & Malpas (2000), 313–50.

Dreyfus, H. L. 2001. "Phenomenological Description Versus Rational Reconstruction". *Revue Internationale de Philosophie* **216**: 181–96.

Dreyfus, H. L. 2004. "A Phenomenology of Skill Acquisition as the Basis for a Merleau-Pontian Nonrepresentationalist Cognitive Science", http://istsocrates.berkeley.edu/~hdreyfus/pdf/MerleauPontySkillCogSci.pdf (accessed 21 November 2012).

Dreyfus, H. L. 2005. "Overcoming the Myth of the Mental: How Philosophers Can Profit from the Phenomenology of Everyday Expertise". *Proceedings and Addresses of the American Philosophical Association* **79**(2): 47–65.

Dreyfus, H. L. 2007a. "The Return of the Myth of the Mental". *Inquiry* **50**(4): 352–65.

Dreyfus, H. L. 2007b. "Response to McDowell". *Inquiry* **50**(4): 371–7.

Dulany, D. E., R. A. Carlson & G. I. Dewey 1984. "A Case of Syntactical Learning and Judgment: How Conscious and How Abstract?". *Journal of Experimental Psychology: General* **113**: 541–55.

Dummett, M. 1993. *The Seas of Language*. Oxford: Oxford University Press

Evans, G. 1975. "Identity and Predication". *Journal of Philosophy* **72**: 343–63.

Evans, G. 1981. "Semantic Theory and Tacit Knowledge". In *Wittgenstein: To Follow a Rule* S. H. Holtzman & C. M. Leitch (eds), 118–40. London: Routledge & Kegan Paul.

Evans, G. 1982. *The Varieties of Reference*. Oxford: Clarendon Press.

Fodor, J. 2008. *LOT 2: The Language of Thought Revisited*. Oxford: Oxford University Press.

Forman, D. 2008. "Autonomy as Second Nature: On McDowell's Aristotelian Naturalism". *Inquiry* **51**(6): 563–80.

Fotion, N. 2000. *John Searle*. Teddington: Acumen.

Gadamer, H.-G. 1992. *Truth and Method*, J. Weinsheimer & D. G. Marshall (trans.). New York: Crossroad.

Gellatly, A. (ed.) 1986. *The Skilful Mind*. Milton Keynes: Open University Press.

Gettier, E. L. 1963. "Is Justified True Belief Knowledge?". *Analysis* **23**: 121–3.

Gibson, J. J. 1977. "The Theory of Affordances". In *Perceiving, Acting, and Knowing*, R. Shaw & J. Bransford (eds), 67–82. Hillsdale, NJ: Lawrence Erlbaum.

Gibson, J. J. 1979. *The Ecological Approach to Visual Perception*. Hillsdale, NJ: Lawrence Erlbaum.

Gill, J. H. 2000. *The Tacit Mode: Michael Polanyi's Postmodern Philosophy*. Albany, NY: SUNY Press.

Gill, J. H. 2010. *Deep Postmodernism: Whitehead, Wittgenstein, Merleau-Ponty, and Polanyi*. Albany, NY: Prometheus.

Ginet, C. 1975. *Knowledge, Perception and Memory*. Dordrecht: Reidel.

Ginsborg, H. 2009. "Was Kant a Nonconceptualist?". *Philosophical Studies* **137**(1): 65–77.

Ginsborg, H. 2011. "Primitive Normativity and Skepticism about Rules". *Journal of Philosophy* **108**(5): 227–54.

Gold, N & D. Harbour 2012. "Cognitive Primitives of Collective Intentions: Linguistic Evidence of Our Mental Ontology". *Mind and Language* **27**(2): 109–34.

Gold, N. & R. Sugden 2007. "Collective Intentions and Team Agency". *Journal of Philosophy* **104**: 109–37.

Goodale, M. A. & A. D. Milner 1992. "Separate Visual Pathways for Perception and Action". *Trends in Neurosciences* **15**: 20–25.

Goodale, M. A. & A. D. Milner 1995. *The Visual Brain in Action*. Oxford: Oxford University Press.

Grene, M. 1961. "The Logic of Biology". In *The Logic of Personal Knowledge: Essays Presented to Michael Polanyi on his Seventieth Birthday, 11th March, 1961*, P. Ignotus *et al.* (eds), 191–205. London: Routledge & Kegan Paul.

Grene, M. 1977. "Tacit Knowing: Grounds for a Revolution in Philosophy". *Journal of the British Society for Phenomenology* **8**(3): 164–71.

Guignon, C. (ed.) 1993. *The Cambridge Companion to Heidegger*. Cambridge: Cambridge University Press.

Hacker, P. M. S. 1972. *Insight and Illusion*. Oxford: Oxford University Press.

Hanna, R. 2005. "Kant and Nonconceptual Content". *European Journal of Philosophy* **13**(2): 247–90.

Hanna, R. 2011a. "Beyond the Myth of the Myth: A Kantian Theory of Non-Conceptual Content". *International Journal of Philosophical Studies* **19**(3): 323–98.

Hanna, R. 2011b. "Kant's Non-Conceptualism, Rogue Objects, and The Gap in the B Deduction". *International Journal of Philosophical Studies* **19**(3): 399–415.

Han-Pile, B. 2005. "Early Heidegger's Appropriation of Kant". In *A Companion to Heidegger*, H. Dreyfus & M. Wrathall (eds), 80–101. Oxford: Blackwell.

Harré, R. 1977. "The Structure of Tacit Knowledge". *Journal of the British Society for Phenomenology* **8**(3): 172–7.

Hattiangadi, A. 2007. *Oughts and Thoughts: Rule-Following and the Normativity of Content*. Oxford: Clarendon Press.

Heck, R. 2000. "Nonconceptual Content and the "Space of Reasons". *Philosophical Review* **109**: 483–524.

Heck, R. 2007. "Are There Different Kinds of Content?". In *Contemporary Debates in the Philosophy of Mind*, J. Cohen & B. McLaughlin (eds), 117–38. Oxford: Blackwell.

Heidegger, M. 1962. *Being and Time*, J. Macquarrie & E. Robinson (trans.). Oxford: Blackwell.

Heidegger, M. 1984. *The Metaphysical Foundations of Logic*, M. Heim (trans.). Bloomington, IN: Indiana University Press.

Heidegger, M. 1988. *The Basic Problems of Phenomenology*, A. Hofstadter (trans.). Bloomington, IN: Indiana University Press.

Heidegger, M. 1997a. *Kant and the Problem of Metaphysics*, R. Taft (trans.). Bloomington, IN: Indiana University Press.

Heidegger, M. 1997b. *Phenomenological Interpretation of Kant's* Critique of Pure Reason, P. Emad & L. Maly (trans.). Bloomington, IN: Indiana University Press.

Hume, D. 1967. *A Treatise of Human Nature*, L. A. Selby-Bigge (ed.). Oxford: Oxford University Press.

Hume, D. 1975. *Enquiries Concerning the Human Understanding and Concerning the Principles of Morals*. Oxford: Clarendon Press.

Ignotus, P. *et al.* (eds) 1961. *The Logic of Personal Knowledge: Essays Presented to Michael Polanyi on his Seventieth Birthday*, 11th March, 1961. London: Routledge & Kegan Paul.

Ismael, J. T. 2007. *The Situated Self*. Oxford: Oxford University Press.

Jha, J. R. 2002. *Reconsidering Michael Polanyi's Philosophy*. Pittsburgh, PA: University of Pittsburgh Press.

Johnson, M. 2007. *The Meaning of the Body*. Chicago, IL: University of Chicago Press.

Jonhannessen, K. S. 1991. "Rule Following, Intransitive Understanding and Tacit Knowledge—An Investigation of the Wittgensteinian Concept of Practice as Regards Tacit Knowledge". In *Essays in Pragmatic Philosophy*, vol. II, H. Hoibraaten (ed.), 101–27. Oslo: Norwegian University Press.

Kane, J. 1984. *Beyond Empiricism: Michael Polanyi Reconsidered*. New York: Peter Lang.

Kant, I. 1987. *Critique of Judgement*, W. S. Pluhar (trans.). Indianapolis, IN: Hackett.

Kant, I. 1996. *Critique of Pure Reason*, W. S. Pluhar (trans.). Indianapolis, IN: Hackett.

Kelly, S. D. 2000. "Grasping at Straws". See Wrathall & Malpas (2000), 162–77.

Kelly, S. D. 2001a. "The Non-conceptual Content of Perceptual Experience: Situation Dependence and Fineness of Grain". *Philosophy and Phenomenological Research* **62**: 601–8.

Kelly, S. D. 2001b. "Demonstrative Concepts and Experience". *The Philosophical Review* **110**(3): 397–420.

Kelly, S. D. 2002. "Merleau-Ponty on the Body". *Ratio* **15**: 376–91.

Krausser, P. 1976. "Kant's Schematism of the Categories and the Problem of Pattern Recognition". *Synthese* **33**(1; Perception I): 175–92.

Kripke, S. 1982. *Wittgenstein on Rules and Private Language*. Oxford: Blackwell.

Kummer, W. 1971. *Primate Societies*. Chicago, IL: Aldine Atherton.

Kusch, M. 2006. *A Sceptical Guide to Meaning and Rules: Defending Kripke's Wittgenstein*. Chesham: Acumen.

Lear, J. 1982. "Leaving the World Alone". *Journal of Philosophy* **79**: 382–403.

Lear, J. 1984. "The Disappearing 'We'". *Aristotelian Society Supplement* **58**: 219–58.

Lear, J. 1986. "Transcendental Anthropology". In *Subject Thought and Context*, P. Pettit & J. McDowell (eds), 267–98. Oxford: Clarendon Press.

LePore, E. & R. Van Gulick (eds) 1991. *John Searle and His Critics*. Oxford: Blackwell.

Lipton, P. 1998. "The Epistemology of Testimony". *Studies in History and Philosophy of Science* **29**: 1–31.

Luntley, M. 2009. "Understanding Expertise". *Journal of Applied Philosophy* **4**: 356–70.

McCleary, R. A. & R. S. Lazarus 1949. "Autonomic Discrimination without Awareness: An Interim Report". *Journal of Personality* **18**(2): 171–9.

McCleary, R. A. & R. S. Lazarus 1951. "Autonomic Discrimination without Awareness: A Study of Subception". *Psychological Review* **58**(2): 113–22.

McDowell, J. 1994. *Mind and World*. Cambridge, MA: Harvard University Press.

McDowell, J. 1998a. *Meaning, Knowledge and Reality*. Cambridge, MA: Harvard University Press.

McDowell, J. 1998b. "Precis of *Mind and World* and Reply to Commentators". *Philosophy and Phenomenological Research* **58**: 365–8.

McDowell, J. 2000. "Towards Rehabilitating Objectivity". In *Rorty and His Critics*, R. Brandom (ed.), 109–22. Oxford: Blackwell.

McDowell, J. 2002. "How Not to Read *Philosophical Investigations*: Brandom's Wittgenstein". Reprinted in his *The Engaged Intellect* (2009), 96–112. Cambridge, MA: Harvard University Press.

McDowell, J. 2003. "Hegel and the Myth of the Given". In *Das Interesse des Denkens: Hegel aus heutiger Sicht*, W. Welsch & K. Vieweg (eds), 75–88. Munich: Wilhelm Fink Verlag.

McDowell, J. 2007a. "What Myth?". *Inquiry* **50**(4): 338–51.

McDowell, J. 2007b. "Response to Dreyfus". *Inquiry* **50**(4): 366–70.

McDowell, J. 2009. *The Engaged Intellect*. Cambridge, MA: Harvard University Press.

Merleau-Ponty, M. 1962. *The Phenomenology of Perception*, C. Smith (trans.). London: Routledge.

Miller, A. 1997. "Tacit Knowledge". In *A Companion to the Philosophy of Language*, B. Hale & C. Wright (eds), 146–74. Oxford: Blackwell.

Miller, A. 2007. *Philosophy of Language*. London: Routledge.

Mitchell, M. 2006. *Michael Polanyi: The Art of Knowing*. Wilmington, DE: Intercollegiate Studies Institute.

Moore, A. W. 1997. *Points of View*. Oxford: Oxford University Press.

Moore, A. W. 2003. "Ineffability and Nonsense". *Aristotelian Society* **77**(suppl.): 169–93.

Mulhall, S. 1996. *Routledge Philosophy Guidebook to Heidegger and* Being and Time. London: Routledge.

Nagel, T. 1986. *The View from Nowhere*. Oxford: Oxford University Press.

Noë, A. 2005. "Against Intellectualism". *Analysis* **65**: 278–90.

Peacock, C. 1983. *Sense and Content*. Oxford: Oxford University Press.

Peacock, C. 1989. "Perceptual Content". In *Themes from Kaplan*, J. Almog, J. Perry & H. Wettstein (eds), 297–329. Oxford: Oxford University Press.

Peacock, C. 1998. "Nonconceptual Content Defended". *Philosophy and Phenomenological Research* **58**: 381–8.

Peacock, C. 2001a. "Does Perception Have a Nonconceptual Content?". *Journal of Philosophy* **98**: 239–64.

Peacock, C. 2001b. "Phenomenology and Nonconceptual Content". *Philosophy and Research* **62**: 609–16.

Pendlebury, M. 1995. "Making Sense of Kant's Schematism". *Philosophy and Phenomenological Research*, **55**(4): 777–97.

Pippin, R. B. 1976. "The Schematism and Empirical Concepts". Reprinted in *Immanuel Kant: Critical Assessments. Volume II: Kant's Critique of Pure Reason* (1992), R. F. Chadwick & C. Cazeaux (eds), 286–303. London: Routledge.

Polanyi. M. 1958. *Personal Knowledge*. Chicago, IL: University of Chicago Press.

Polanyi. M. 1959. *The Study of Man*. London: Routledge & Kegan Paul.

Polanyi. M. 1966. "The Logic of Tacit Inference". *Philosophy* **41**(155): 1–18.

Polanyi. M. 1969. *Knowing and Being: Essays by Michael Polanyi*, M. Grene (ed.). London: Routledge & Kegan Paul.

Polanyi. M. 2009. *The Tacit Dimension*, A. Sen (foreword). Chicago, IL: University of Chicago Press.

Poston, T. 2009. "Know How to be Gettiered?". *Philosophy and Phenomenological Research* **79**: 743–47.

Pritchard, D. 2007. *Epistemic Luck*. Oxford: Oxford University Press.

Prosch, H. 1986. *Michael Polanyi: A Critical Exposition*. Albany, NY: SUNY Press.

Ramsey, W. M. 2007. *Representation Reconsidered*. Cambridge: Cambridge University Press.

Reber, A. S. 1976. "Implicit Learning of Synthetic Languages: The Role of Instructional Set". *Journal of Experimental Psychology: Human Learning and Memory* **2**: 88–94.

Reber, A. S., A. Allen & S. Regan 1985. "Syntactical Learning and Judgment, Still Unconscious and Still Abstract: Comment on Dulany, Carlson, and Dewey". *Journal of Experimental Psychology: General* **114**: 17–24.

Rietveld, E. 2008a. "Situated Normativity: The Normative Aspect of Embodied Cognition in Unreflective Action". *Mind* **117**: 973–1001.

Rietveld, E. 2008b. "Unreflective Action: A Philosophical Contribution to Integrative Neuroscience". ILLC Dissertation Series DS-2008-05. PhD thesis, Department of Philosophy, University of Amsterdam.

Rietveld, E. 2010. "McDowell and Dreyfus on Unreflective Action". *Inquiry* **53**(2): 183–207.

Rizzolatti, G. & C. Sinigaglia 2007. "Mirror Neurons and Motor Intentionality". *Functional Neurology* **22**(4): 205–10.

Rorty, R. 1971. "Verificationism and Transcendental Arguments". *Noûs* **5**: 3–14.

Rorty, R. 1979. *Philosophy and the Mirror of Nature*. Princeton, NJ: Princeton University Press.

Rorty, R. 2000. "Response to Ramberg". In *Rorty and His Critics*, R. B. Brandom (ed.), 370–77. Oxford: Blackwell.

Rouse, J. 2000. "Coping and Its Contrasts". See Wrathall & Malpas (2000), 7–28.

Rouse, J. 2005. "Mind, Body, and World: Todes and McDowell on Bodies and Language". *Inquiry* **48**: 38–61.

Rust, J. 2009. *John Searle*. London: Continuum.

Ryle, G. 1929. "Review of *Sein und Zeit*". *Mind* **38**(151): 355–70.

Ryle, G. 1929–30. "Are There Propositions?". In *Proceedings of the Aristotelian Society* **30**: 91–126.

Ryle, G. 1931. "Mr Ryle on Propositions: Rejoinder". *Mind* **40**(159): 330–34.

Ryle, G. 1945–6. "Knowing How and Knowing That". *Proceedings of the Aristotelian Society* **46**: 1–16.

Ryle, G. 1949. *The Concept of Mind*. London: Hutchinson.

Schacter, D. L. 1987. "Implicit Memory: History and Current Status". Journal of Experimental Psychology: Learning, Memory, and Cognition, **13**(3): 501–18.

Schaper, E. 1964. "Kant's Schematism Reconsidered". *The Review of Metaphysics* **18**(2): 267–92.

Scott, D. 1985. *Everyman Revived: The Common Sense of Michael Polanyi*. Lewes: Book Guild.

Scott, W. T. & M. X. Moleski 2005. *Michael Polanyi, Scientist and Philosopher*. New York: Oxford University Press.

Searle, J. 1983. *Intentionality*. Cambridge: Cambridge University Press.

Searle, J. 1991. "Response: The Background of Intentionality and Action". In *John Searle and His Critics*, E. LePore & R. Van Gulick (eds), 289–300. Oxford: Blackwell.

Searle, J. 1992. *The Rediscovery of Mind*. Cambridge, MA: MIT Press.

Searle, J. 1995. *The Construction of Social Reality*. London: Hutchinson.

Searle, J. 2000. "The Limits of Phenomenology". See Wrathall & Malpas (2000), 71–92.

Searle, J. 2001–2. "Neither Phenomenological Description Nor Rational Reconstruction: Reply to Dreyfus". *Revue internationale de philosophie* **216**: 277–297

Searle, J. 2010. *Making the Social World: The Structure of Human Civilization*. Oxford: Oxford University Press.

Sellars, W. 1954. "Some Reflections on Language Games". *Philosophy of Science* **221**(3): 204–28.

Sellars, W. 1962. "Time and the World Order". In *Minnesota Studies in the Philosophy of Science*, vol. III, H. Feigl & G. Maxwell (eds), 527–616. Minneapolis, MN: University of Minnesota Press.

Sellars, W. 1968. *Science and Metaphysics*. London: Allen Lane.

Sellars, W. 1978. "The Role of the Imagination in Kant's Theory of Experience". In *Categories: A Colloquium*, H. W. Johnstone (ed.), 231–45. University Park, PA: Pennsylvania State University Press.

Sellars, W. 1997. *Empiricism and the Philosophy of Mind*, R. Rorty (intro.), R. Brandom (study guide). Cambridge, MA: Harvard University Press.

Sen, A. 2009. "Foreword". In *The Tacit Dimension*, M. Polanyi, vii–xvi. Chicago, IL: University of Chicago Press.

Sennett, R. 2008. *The Craftsman*. London: Penguin.

Shieber, J. 2010. "On the Possibility of Conceptually Structured Experience: Demonstrative Concepts and Fineness of Grain". *Inquiry* **53**(4): 383–97.

Smith, B. (ed.) 2003. *John Searle*. Cambridge: Cambridge University Press.

Snowdon, P. 2004. "Knowing How and Knowing That: A Distinction Reconsidered". *Proceedings of the Aristotelian Society* **104**: 1–29.

Sosa, E. 2007. *A Virtue Epistemology: Apt Belief and Reflective Knowledge*. Oxford: Clarendon Press.

Speaks, J. 2005. "Is there a Problem about Nonconceptual Content?" *Philosophical Review*, **114**(3): 359–98.

Stanley, J. 2011a. *Know How*. Oxford: Oxford University Press

Stanley, J. 2011b. "Knowing (How)" *Noûs* **45**: 207–38.

Stanley, J. & T. Williamson 2001. "Knowing How". *Journal of Philosophy* **97**: 411–44.

Strawson, P. F. 1959. *Individuals*. London: Methuen.

Strawson, P. F. 1966. *The Bounds of Sense*. London: Methuen.

Strawson, P. F. 1970. "Imagination and Perception". In *Experience and Theory*, L. Foster & J.W. Swanson (eds), 32–54. Amherst, MA: University of Massachusetts Press.

Stroud, B. 1968. "Transcendental Arguments". *Journal of Philosophy* **65**(9): 241–56.

Stroud, B. 1991. "The Background of Thought". In *John Searle and His Critics*, E. LePore & R. Van Gulick (eds), 245–58. Oxford: Blackwell.

Taylor, C. 1980. "Understanding in Human Science". *Review of Metaphysics* **34**(1): 25–38.

Tolman, E. C. 1932. *Purposive Behavior in Animals and Men*. New York: Appleton-Century-Crofts.

Toribio, J. 2008. "State versus Content: The Unfair Trial of Perceptual Nonconceptualism". *Erkenntnis* **69**(3): 351–61.

Travis, C. 2007. "Reason's Reach". *European Journal of Philosophy* **15**: 225–248.

Tsohatzidis, S. (ed.) 2007. *John Searle's Philosophy of Language*. Cambridge: Cambridge University Press.

van Grunsven, J. 2008. "Possibilities of Action in Heidegger and Merleau-Ponty: A Critique of Hubert Dreyfus's and Sean Kelly's Approach to Unreflective Freedom". *Women in Philosophy Annual Journal of Papers* **4**: 42–56.

Weber, M. 1946. *Essays in Sociology*, H. H. Girth & C. Wright Mills (eds, trans.). New York: Oxford University Press.

Wiggins, D. 1975. "Deliberation and Practical Reason". *Proceedings of the Aristotelian Society* **76**: 29–51.

Williams, B. 1981. "Wittgenstein and Idealism". In his *Moral Luck*, 144–63. Cambridge: Cambridge University Press.

Williams, M. 1991. *Unnatural Doubts*. Oxford: Blackwell.

Wittgenstein, L. 1953. *Philosophical Investigations*. Oxford: Blackwell.

Wittgenstein, L. 1969. *On Certainty*. Oxford: Blackwell.

Wrathall, M. & J. Malpas (eds) 2000. *Heidegger, Coping and Cognitive Science*. Cambridge, MA: MIT Press.

Wright, C. 1986. "Theory of Meaning and Speaker's Knowledge". In his *Realism, Meaning and Truth*, 204–38. Oxford: Blackwell.

Zhenhua, Y. 2002–3. "Tacit Knowledge/Knowing and the Problem of Articulation". *Tradition and Discovery: The Polanyi Society Periodical* **30**(2): 11–22.

Zhenhua, Y. 2004–5. "Kant's Notion of Judgment from the Perspective of the Theory of Tacit Knowing". *Tradition and Discovery: The Polanyi Society Periodical* **31**(1): 24–35.

INDEX